The Twenty-First Century

Technology's Impact on Academic Research and Law Libraries

The Twenty-First Century

Technology's Impact on Academic Research and Law Libraries

Betty W. Taylor
Elizabeth B. Mann
and
Robert J. Munro

G.K. Hall & Co.
Boston, Massachusetts

THE TWENTY-FIRST CENTURY: TECHNOLOGY'S IMPACT
ON ACADEMIC RESEARCH AND LAW LIBRARIES

BETTY W. TAYLOR, ELIZABETH B. MANN,
ROBERT JOHN MUNRO

Copyright 1988
by G.K. Hall & Co.
70 Lincoln Street
Boston, Massachusetts 02111

All rights reserved

No part of this book may be reproduced without
the written permission of the publisher.

Library of Congress Cataloging-in-Publication Data

Taylor, Betty W.
    The twenty-first century: technology's impact on academic
research and law libraries / Betty W. Taylor, Elizabeth B. Mann,
Robert J. Munro.
    p. cm. -- (Professional librarian Series)
    Bibliograpy: p.
    ISBN 0-8161-1882-5.
    1. Libraries, University and college--Automation. 2. Research
libraries--Automation. 3. Law libraries--Automation. 4. Library
science--Technological innovations. 5. Library science-
-Forecasting. I. Mann, Elizabeth B. II. Munro, Robert John.
III. Title. IV. Series.
Z675.U5T33 1988
027.7--dc19   88-12667
                                                                   CIP

Contents

Preface *vii*
1. Contemporary Forecasts, 1980-87 *1*
2. Introduction to the Issues *25*
    Impact of Technology on Information Publication *25*
    Library Collections and Automated Information *27*
    Budgeting *28*
    Payment for Electronic Information Access *32*
        Faculty *34*
        Students *34*
        Library Patrons (Other than Faculty and Students) *35*
    Personnel *36*
    Computer Equipment *37*
3. Findings of the Questionnaire *41*
    Purpose and Methodology *41*
    Findings *44*
        Impact of Technology on Information Publication *44*
        Library Collections and Automated Information Access *52*

    Budgeting *55*
    Payment for Automated Information Access *58*
      Faculty *58*
      Students *59*
      Library Patrons (Other than Faculty and Students) *60*
    Personnel *60*
    Computer Equipment *62*
4. Conclusions *65*
    Scenario for the Academic Research Library by the Year 2000 *67*
    Scenario for the Law Library by the Year 2000 *71*
    Scenario for Libraries beyond the Year 2000 *74*
    Authors' Commentary *77*

Selected Bibliography *87*

Appendixes *109*
    A. Questionnaire with Frequencies of Respondents' Opinions *109*
    B. Respondents' Opinions Expressed in Cross-tables *123*
    C. Statistically Significant Differences in Respondents' Opinions *163*
    D. Selected Comments of Respondents *185*

The Authors *235*

Preface

The intent of this report is to present our findings and analysis on the impact of technology on the future of academic research and law libraries and fiscal planning in the last decade of the 1900s and the 2000s. The data that support these findings and analysis were garnered from a survey instrument of approximately 150 questions completed by 224 respondents. The respondents who represented the "worlds" of the Association of Research Libraries (ARL) librarians, law librarians, college of law deans, scientists, library science professors, and networkers responded to questions in six areas: (1) impact of technology on information publications, (2) library collections and automated information access, (3) budgeting, (4) payment for automated information access, (5) personnel, and (6) computer equipment. The opinions of the respondents provided the authors with a view of the present reality and a mix of attitudes and predictions that suggested realistic futures. The futures that are suggested by the data in chapter 3, "Findings of the Questionnaire," are more fully developed in chapter 4, "Conclusions."

Chapter 1, "Contemporary Forecasts, 1980-87," and chapter 2, "Introduction to the Issues," are preliminary in nature. The reader will want to concentrate on chapter 3 for analysis of how the five respondent groups reported their opinions on the issues. This in turn is background for the futuristic analysis in chapter 4. The reader will have occasion to turn to the appendixes to read the questionnaire in full and the statistical analyses. The authors have also included selected personal comments written by the respondents on the questionnaire in Appendix D. These comments make for fascinating reading.

The authors are indebted to a number of people whose assistance was invaluable in the development of the questionnaire and analysis of our findings. We especially thank Professor M. A. Ferguson and her graduate assistant, L. Donner, who devoted much time and effort in critiquing the questionnaire and preparing the statistical tabulations; those who read the first draft of questions and responded both to the substance and form, particularly Dr. Linda Crocker of the College of Education of the University of Florida and Dr. Art King of the College of Dentistry of the University of Florida; Nolan Pope, assistant director for systems, University of Wisconsin, formerly from the University of Florida, who offered perceptive comments in the development of this proposal; Max Willocks, assistant director for public services, University of Florida; and Ms. Debra W. Walk, former graduate assistant to Dr. Elizabeth B. Mann, who compiled the bibliography. We are most appreciative of the tireless efforts that our staff at the University of Florida Legal Information Center devoted to this project with special mention of Mavis Green, Joan Hamby, and Amy Martin. Mark Bergeron, assistant in computer instruction, resources and operations at the College of Law of the University of Florida, produced the pie charts for chapter 3.

1
Contemporary Forecasts, 1980-87

In this chapter we have sought to construct a survey of prophecies and forecasts concerning the library of the future made during the period 1980-87. We have restricted ourselves to the present decade since forecasts through 1979 were covered in *The Impact of a Paperless Society on the Research Library of the Future* (1980), a report prepared by Frederick Lancaster, Laura Drasgow, and Ellen Marks for the National Science Foundation. These researchers noted the hazards of prophecy:

> Forecasting, to be sure, is a difficult enterprise. The forecaster must recognize that part of the future that is unknowable and must be prepared for unexpected changes and events which cannot be anticipated. For a library forecast to be both integrated and as realistic as possible, the forecaster must attempt to systematically take into account all aspects that can be anticipated. This requires an understanding of known or expected changes in its environment.[1]

Even given the pitfalls of predicting the future, however, several persons have braved this path and presented their ideas of the future of the library and the profession as technology and the paperless society evolve. Frederick W. Lancaster, Donald King, James Thompson, Richard Boss, Mary Wolfe, and Vincent E. Giuliano are frequently cited as predictors of the future of libraries in general, as well as Betty W. Taylor who has focused on law libraries.[2]

In the report prepared for the National Science Foundation, Lancaster, Drasgow, and Marks presented and discussed a "scenario depicting the research library in the year 2001." The scenario predicted the decline of the library as an institution but an increase in the importance of the information professional. The focus of this research was on the "possible future developments in the publishing industry and the likely impact of these developments on research libraries." Representative samples of librarians, publishers, and technologists were surveyed in a Delphi study, which confirmed "the probable conversion from print on paper publishing to electronic publishing in the case of indexing/abstracting services, scholarly journals, reference books, patents, technical reports, standards and specifications, and dissertations." It was predicted that "a substantial move into this conversion will have occurred by the year 2000."[3]

Although automation has taken a firmer hold on library operations and services, the funding for the up-dating of library technology and the expansion of its use has not been forthcoming for several reasons. In many cases the initial outlay for automation was viewed and planned as a one-time expenditure. Indeed, little or no future funding was contemplated in most situations. Moreover, while libraries have been struggling with applications of technology to functions and services, economic conditions have resulted in decreased funding for their operations. Therefore, librarians have been faced with the problem of deciding what to trim and what to eliminate, while still embracing the new technology and providing their users with good service.

A 1978 American Library Association publication, *Into the Information Age,* prepared by the Arthur D. Little firm, described the library's economic plight thus:

> It's a strange world where "It takes all the running you can do to stay in the same place" but it is indeed a lucky library of any type that can stay in the same place. That the rate of increase in

library costs exceeds the rate of inflation in the U.S. (as a general rule) is not secret. It is also no secret that very many (if not most) libraries have been unable to secure operating budget increases commensurate with inflation. Thus, there has been--since the early 1970's and growing more intense by the year--massive economic pressure on libraries. This pressure is experienced differently by different library sectors (college, public, special, major research libraries, etc.), but essentially is forcing all sectors into cutting staff, buying fewer materials, maintaining shorter hours or otherwise seeking operational economies. Given fixed or even declining budgets in the face of relentless inflation and escalating personnel costs, there is in many library sectors less and less money for purchases of materials. Simultaneously, the variety of materials published, their prices, and the demand for them are growing. With the exception of specialized industrial libraries and information centers and government libraries, the parent institution in which a library is situated (e.g., a city government, a college or university, a school system) itself is experiencing significant difficulty in finding the financial resources to provide for its operations, and the library priority is usually among the least urgent for attention. The recent national inventory of library resources study, sponsored by the National Commission on Libraries and Information Science, reveals a shortfall in 1975 of $5 to $6 billion in library funding.[4]

The situation has not improved in the ten years since this study was made. Libraries have been attempting to operate while experiencing significant decreases in the level of financial support, but they have not been able to maintain their collections nor their services at the same level. Budgets have not kept pace with the hefty price increases of journals and books. (The prices of scholarly journals and books continue to rise at an average rate of 15% per year.) Another element of the problem faced by libraries is that the number of books and journals produced worldwide has also continued to accelerate. Add to this the problem of financing automated functions and services, and it is clear that library administrators have been confronted with some difficult decisions.

M. Carl Drott of the Drexel University School of Library and Information Science predicted in 1981 that "in the next decade, the automation of libraries will be affected by conflicting trends. Computer hardware costs will drop dramatically. Especially affected will be small computers with large quantities of memory. This is a type of machine well suited to the needs of individual libraries. Rising cost of programming and the high costs of financing will slow new system development. Especially hard hit will be custom systems designed for a single library." He also stated, "The growth of automation in all parts of society will give libraries many more options as to what and how to automate. The spread of computers will also offer more reason to add computers and software to library collections. In both the use and acquisition of computers, libraries will tend to follow society. But computer progress will be so rapid that even followers will be able to set a rapid pace."

It was Drott's opinion that "in the final analysis, human adaptability will be the limit on automation. . . . Humans rather readily adapt to automation which supports or simplifies current work processes. These will be the areas of fastest growth. Completely new information processes will require much greater human adaptation. We can expect that such innovations will be accepted at a much slower pace."[5]

Thus librarians, confronting inadequate budgets, ever-increasing proliferation of information and pressure to embrace more fully the new technologies have come to question the future of libraries. Some futurists and technologists have even predicted their demise. In fact, predictions made since the 1960s that books and libraries were becoming obsolete because of new technologies have continued more vociferously in the 1980s with the rapid development of newer technology and the appearance of companies selling information tailored to the needs of the particular user.

Vincent Giuliano, a former dean of a library school and consultant for Arthur D. Little, Inc., on technology and organizations, stated in 1979:

> Libraries are simply not Information Age institutions, unpleasant though that might be to contemplate. Communication, currency, and ready access to information are crucial in the Information Age. In libraries the emphasis is on the collection of information, organization and preservation of the collection in relatively static form (e.g. books and periodicals), not on the process of communication. The library emphasis is more on having than communicating, more on preserving older material than quickly accessing newer material. Communication means are primitive; a patron must physically come to the library to get service in most instances; the delay in obtaining material, say through interlibrary loan, may be weeks or months.[6]

Additionally, he pointed out:

> Information that counts flows around libraries, not through them. When information does flow to a library, more often than not, it stops there. Use of new information technologies by libraries is usually oriented only towards helping with the existing functions and form of the library. It does not address the issue of functional obsolescence. Most library automation revolves around the cataloging and bibliographic control functions. Such automation misses the major point; it is like seeing the major implication of steam power for shipping to be in the use of steam winches to haul sails on clipper ships. Those steam winches are useful, but they did not save the clipper ships. The ships built around the steam engines left the sailing ships functionally obsolete, steam winches making no difference. Modern information institutions, like the online database publishing utilities, are making libraries obsolete. Automation of cataloging and bibliographic functions will not save libraries; it may, in fact, speed their demise.[7]

On the other hand, Richard De Gennaro, director of the New York Public Library and formerly director of libraries at the University of Pennsylvania, challenged Lancaster, Giuliano, and other technologists and futurists and stated in 1982:

> I conclude that libraries are and will continue to be a critical link in the chain that produces, preserves, and disseminates the knowledge that has created and sustains our information society.

> The information industry is not making libraries obsolete. Rather, it is revitalizing them with new technology and services. Libraries, in turn, nourish that industry with the knowledge resources it needs while providing a vital and ready initial market and distribution system for its new services and products. Libraries are becoming more, not less, important in our information society even though their relative share of the total information market is declining.
>
> Technology in the hands of businessmen and librarians has been responsible for the enormous growth and expansion of libraries that has occurred since Gutenberg invented movable type and started mass-producing printed books in 1452. The coming of computer and related electronic technologies in the last two decades represents a development of similar magnitude and significance. The difference is that the development and effects of printing technology took centuries to unfold while the development and effects of electronic technology are compressed into decades and are transforming our entire technological society.
>
> Gutenberg's invention made libraries as we know them necessary and possible. It is already a fact that our electronic computer technology is making new kinds of electronic 'libraries' or data banks necessary and possible, but whether or when it will make Gutenberg-type libraries obsolete, nobody really knows. In the meantime, those charged with the stewardship of libraries should be assured that librarians and businessmen are using electronic technology to give libraries the enhanced capabilities they need to continue to function effectively in the present mode and to make the transition to new and as yet unknown future modes."[8]

Brigitte Kenney, in describing a scenario for the future, wrote the same year:

> Libraries will cease to be places and instead will be organizations of people, working at home much of the time, and providing the expertise necessary to help users with the confusing variety of differing and competing technologies, and with searching and retrieving from the many electronic data stores throughout the U.S. and, eventually, the world. There will still be a need for

large research collections of printed materials as well as small, quickly changed, collections of popular entertainment-type reading materials. The large collections will continue to be staffed by scholar-librarians, subject specialists all, who will provide interpretation and access to the collections. These same libraries will also be used by a national library resource system to provide facsimile copies of scholarly materials. . . . Paper will not disappear but it will often be the end product of an electronic search of a database; search results can be printed out if desirable.[9]

Kenney's scenario further predicted that

librarians will become information professionals; they will realize that they are in the information business, that all forms of information are legitimate concerns, and that to make the many and varied resources available to their publics is their most important job.

Moreover, information professionals both inside and outside libraries will become increasingly skilled at guiding their clients to the information needed, be this a community database or a remote information source. They will become adept at repackaging information to suit individual needs. They will be more appreciated and better rewarded than they were in the days before information technology made their tasks much easier, but at the same time increased the complexity of information sources at all levels. There is no doubt that many information professionals will meet this challenge; those who do not will be obsolete.[10]

Julius Marke, writing in 1981, foresaw a change in the role of the law librarian and the library staff as it related to the teaching process of the law school.

The trend to problem method seminars involves research in depth and writing problems in areas of concentrations. As a result, new demands are being made on the library for larger collections of specialized materials. This can result in the law librarian and law library staff becoming more intimately involved with the law school curriculum as the faculty and students place even more reliance on their specialized knowledge in legal research. Library personnel may be called on to participate in team teaching, especially in the problem-solving seminar courses in which the specialist's contribution is stressed."[11]

He anticipated that the future law librarian would

play a significant role by being a highly trained and skilled professional, knowledgeable not only in the instruction of how to use LEXIS and WESTLAW, but also the online bibliographic search services which the student with the problem-oriented course would need recourse to. In a way, this professional will be a traffic director for these purposes. I can see the law librarian and the law library staff involved in legal research in the grand manner--supervising and planning great information retrieval systems--and taking a leading role in the legal research activity of the future."[12]

James Thompson, in his book *The End of Libraries*, hypothesized that sheer size of collections, the inadequacies and vagaries of systems of classification, the very nature of the book itself, and the attitudes of librarians may all lead to the extinction of libraries. He predicted that continued inertia will result in libraries becoming archives of little-used materials and recommended that librarians redirect their mission from collection building to that of building information user linkages.[13]

Meredith Butler reviewed the literature through October 1983 on electronic publishing and its impact on libraries and correctly pointed out that "the literature on electronic publishing is increasing daily. . . . Electronic technology is the future, if not the only future, for libraries. It will be imperative for knowledgeable, well-informed librarians to plan that future."[14]

In 1984 De Gennaro, although noting that "there are a number of articulate spokesmen for a point of view which holds that information in electronic form will put an end to all but the most popular books, journals, and libraries by the year 2000," stated:

It is obvious that information technology is already beginning to change publishing and libraries and those changes will accelerate in the future, but no one can foretell yet whether or when technology will make books and libraries obsolete. The practical reality is that users continue to need libraries and librarians must meet those needs with the resources and technologies that are now available. We have no choice but to assume that print materials will continue to coexist along with information in electronic form for at least another two decades--that is the rest of our working lives for most of us. The role of librarians, in the future as in the past, will be to carry out the library function, i.e., to decide what information to collect and preserve, how to organize it, and how to make it freely available to those who need it. The library function is vital to society, but it is not profitable and we cannot rely on the commercial sector to perform it.

Many, perhaps even most, librarians will work outside libraries in the electronic future, but librarians who now work in libraries cannot and should not abandon their libraries to become information brokers or turn their libraries into information businesses. The job of librarians is to guide their libraries through a major transition from the collection-centered institutions that they are today to the access and service-oriented institutions that they must and, I believe, will become in the next two decades.[15]

He went on to observe that

for the library to maintain its position as the university's principal information resource and service, it will have to play a leading role in this technological revolution. In this electronic future, information will proliferate and become more ephemeral and the task of bringing it under control will become more difficult and more vital. Thus, the new information processing technologies will increase the importance and enlarge the role and capabilities of the academic library.

The challenge to librarians in the decade ahead is two-fold: 1) to automate their public catalogs and internal operations and develop the capacity to deal with large quantities of information in a variety of new electronic forms, and 2) to continue to

> strengthen and provide for growth of their traditional collections and services.
>
> The challenge to those who fund libraries is to provide the financial resources that will be needed to accomplish this two-fold task.[16]

He concluded from this that

> our task as librarians is to convince our backers and funders to invest the large sums of money needed to add this electronic dimension to our libraries. We cannot bootstrap our libraries into the electronic age. When we first started using computers in libraries 20 years ago, we thought we would save money. Then we thought automation would at least reduce the rate of rise of library costs, but even this is proving to be illusory as the demand for new and more sophisticated systems and services increases. We are no longer merely automating our internal operations, we are providing new user services and access to a broader range of resources both traditional and electronic. As these new services become more efficient and more widely known, demand for them will increase, and while the unit cost of providing any given service will decline, the total cost of satisfying the increased demand will go up.[17]

Lengthy discussions have concerned the kinds of personnel that will be needed in the library of the future. Perhaps the most dire prediction here has been the demise of technical services. Maurice J. Freedman has discussed the use of automation as it relates to this area. He raised questions that relate to the responsibilities of the professional and paraprofessional staff, stressing that

> the paraprofessional's work may shift as technology shifts, but the paraprofessional, as well as the clerk, will also be kept on the job and perform many more of their duties with some form of data processing equipment. Most of the paper records and files will be replaced with machine files. As long as response time for some of the networks is as bad as it has been at times, the paraprofessionals will be kept occupied, if not always busy. It is conceivable that automation will reduce the time required to

perform specific tasks of paraprofessionals, and some staff time may be reallocated.[18]

He noted further that

> the work of a professional librarian is professional. It requires the exercise of judgment based on education, experience, and understanding of the individual's specific responsibility, all in the context of the library's overall mission. The professional will, of course, routinely work and interact with some form of computer and the computer will enhance the professional's performance by creating options totally unavailable with manual files and with the computer's capability at the professional's fingertips the decision-making should be enhanced.[19]

Freedman then gave the following advice: "As for controlling the future, a librarian should stay on top of developments without being blinded by the glitter of technology or seduced by its siren song." And he added a note of caution: "The future of automated technical services in libraries presented here is fundamentally a rosy one, but the reality still visible is that the promise of automation, at least for some libraries, is, as yet, unfulfilled or compromised."[20]

Visualizing another scenario, Richard Boss predicted that

> by 1990, the majority of medium-sized and large libraries in North America will be automated; by the end of the century a majority of all but school libraries will have implemented systems. Libraries will not be paperless, however. Acquisitions decisions will be based on extensive management information about library users and patterns of collection use, ordering will be done online, and funds accounting will be done automatically. Shared cataloging will be a by-product of shared bibliographic databases mounted on bibliographic utility systems or distributed on videodisk or optical digital disk.
>
> Online patron access catalog and circulation control functions will be commonplace because they have the greatest potential value for users. The user will be able to access both the holdings and current availability status of materials in an entire library system from a terminal in any library location or from the home

or office using a computer terminal or a television receiver adapted for videotext. Automation will also have extended to the library office.

Libraries will continue to have collections of printed books and journals, but a significant percentage of statistical and directory data will be accessed through computer terminals, as will almost all bibliographic data. A librarian will have to be skillful in both the printed and electronic media to serve patrons well.

Libraries will face commercial competition, from electronic systems such as videotext to information brokers who respond to telephone queries for a fee. Most people will probably use several suppliers to satisfy their information needs. They will make their choices based on ease of use, speed of response, and cost to the user. Libraries may remain the least costly alternative, but they may find it difficult to compete in ease of use or speed of response unless librarians become highly effective managers of technology.[21]

Clyde Hendrick, a graduate school dean, speaking to a university library group in late 1985, discussed his vision of the library of the future.

The library will still exist in the next century. It will not only exist, but it will become increasingly important in the life of the university community and the wider society. The doomsayers who predict the dispersion or demise of the library are wrong. As knowledge continues to multiply, the need for expertise--to collect, categorize, store, sort, retrieve, and advise and comfort bewildered users--will also multiply.

The library of the twenty-first century will become much more diverse in its activities. Books will undoubtedly continue to exist throughout the new century, but the media available for recording and transforming knowledge will increase substantially, perhaps in ways not now foreseen. The proliferation of media, plus the increasing specialization and complexity of knowledge, suggests that the library will become a much more complex social institution. The keepers of the treasure house, the professional librarians, will also have to become both more of a generalist and more of a specialist in the many areas that will develop. In the next century the librarian will work almost entirely with the intellect. The tedious muscle work of yesterday and today will be done by machines and nonprofessional staff. Of course the librarian will have to administer those machines and staff. Thus librarians will become administrators of the science of knowledge, or, in short, administrative/knowledge scientists.

Commensurate with this enlarged role for the librarian, the university library as a social system must become a true power center in the university community. To do so, it must assert its own status as social system much more strongly than it does now or has in the past. At the same time, the library must permeate other sectors of the university more fully than is now the case.

In summary, my vision is that the library must move from the posture of beautiful but somewhat passive treasure house to the active role of knowledge mediator for the society. As a matter of fact, I believe that the continued viability of a coherent society depends on such a proactive role for the library. Without a central mediating force to channel the knowledge explosion, we will all be lost in the spiraling fragmentation of information chaos.[22]

Peter Briscoe and others pointed out in 1986 that

As a social institution the library has existed for at least twenty-six hundred years--three times longer than the university. Significantly, the first known library--Ashurbanipal's in Nineveh, which flourished in the seventh century B.C.--performed the same basic functions as a library today. It (a) assiduously collected written texts from throughout the known world; (b) cataloged and classified them by subject; (c) conserved records by recopying; (d) used them to answer the king's questions (reference); and (e) provided him and a few other high officials with something to read (circulation).

Functionally, the library has been well-defined and stable from its outset. History records changes in the locations, numbers, and sizes of libraries and in their types of clientele, sources of funding, subject specializations, prevailing media, technologies, and practices. But the institution's fundamental work seems to have remained the same. This should be kept in mind whenever one thinks about the library of the future. Nevertheless, a number of observers believe that the library will undergo drastic changes within the next twenty to thirty years. The most outspoken, F. W. Lancaster, flatly states that "I see little future for the library" and predicts it will be both "disembodied" and "bypassed" by technological developments.[23]

This article projected into the future the role of the library as a social institution. But it first pointed out three trends in the environment that "appear likely" to affect both the role of the librarian and the nature of the library as an institution: the growth of an information industry, the proliferation of computer terminals in homes and offices, and a gradual shift in publishing from print to electronic media.[24]

The authors also examined the question of whether the library of the future will be an institution of knowledge or a broker of information.

> Probably the most critical strategic decision a library will make in the next ten to twenty years is its definition of itself. As an institution it has been unique for twenty-six hundred years; as a broker, it will likely join a mob. Information and knowledge are not mutually exclusive concepts. They are the extremes of a continuum, or the beginning and end of a process. Knowledge subsumes information, but the converse is not true. By extension, a knowledge institution can include an information-brokering function, but not the other way around.[25]

Finally, Briscoe and his coauthors asserted:

> One thing is certain. Technology has already changed the traditional way in which libraries operate, and this trend will continue. But how it continues, what direction it takes, and how those in libraries apply available technology is up to them. Above all, librarians must not let technology be the dictator. The library needs to persist in its role as a knowledge institution--mankind's archive and encyclopedia--while providing the necessary services of an information broker: computer literature searching, information retrieval, and document delivery.[26]

Contemporary Forecasts, 1980-87

Frank Newman, president of the Education Commission of the States, in a report issued September 1985 by the Carnegie Foundation for the Advancement of Teaching, called for a fundamental reexamination of the effectiveness of existing educational programs and the crafting of new policies to meet society's changing needs. The report covered a wide range of policies in higher education, and the research library was not omitted. A few excerpts follow.

> Research in every field depends on the availability of the latest knowledge (data, analysis, ideas). As research has accelerated, the available knowledge has grown at an incredible rate--the well documented "knowledge explosion." The expansion in the numbers of research universities has meant a parallel expansion in the numbers and quality of research libraries. Two major problems now face research libraries--the costs of providing for their users a huge and growing array of books, scholarly journals, government documents, and other works; and the confusion brought about by the advent of widespread electronic information. Both demand fundamentally new ways of thinking about the function of the library.
>
> What is now plain is that even the wealthiest research libraries cannot hope to acquire and maintain all of the scholarly materials now available. As Robert Rosenzweig put it, "It is now commonly accepted that such completeness is unattainable for a single library (only the Library of Congress comes close to having such an aspiration) and that cooperation among libraries is essential to provide scholars and others with the products of the 'knowledge explosion' of the past few decades." The problem has moved beyond even this level, as profound as that is, and a fundamental and wrenching shift lies ahead for research libraries.[27]

Newman's report posed three crucial problems:

> In the traditional method of providing access to materials, the research library acquires the material outright and then makes it available to scholars essentially free of charge. The large bulk of research library costs are for the acquisition, cataloguing, and maintenance of this material. Now, a number of data bases are available to libraries but when the library gains access there is most often a charge which is passed on to the user. The result is

15

to discriminate in favor of acquired as opposed to accessed material, and to discriminate in favor of the haves as opposed to the have-nots.

Library personnel, while now fully competent to handle the library automation that has taken place, have neither the education nor the emotional commitment to prepare for the shift in outlook required to change from owning, cataloguing, and lending, to becoming electronic data sleuths ready to link a student or faculty member to someone else's data bank. Moreover, the time has come for information specialists to learn more about the needs of libraries.

The old, hard copy system of library materials provides important services such as indexing to scholars. While there are some newly available indices to certain electronic data bases, most notably those that are available commercially, the large majority are simply hidden from sight. One great loss is that information used in one field, or even a subfield, is not available to researchers in other fields who are not aware of its existence. Another service is the control of quality through such steps as the refereeing of journal articles. A third service is the provision of an accessible, orderly historical record. For many of the electronic data in the most critical research areas, none of these is available.[28]

The report indicated that

the basic problem is that the research community, and much of the rest of the society, is moving beyond the capacity of the research library. It is time to shift from the main emphasis on acquisition to an emphasis on access. Perhaps it is time to stop calling these centers "libraries." Time is important. The problems of access, indexing, cost structures, and quality could easily get out of hand.

It is not clear how to achieve an evolution to a new system, or even how a new system would function. One thing is clear, however: The federal government will surely be involved. It has a major stake in the existence of an efficient system with rapid exchange of the latest information so that American research and American industry can gain a competitive edge. And only the federal government is likely to have the resources and clout necessary for the transition.

> A working group from the key academic, library, and governmental organizations should be formed and charged with the task of proposing the model for the next generation of scholarship information systems."[29]

It appears that some administrators and library leaders have also been thinking along these lines. In April 1986 Patricia M. Battin was named vice president and librarian at Columbia University. As Columbia's "computer czar," she stated that she wanted to "open a one-stop information shopping center at Columbia University. Scholars," she said, "should not have to go to the library for information stored in books and journals, then to the computer center for information stored electronically--and afterward have to figure out on their own how to use their computers to organize the information they have collected."[30]

Battin pointed out that "librarians don't organize books; they organize knowledge and ways to gain access to the knowledge." They have long known how to do this, but now, she said, they

> have also become expert at organizing and gaining access to information stored on computers. Such knowledge is vital to scholars, who are trying to cope with masses of information stored both on paper and in computers, and also trying to learn how to take advantage of computer technology in their work.
>
> They need discipline-specific information, not only to take advantage of information in books and journals, but also to enable them to use on-line data bases and find software that will help them organize their data. "Different disciplines need their information organized in different ways."
>
> Research librarians, who tend to specialize in one discipline, are today the best source of discipline-specific information about research resources."[31]

The Twenty-First Century

According to the story about Battin in the *Chronicle*, her position gave her the responsibility to develop a new concept--the Scholarly Information Center. The needs of scholars will change, she said, and "we don't know what services will be necessary. New capabilities will mean new needs. We'll have to do some broken-field running to respond to needs as they change." She continued, "We are trying to find the best institutional structure to bring together support services for scholars so we don't create barriers."[32]

It was approximately ten years ago that Frederick W. Lancaster first talked about a paperless electronic information society. He is the most frequently cited author in the library field who is writing about this subject. In his 1982 publication *Libraries and Librarians in an Age of Electronics* he pulled together his extensive writing to present a coherent whole, and in late 1985 his article "The Paperless Society Revisited" appeared in *American Libraries*. In the article he reassessed his earier predictions in terms of what had transpired in the past decade.

> On the whole, I believe that the evolution is proceeding more rapidly than I expected a decade ago. Personal computers are becoming commonplace, and electronic mail is spreading into more and more communities of users. Video-tex techniques are putting a variety of electronic information sources directly into at least some of our homes.
>
> That so much has taken place in the last 10 years is all the more remarkable considering that very few true electronic publications exist as yet. Clearly, the printed book is not threatened by the types of publications now available in electronic form. How could it be, for most of the electronic products are merely printed books displayed electronically. An electronic encyclopedia could and should be much more than printed pages viewed on a terminal. The same must be said for the science journal. True electronic publication implies that authors would compose for a different medium and, in so doing, would no longer be constrained by the static limitations of the printed page.

When the true capabilities of electronics are employed to convey information or inspiration, we can expect that completely new communication forms will emerge. Such capabilities would include the use of sound, moving pictures, and electronic analog modeling. These capabilities may well lead to new forms of art and imaginative literature. Electronic painting and electronic poetry already exist, and, though it may now be hard to accept, there is no real reason to expect that people will still be writing novels a hundred years from now.

What I am suggesting, then, is that the printed book will be replaced by something quite different from anything we have yet seen, and this will occur because the medium replacing it will be widely perceived to be better.

The replacement of print on paper is not inevitable. That is, society could presumably choose to reject the transition. However, we are so far along the road toward a paperless society that it is difficult to see what might occur that would permanently reverse the trend.

Let me conclude with a further point of clarification. The fact that I have written about an electronic future does not necessarily mean I endorse such a future or that I enthusiastically look forward to it. A new technology may improve an existing situation but bring with it its own set of problems. It can be used to benefit society or to impair it. The impact is determined by the qualities of the humans who exploit it, rather than by properties inherent in the technology itself.[33]

A publication in 1982 that stimulated widespread examination of changing information practices and libraries came from outside the library and education community. No book since *Future Shock* has caused as much discussion of America today and its future as John Naisbitt's *Megatrends: Ten New Directions Transforming Our Lives*. Naisbitt details America's shift from industrial production to the provision of services and information.

Naisbitt lists five key points that he considers the most important things to remember about the shift from an industrial to an information society:

> The information society is an economic reality, not an intellectual abstraction.
>
> Innovations in communication and computer technology will accelerate the pace of change by collapsing the "information float."
>
> New information technologies will at first be applied to old industrial tasks and then, gradually, give birth to new activities, processes, and products.
>
> In this literacy-intensive society, when we need basic reading and writing skills more than ever before, our education system is turning out an increasingly inferior product.
>
> The technology of the new information age is not absolute. It will succeed or fail according to the principle of high/tech high touch.[34]

Naisbitt pointed out that "we are drowning in information" and that unorganized and uncontrolled information is not a resource in an information society.[35]

> Information technology brings order to the chaos of information pollution and therefore gives value to data that would otherwise be useless. If users--through information utilities--can locate the information they need, they will pay for it. The emphasis of the whole information society shifts, then, from supply to selection.
>
> This principle is the driving force behind the new electronic publishers who provide on line data bases, communication channels for sorting through and selecting. These new businesses are selling medium, not information as such.[36]

Some of Naisbitt's predictions are of particular interest to the library profession. After stressing the importance of the computer and the new technology that will connect the information seeker with the source of that information, he forecast the long-range growth of information occupations and pointed out that with the rapid changes to come we cannot expect to remain in the same job or profession for life--we will seek retraining over and over.

The utility of forecasts to the study of the future of libraries, as is true of any forecasts, does not necessarily reside in their being totally accurate representations of the future. The future is inscrutable, and those who offer predictions should do so with respect and caution. The importance of predictions of the future is that, if evaluated critically, they can assist decision makers in long-range planning. They can bring new dimensions, new horizons, and innovations to the decision-making process. That a futurist may prove over time to be accurate is, in the final analysis, not the most important goal of prediction; it is rather that in the examination of old ideas we are impelled to avoid the habit of the ostrich, who hides its head in the sand.

Notes

1. Frederick W. Lancaster, Laura Drasgow, and Ellen Marks, *The Impact of the Paperless Society on the Research Library of the Future* (Urbana: University of Illinois, Graduate School of Library Science, 1980), 8.
2. In 1981 Betty W. Taylor, addressing a group of legal educators on the future of law school libraries, said:

   Libraries of the future must house nontraditional as well as traditional library resources, combining the warehouse of law books with electronic devices that tap the information resources of the world. . . . As use of rich resources in automated form takes precedence over lesser-used materials in hard copy, librarians will be faced with conflicting priorities as demands for information increase simultaneously with decreasing book budgets. Allocations for access to information databases will grow disproportionately. . . . In the future more funds will be devoted to participation in networks and accessing databases than on books or people. It will be an uphill battle. . . . Already librarians protest that they cannot afford to subscribe to automated systems. In reality they cannot afford to do otherwise when benefits and costs are compared.

By the end of this decade most legal information centers will be totally automated for both public and technical services. Legal information centers or law libraries will subscribe to [national and international databases]. . . . More than likely, every faculty member will have a terminal in the office and . . . a second one at home. Terminals will be scattered throughout the library. Some carrels will be equipped with them. Perhaps students will bring terminals to school. One educator has suggested that libraries will have terminals at the circulation desk for patron checkout and suggests that the library should have terminals for every student" (Betty W. Taylor, "The Future of Law School Libraries," in *Conference on Legal Education in the 1980's Proceedings, November 12-14, 1981.* Cosponsored by the A.B.A. Section of Legal Education and Admission to the Bar and New York University School of Law [Chicago: American Bar Association, 1982], 84-102).

3. Lancaster, Drasgow, and Marks, *Impact of Paperless Society*, report documentation, n.p.
4. Vincent Giuliano, Martin Ernst, Susan Crooks, and James Dunlop, *Into the Information Age: A Perspective for Federal Action on Information* (Chicago: American Library Association, 1978), 108.
5. M. Carl Drott, "Automation in Libraries: The Decade to Come," *Show-Me Libraries*, October-November 1981, 51.
6. Vincent E. Giuliano, "A Manifesto for Librarians," *Library Journal*, 15 September 1979, 1838.
7. Ibid., 1839.
8. Richard De Gennaro, "Libraries, Technology, and the Information Marketplace," *Library Journal*, 1 June 1982, 1054.
9. Brigitte L. Kenney, "Library Information Delivery Systems: Past, Present, and Future," *Drexel Library Quarterly* 16, no. 4 (Fall 1981):61.
10. Ibid., 62-63.
11. Julius J. Marke, "Law Libraries in the Eighties," in *Conference on Legal Education in the 1980's Proceedings, November 12-14, 1981.* Cosponsored by the A.B.A. Section

of Legal Education and Admission to the Bar and New York University School of Law (Chicago: American Bar Association, 1982), 111.
12. Ibid., 112.
13. James Thompson, *The End of Libraries* (London: Bingley, 1982).
14. Meredith Butler, "Electronic Publishing and Its Impact on Libraries: A Literature Review," *Library Resources and Technical Services* 28 (January-March 1984):57.
15. Richard De Gennaro, "Shifting Gears: Information Technology and the Academic Library," *Library Journal*, 15 June 1984, 1204.
16. Ibid., 1205.
17. Ibid., 1208.
18. Maurice J. Freedman, "Automation and the Future of Technical Services," *Library Journal*, 15 June 1984, 1202.
19. Ibid., 1202.
20. Ibid., 1203.
21. Richard W. Boss, "Technology and the Modern Library," *Library Journal*, 15 June 1984, 1189.
22. Clyde Hendrick, "The University Library in the Twenty-First Century," *College and Research Libraries*, March 1986, 127-28.
23. Peter Briscoe, Alice Bodtke-Roberts, Nancy Douglas, Michele Heinold, Nancy Koller, and Roberta Peirce, "Ashurbanipal's Enduring Archetype: Thoughts on the Library's Role in the Future," *College and Research Libraries*, March 1986, 121.
24. Ibid., 122.
25. Ibid., 123.
26. Ibid., 124.
27. Malcolm G. Scully, "Nation Is Urged to Link College with Civic Goals," *Chronicle of Higher Education* 31, no. 3 (18 September 1985):28.

28. Ibid., 28.
29. Ibid., 28-29.
30. "Columbia U's Head Librarian Is Now Managing Academic Computing, Too," *Chronicle of Higher Education* 32, no. 6 (9 April 1986):39.
31. Ibid., 39.
32. Ibid., 40.
33. F. W. Lancaster, "The Paperless Society Revisited," *American Libraries*, September 1985, 555.
34. John Naisbitt, *Megatrends: Ten New Directions Transforming Our Lives* (New York: Warner Books, 1982), 19.
35. Ibid., 24.
36. Ibid., 24-25.

2
Introduction to the Issues

Libraries of the future undoubtedly will differ from today's libraries. Technology is rapidly changing information delivery through on-line systems and floppy disks, and more dramatic developments loom on the horizon, as more information is packed into smaller devices such as optical, digital, video, compact, and laser disks. Combining the traditional manual methods of delivering library services with electronic devices challenges today's librarians. They are confronted with ever-increasing numbers of more costly printed publications competing for budget dollars with the computer services that are in high demand by students and faculty.

Impact of Technology on Information Publication

To plot for the development of libraries in the future, planners must project the needs for and availability of information resources, financial support, personnel, and physical facilities. Formerly, administrators planned for growth by estimating a percentage increase in the budget that accounted for an inflation factor and projecting for specific acquisitions. That method is far less practical today, for technological advances have rendered those principles less viable in the electronic information era. Yet planners must craft some predictions of what technological factors will influence library planning. And complicating the picture is the fact that various library planners project differing influences and place extremely wide values on the variables.

To determine if there is any consensus about the impact of technology on information publishing for library planning and budgeting purposes, we designed a series of questions to elicit views on information formats from key decision makers.

As more and more information appears in electronic databases, questions are raised about the continued simultaneous publication of identical or similar information in hard-copy form. Will all hard-copy information eventually be available in machine-readable form? Will preferences emerge for one of the formats? If so, how widespread will that preference be?

The book will continue to exist despite technological advances. Given this fact, there must be a book budget, a building to house the books, and personnel to administer the collections. This is not to say, however, that all information will continue to be published in the book format. Thus, one of the questions to which an answer was sought was: can we develop some rule of thumb stating that books to be read from cover to cover will continue to be in popular demand, will be published well into the twenty-first century, and will be maintained in libraries? Will those resource materials in which only small segments of the whole are consulted coexist in the future in hard copy, microform, video, and electronic formats? At some time near the turn of the century or later will information stored in these various media be available in electronic format only? Agreement on answers to these questions could have a major impact on planning for the size of book and electronic collections, budgets, physical facilities, and personnel in the future.

Another extremely important series of questions relates to library patrons. Where will they seek information? Will they continue to see the library as the resource center for all their information needs, thus belying the forecasts that doom the library as an institution? If information becomes available on-line, will they use that medium? Will they travel to the library for assistance and equipment in using the electronic format? Will they become proficient in computer use and prefer to access information through their personal computers elsewhere, either accessing the library directly on-line or bypassing it altogether? Will they consider the library as a consulting service and call for advice about accessing information databases? Will the cost of on-line information be targeted for access by those individuals and libraries with limited financial resources? Is it likely that other technological innovations will appear to create more complex issues? Will the mission of libraries be the same or modified or changed completely in the future?

Library Collections and Automated Information

A question preoccupying librarians and library users alike is what impact automation will have on the library collection. Some futurists predict scenarios involving libraries without walls, electronic information on-line, and users with terminals or personal computers accessing data from offices, classrooms, laboratories, homes, or even wristwatches. In such an environment, how can librarians plan for the future of an existing library? Should acquisitions continue on the present track? Should librarians anticipate a demand for more information on-line and less in hard copy, or more in hard copy and the same or less on-line?

If the amount of on-line information continues to grow, should hard copy acquisitions be reduced? Should only one copy be maintained as a backup? Could that copy be a microform copy or some type of storage disk? As time goes by will librarians reduce the number of copies of bound volumes in favor of on-line information? What about accreditation standards that require specific titles in the library? Will access to on-line information satisfy those requirements? Is there a trend in this direction? Is it desirable? If there is a trend to reduce hard-copy acquisitions of basic library materials, what percentage reduction will there be by the year 2000? Is this desirable?

What will be the impact of technology on library collections? Annual acquisitions decisions as to hard-copy accumulation and electronic information subscriptions will have an overall effect upon the collection. Will there be an intentional reduction in the hard-copy collection? Is there a trend toward eliminating frequently used basic library materials when those materials are available to faculty and students on-line? Is this desirable? What will be the impact by the year 2000?

Major microform collections are maintained by academic and law libraries. How will they be affected by the newer information storage technologies? Should microform purchases continue? At the present rate? At a slower pace? Will information now stored on film be supplemented or supplanted by information on disks? How will costs of microform compare with other storage media? Will microform disappear from libraries by the turn of the century?

Budgeting

Equally important to administrators is the concern about the impact of technology on library budgets. Is electronic information more expensive or less expensive to lease or purchase? Can libraries afford to supply access to individualized information in both books and computerized formats?

Allocating resources for electronic information is one of the more challenging experiences facing librarians today. Balancing expenditures for traditional-type library materials with the new technological resources requires librarians to tread a very fine line, recognizing their obligation both to maintain standard titles and to offer the new resources as well. Conservative faculty and students may be monitoring electronic information expenditures, weighing any excesses they deem to have jeopardized the acquisition of library materials important to them, while the technology enthusiasts apply pressure to provide more access to the new information services.

Introduction to the Issues

In an earlier study conducted by Betty Taylor, it was found that electronic information

> accounts for low percentages of the over-all law library materials, personnel, and expense budgets, ranging from a low of 0% in some schools to a high of 10.6% in one school in the 1983-84 fiscal year. But with the rapid growth and expansion of computerized information services, increased funding for automation raises new problems for law library directors and law school administrators regarding access of information, apportioning costs, and accountability for expenditures accompanied by no apparent limitation on the potential resources the law library will be expected to offer its patrons.
>
> Law school librarians and administrators are acutely aware of the developing dilemmas, because of the availability of substantial segments of original source materials in full text databases. . . . WESTLAW and LEXIS are subscription-based services charged by an annual educational rate, thus the costs are controllable. . . . What happens budgetarily when the control through terminals is lost to personal computers, the access unlimited, and access charges incurred at the per connect hour rate? . . .
>
> Most law school libraries report a marked increase in their computer expenditures in recent years. There is every indication that libraries are investing moderately in informational and bibliographic systems, but there is a gradual upward trend in total expenditures.[1]

Accompanying the instant questionnaire was a request that law librarians submit their expenditures for cataloging, bibliographic, and full-text computer services from the initiation of the services to the present. For the period prior to 1979-80 there are no published statistics available. Fifty law schools submitted this information, but no librarian reported expenditures prior to 1975-76. The known expenditures submitted by 29% of existing law schools for computer services were $20,000 for all law school libraries in 1975-76; $103,000 in 1976-77; nearly $295,700 in 1977-78; and close to $755,000 in 1978-79. Published figures indicate that by the end of fiscal 1979-80, 97 law libraries expended $1,812,523. In the five-year period between 1979-80 and 1985-86 total computer services expenditures increased nearly $1 million annually and rose to $7,335,056. In most cases these figures do not reflect equipment or development costs for local computerized systems or costs not directly associated with on-line services that are paid by the law school and not the library.

> Comparisons among law school libraries yield no discernible pattern as yet, although there may be some relationship between collection size and expenditures for computerized bibliographic services since ten of the 20 largest computer spenders rank among the largest 26 libraries in size. No apparent relationship exists between the top computer information retrieval spenders and the quantity of locally available information resources, for eight of the 20 big spenders rank among the top 27 law libraries in size. Similarly, eight of the big computer retrieval spenders also have budgets for library materials that rank among the top 30 law libraries....
>
> The average law library was spending $20,000 on computer services in 1979 and by 1984 that amount had increased to $35,000. These figures indicate the need to project greater increases in the law library budgets in the future as more data and databases become available.[2]

Laser disk technology is rapidly becoming popular in law libraries but predicting its impact on budgets is difficult. The new products on the market are rather costly, but as the demand increases, the prices probably will decline; the costs, however, are likely to be offset by the increase in products available. "One thing is certain--computerized services costs will increase in the future," and budgets must adjust to the changing environment.[3]

Librarians usually retain the right to control their libraries' information resources, and they view electronic information as no exception to the accepted policy. Since they are held accountable for the budget, most feel they must have major control over policy as well as maintenance. It is customary, however, to provide an institutional vehicle for faculty input, and in fact, law school accreditation standards mandate that faculty have a voice in the library operation.

Libraries are the laboratories of institutions and are used intensively by various groups of patrons, who feel a sense of ownership, possessiveness, and protectiveness toward their books or information services. Policies in conflict with perceived notions of library content management and organization can disturb faculty and student complacency about their library. Therefore, most faculty and students want to exercise some control to ensure that library operations continue to meet their needs. Decisions by librarians to spend more or less funds on hard copy in comparison with electronic information are likely to arouse interest. Thus, to channel this interest in the right direction, librarians may prefer to form faculty committees to recommend general policy.

Budgeting for electronic information services has evolved in different ways in different libraries. Some institutions are spending substantial funds, whereas others are investing minimal amounts for access to computer-generated information. Some directors budget regular library funds; others request special funds for that purpose. Identifying appropriate accounts for expenditures may present problems in institutions that require a distinction between expenses for expendable or capital items. Budgeting for information access in the future will become more problematic as costs, access, and popularity increase within a fluctuating economy.

In those law libraries where book budgets are adequate and flexible, subscriptions for LEXIS, WESTLAW, LEGALTRAC, and other services are often paid from regular library funds. But those law librarians who consider their budgets taxed already for traditional-type materials may request and receive separate budgets to accommodate automated services. There are advantages and disadvantages to both types of systems. When subscriptions to electronic information are paid out of regular library funds, the costs are less obvious, but the book budget may suffer if the budget becomes static or decreases while electronic services costs increase because of expanded contents or numbers of databases. When electronic information subscriptions are paid out of separate funds, they stand out as budgetary items and may be subjected more readily to change or deletion. When specific sums are allocated, it would be more difficult or virtually impossible to add new services during the year without some flexibility that allows for the transfer of funds from one account to another. Our questionnaire was designed so that respondents could express opinions about or preferences for combined or separate budgeting for electronic information.

Payment for Electronic Information Access

Librarians' efforts to encourage faculty and student use of computers to access information databases have contributed to the popularity of computers in the academic, research, and special library environment. Initially, in many schools, faculty, students, and librarians were offered free time or research and development funds to experiment with building and accessing different types of databases. Consequently, there was little or no emphasis on or tracking of access and usage costs. At some schools, computer scientists were eager to promote the librarians' acceptance because library patrons were potentially large, discipline-specific user groups with a sizable information power base.

Over the years librarians became avid users of computer systems and active generators of information in the electronic format for the benefit of library patrons. Librarians helped persuade the world of patrons to accept the advantages of electronic information, and now patrons have joined the throng of enthusiastic users.

As librarians, who have brought libraries into the technological world, become critical promoters and users of information databases, they carry a larger share of the financial burden to information access. University faculty often see the library budget as a consistent source of funding, justifiably expended on access to information databases. Library patrons reason that the library purchases information in hard-copy

Introduction to the Issues

books to circulate to its readers and that the patrons have a right to expect information delivery in the new format, also.

On the other hand, librarians examine their budgets in relation to the costs that patrons could generate for specific, individualized information. They shudder to think of how rapidly the accumulated costs could deplete the budget if the entire readership suddenly demanded free access to information in any format.

At a 1979 White House Conference on Library and Information Services the highest priorities stated in the resolutions passed by delegates were to provide "free and full access to information" (Resolution A-1) and to "affirm that all persons should have free access, without charge or fee to the individual, to information in public and publicly supported libraries" (Resolution A-2). The ground swell for these statements came from the state conferences that generated the basic principles of free access to information. Of course, at the time, few librarians could guess what that would mean in terms of budgets.

Many articles in the library literature today reflect the concern of librarians about payment for information searching and printing. More and more frequently librarians ask the basic question: "Who pays?" This seems like history repeating itself! Early libraries required payment of fees for use; later the concept of "free" libraries opened up access to patrons without direct costs. Now that individualized information costs for on-line information could be way out of proportion in comparison with an ordinary library book budget, librarians again are contemplating fees to support computer access to information.

Outspoken librarians write papers and give speeches on the pros and cons of user fees--but which group reflects the thinking of the majority? In an attempt to define the attitudes of the groups we surveyed toward user payment of computer costs, we drafted six questions to determine what the opinions are generally toward three segments of users: faculty, students, and library patrons other than faculty or students.

FACULTY

In research institutions, the faculty is an exclusive priority group. Top performers are attracted to universities by rich resources. They expect perquisites to be offered to entice them to teach and conduct research at prestigious schools. Among those special benefits may be access to computer facilities, information databases, and computer professional support. How should faculty be treated in their use of electronic information? Should access be offered free or at a limited cost? The next question follows: if the access for faculty is free or low priced, who bears the cost? Some colleges and departments receive grant or development funds that enable the faculty to gain access to the information they need without regard to the cost, but charging expenditures back to outside fund accounts is transparent to the faculty member. Many institutions absorb the costs for access or the faculty members simply do without the services.

In law libraries LEXIS and WESTLAW access charges are based on an annual subscription rate, and access is furnished free of per-use charge to law school users. Access is available in faculty or home offices on a free password arrangement or at a low cost. Law faculty recognition of the value of accessing other databases is only beginning to emerge; therefore, at the moment most law librarians are merely speculating about potential costs for faculty computer access. On the other hand, some law schools have allocated substantial funds for faculty computer access to information, and usually information retrieval costs can be met within these resources.

STUDENTS

Payment of costs for student access to computerized information raises entirely different issues than those related to faculty or noninstitutional library patrons: questions concerning the sheer numbers of students, types and competency of computer access, ability of institutions to absorb the costs, the legality of assessing computer costs within student tuition and activity fees, and a myriad of other budgeting and accounting matters arise.

Divergent views are expressed by those associated with providing computer services to students. One view emphasizes the student need for access to information, the desirability of promoting computer literacy and teaching computer use to explore in-depth resources, equality of access, and problems of inability to pay. In a contrary view, budget managers see the magnitude of the cost, feel that students would overtax a free-use system, and seek a solution through tuition, fees, computer assessments, outside public or private participation, or some combination of these.

On the other hand, law students, benefiting from institutional absorption of costs and educational rates, have free use of computer access at least to the two major databases of LEXIS and WESTLAW. This arrangement works well in the legal community where law firms subsidize the educational rates for access to databases. Similar arrangements do not apply in the academic research environment. The costs to a large library of continuous free availability of databases used by thousands of students would be staggering.

Many institutions are currently struggling with internal aspects of student computer services: namely, access to computing centers for academic programming activity directly related to class assignments and to library bibliographic databases listing local holdings. Free student access to databases beyond the campus is another uncharted dimension.

LIBRARY PATRONS (OTHER THAN FACULTY AND STUDENTS)

Providing information access to those not directly associated with an institution obviously is not a high priority item with institutional administrators. Many of these patrons use research libraries by acquiescence or privilege rather than by right, and most academic librarians do not assume any responsibility for purchasing materials that may be desired or needed by noninstitutional patrons.

The series of questions on this user group was designed to determine if there was any sense of obligation to a segment of library users for access to information. Accessing information in hard copy is different from use of microform collections, for example, which often contain unique materials not available in any other format in the library. Microforms and books pose no additional substantive cost problem beyond the initial acquisition; therfore, the patron may use the microform facilities without generating any further expense.

But what about information that is available only in the computerized format and its retrieval incurs a cost? In the absence of providing the information in a convenient (noncosting) format, does a library have an obligation to furnish access to the information free of charge to an individual not directly associated with the institution?

In law schools these questions reflect real concerns. Contributing alumni and friends consider themselves part of the law school community. How should librarians respond to their inquiries about access? Should the response be any different to a nonassociated, noncontributing group needing access to legal information that is otherwise unavailable in the vicinity? Should a fee to use the library provide access to electronic information as well?

The often-raised issue of who pays the cost of accessing electronic information, particularly information that is available only in on-line format, remains unresolved. Thus, budgetary planning for the next five years and projecting expenditures to the year 2000 necessitates creative solutions to perplexing problems.

Personnel

As the emerging concept of on-line cataloging became reality, administrators offered a vision of one cataloger in the country preparing a bibliographic record for an on-line database with catalogers from all other libraries updating that record. No card catalog maintenance would be necessary, further reducing staff needs. Technological advances in optical scanning, barcoding, automated book storage and retrieval, and laser disks would soon displace the need for a large professional and support staff. In short, it was projected that a substantial reduction of library personnel would accompany increased automation.

Catalogers, however, are still gainfully employed and are retaining their valuable positions in libraries. Although it seems logical for administrators to expect automation to have an impact on numbers of personnel, particularly in the technical services, this has not yet happened. On the contrary, the detail involved in inputting complete data on-line from a number of different sources sustains a requirement for larger staffs, not smaller. In some libraries reassignment of duties to public services has created a change in responsibilities but not in numbers. So far, there seems to be little or no substance to any claim that automation directly reduces the numbers of library staff essential for an effective operation. The changes may occur down the road, however, as libraries become fully integrated into on-line systems and concentrate on current rather than retrospective activities.

Traditionally, library administrators have hired graduates with master's degrees in library science (M.L.S.) and have paid them on a professional salary scale. Now, the technical nature of integrated library systems and information access has created a need for computer specialists. Questions of qualifications, titles, ranks, and compensation will become more pressing as new computer systems are introduced into libraries and departmental units.

Reaction to personnel issues was solicited for projections on staff support requirements in future years.

Computer Equipment

Acquiring computer equipment and furnishing computer facilities have presented college and university administrators with particularly difficult challenges. They must accumulate the financial resources for purchasing expensive equipment and face the uncertainties of brand names, quality, life span, obsolescence, peripherals, software, supplies, and furniture. Moreover, equipment requests can be virtually limitless.

Imaginative administrators have received much publicity and credit of late for their innovations in providing the computer resources to improve educational opportunities for their students. Brown University and Carnegie-Mellon University were among the first institutions to ensure that students have individual access to computers throughout their years in higher education. Each year additional schools announce programs to support equipment acquisition for students through tuition, public appropriations, or private support.

Questions were asked about student access to computer equipment to determine if a trend could be discerned for more individualized access to computers and to asses the extent of institutions' responsibility to provide full access to computing facilities. A prime question is whether or not colleges and universities have an obligation to furnish students with computers. Or do they classify personal computers similarly to typewriters, expecting that, generally, students will own their own? Such ownership could reduce the numbers of computers that libraries need to furnish for information access.

Faculty computer support is another area of growing interest to both faculty desiring the support and administrators who must procure the funds. Faculty involved in computer-assisted instruction must have access to computers in order to prepare instructional programs, conduct tests, and evaluate student performance. Issues concerning access to computer equipment are very real in the computer environment. Equipment purchase policies may vary widely among institutions, but the focus of our questions on faculty access to terminals or personal computers was designed to elicit projections about an institutional responsibility to furnish equipment to faculty without cost.

A related question concerns the obligation to furnish faculty with personal computers for word processing. Logically, personal computers could be furnished on the same basis as office furniture, books, and so on. But depending upon the institution, there may not be sufficient funds to make this guarantee to every faculty member, and a program would have to be designed to phase in a faculty enhancement plan.

In law schools, equipment acquisition seems to be accelerating. Of 104 schools responding to a 1984 survey conducted by the American Bar Association, 100 reported acquisition of computers. Sixty-eight schools provided at least 1 computer for the faculty, and 12 schools provided more than 15 computers. Undoubtedly, these figures would change substantially if schools were surveyed again.[4]

Increased acquisition of highly complex computer equipment for use with electronic information systems may generate a need for technical staff--either professional librarians who have acquired the specialization or computer-trained persons. Coping with the new technology in the traditional library and departmental environment poses many new issues for administrators and librarians alike.

Notes

1. For further comments, see Betty W. Taylor and Dan F. Henke, *Automation in the Law School, including Law Libraries* (New York: Glanville, 1986).
2. Ibid.
3. Ibid., p. 52.
4. Ibid. Detailed information on expenditures for electronic information are included in this publication. See also Betty W. Taylor and Dan F. Henke, *Budgeting for the Law School Library* (Dobbs Ferry, N.Y.: Glanville, 1981).

3
Findings of the Questionnaire

Purpose and Methodology

This study was conducted by investigators at the Legal Information Center of the University of Florida. Principal investigators were Prof. Betty W. Taylor, Dr. Elizabeth B. Mann, and Dr. Robert J. Munro. The project, a mail survey, was designed to determine opinions on the impact of technology on the academic research libraries and law school libraries. The Communication Research Center, College of Journalism and Communications, University of Florida, assisted with questionnaire construction, revision, pretesting, and administration and data analysis.

In September 1984, the Communication Research Center (CRC) was contacted by Dr. Munro for assistance in developing a research grant proposal. Professor Taylor, director of the Legal Information Center, University of Florida; Dr. Mann, professor, School of Library and Information Science, Florida State University; and Dr. Munro were designing a study of the impact of new computer technologies on libraries. Following a meeting with Dr. Munro, Professor Taylor, and Professor Mann on September 18, 1984, the CRC director, Dr. M. A. Ferguson, refined the proposal and developed a budget estimate to cover the questionnaire costs. After minor revisions to the proposal and the budget, the principal investigators submitted their grant proposal to the Council on Library Resources, Washington, D.C., on October 8, 1984, under the Librarian/Faculty Program.

On December 4, 1984, the Council on Library Resources notified the investigators that they had approved their proposal. Thus began a series of meetings among the CRC director, the research assistant, and the principal investigators to develop and pretest a reliable and valid measuring instrument.

Initially the Legal Information Center drafted the questions and the CRC staff made suggestions for changes in the instrument to facilitate data entry and ensure the reliability and validity of the study.

The reliability of an instrument refers to "that quality of measurement method that suggests that the same data would have been collected each time in repeated observations of the same phenomenon."[1] Validity is "the capacity of a measuring instrument to predict what it was designed to predict."[2] To enhance reliability and validity, the questionnaire was pretested a number of times, both with colleagues of the investigators and with College of Journalism and Communications faculty and staff.

Using the results of these extensive pretests, the principal investigators and the CRC staff met to determine the survey format. The final version of the questionnaire comprised 51 questions, most with three responses per question. Both closed- and open-ended items were included. For the closed- and open-ended questions, five-point Likert-type scales were used, with agreement categories ranging from "Strongly Agree" to "Strongly Disagree" and with desirability categories ranging from "Very Desirable" to "Very Undesirable." In addition, many questions asked when a particular event is likely to happen, with a scale ranging from 1990 to post-2000 and never.

The questionnaire with a cover letter explaining the purpose of the study was mailed out on April 20, 1985, to a total of 740 potential respondents in seven categories: library

Findings of the Questionnaire

science professors, scientists, library networkers, publishers, Association of Research Libraries (ARL) directors, law deans, and directors of law libraries. To identify group membership upon return, each group received questionnaires on a different color of paper.

The total number of respondents was 224 for an overall response rate of 30.3%. The final sample consisted of the following proportions in rank order: law library directors, 33.5 %; ARL directors, 19.6%; law deans, 19.2%; scientists, 14.7%; library science professors, 8.0%; library network members, 3.6%; and publishers, 1.3%. Half of the responses were from law deans and law librarians.

Table 1 indicates the number of questionnaires mailed to each group and the response rate.

Table 1

Number of Questionnaires Mailed and Response Rate by Group

	Number Mailed	Number Received	Response Rate
Law Library Directors	190	75	39.5%
Deans	175	44	25.5
Scientists	165	33	20.0
ARL Directors	120	44	36.7
Library Science Professors	35	18	51.4
Publishers	30	4	10.0
Library Networkers	25	8	32.0
	740	224	30.3%

Readers of this report should be cautioned about the external validity of the findings, which refers to the generalizability of findings to some larger population. As can be observed in Table 1, the response rate varied widely for the different groups, ranging from 10% for publishers to about 51% for library science professors. Given this variation, it is difficult to estimate the generalizability of the findings.

As the surveys were returned, the closed-ended responses were coded and all data were entered into the computer by CRC staff. After the data were entered, each entry was checked for mistakes and analysis began.[3] All data analyses used SPSSX (Statistical Package for the Social Sciences).[4]

The particular SPSSX programs used were: Frequencies (for descriptive statistics), Crosstabs (for chi-squares and contingency tables), and Oneway (for analysis of variance).

After examining the descriptive statistics, the principal investigators decided to delete the publishers' group (with 4 respondents), and collapse members of the library network (8 respondents) and library science professors (18 respondents) into one group for future analyses. Analyses then continued with these collapsed groups to examine differences in responses across the groups.

In reviewing the following analyses of the responses to the questionnaire, the reader should note that each discussion is labeled with the respective question. For example, "Q1A" refers to the first question in the questionnaire and the "A" refers to the subsection that relates to agreement with the question, whereas "Q1B" and "Q1C" refer to the issues of desirability and event time. The reader should refer to Appendix A for the text of the questions and to Appendixes B and C for a detailed breakdown of the statistical data. It should also be kept in mind that the pie charts relate to the preceding discussion.

Findings

IMPACT OF TECHNOLOGY ON INFORMATION PUBLICATION

The respondents by a very large majority (89.7%) agreed or strongly agreed that publication of printed books will continue to increase in the future despite the increase of publication of information in computerized and multimedia formats (Q1A). With regard to the desirability of this trend, 75.8% of the respondents found the trend to be very desirable or desirable (Q1B). Law deans' and directors' scores differed significantly from those of library science professors and networkers who agreed more with the trend. As for the trend's eventtime, the respondents chose a long-term duration of the trend by nearly a 2 to 1 ratio (Q1C). A small group of law deans favored the 1990 category.

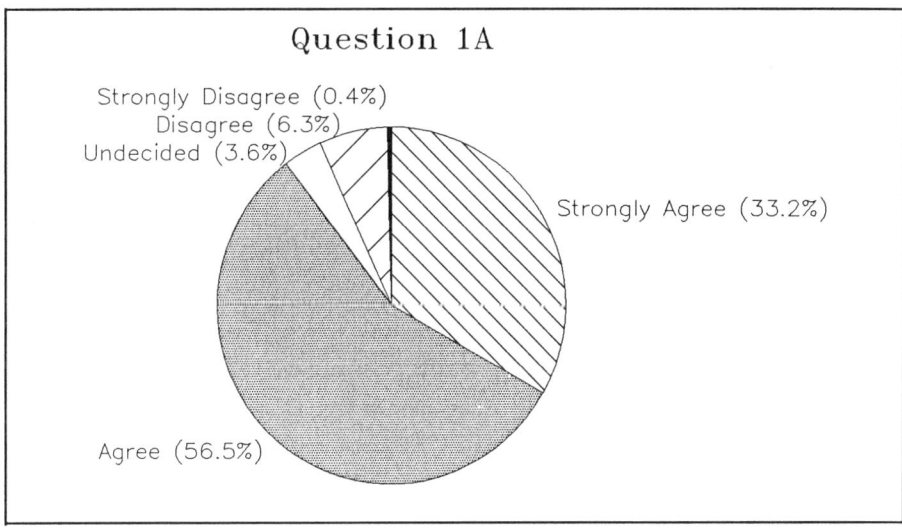

Question 1A

Strongly Disagree (0.4%)
Disagree (6.3%)
Undecided (3.6%)
Strongly Agree (33.2%)
Agree (56.5%)

The respondents by a slight majority (56.8%) agreed with the assertion that book collections of the libraries of the future will be reduced in size as more information becomes available in computerized and multimedia formats (Q2A). All respondent groups chose this conclusion except ARL directors whose scores significantly differed from those of scientists, law deans, and law library directors. ARL directors were least in agreement with the trend. In regard to desirability, 58.2% of the respondents expressed a pattern similar to that of "agreement" (Q2B), with some respondents, particularly ARL directors and law librarians, moving from the undesirable to the undecided category. Of the respondents, 43% chose a long-term direction for the event time with 27 "nevers" (Q2C). The scientists chose an earlier duration, the library science professors and law deans split, and ARL directors and law librarians chose a longer duration period.

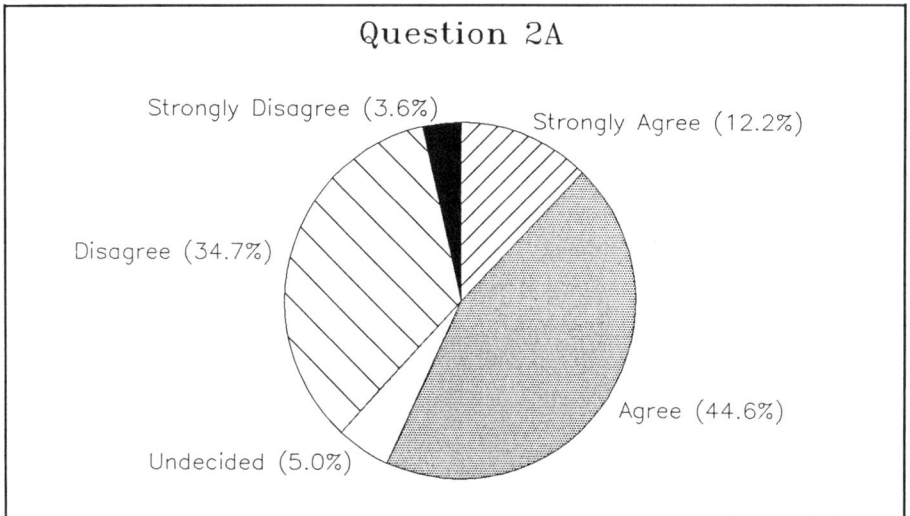

The respondents (57.7%) agreed that in the future more people will buy the information they want to read in a computer-based format and will borrow less from a library (Q3A). Strongly supported by law librarians, law deans, and scientists, the assertion split library science professors and was disfavored by ARL directors, who scored significantly differently from scientists and law librarians. On desirability, the respondents split widely (Q3B). Where 23 respondents were undecided on agreement with the assertion, the figure of undecided increased to 59 on desirability. ARL directors and library science professors found the asserted trend to be more desirable than did the other groups. In contrast to the previous question, the respondents expected the trend to occur earlier.

Findings of the Questionnaire

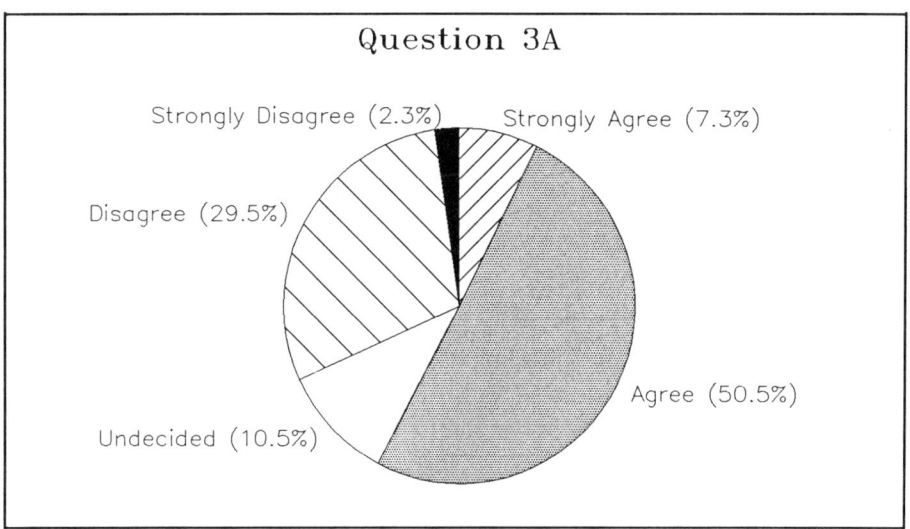

The assertion that in the future the services that libraries provide to patrons will be predominantly guidance in retrieving information in the nonbook format received a very negative response (Q4A). ARL directors disagreed the most, differing significantly from scientists, law deans, and law librarians. On desirability, the respondents moved to a slightly less negative position (Q4B). With 39 "nevers," the respondents expected the event(s) to occur over a longer period of time (Q4C).

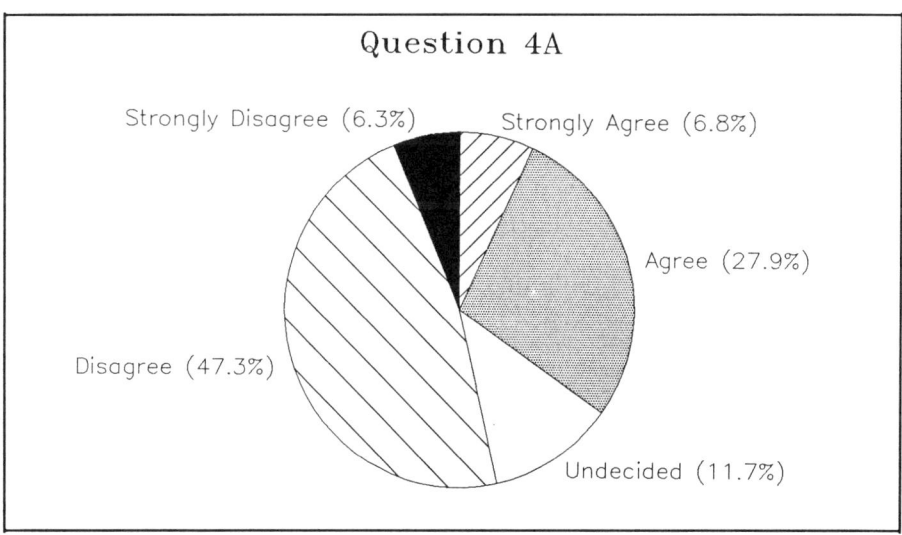

THE TWENTY-FIRST CENTURY

By a very strong majority (76.4%), the respondents agreed or strongly agreed that microfilm will be replaced by a form of computer-generated technology (Q5A). Library science professors, who strongly agreed, scored significantly differently from law librarians. The respondents' views on the desirability criterion reinforced this position (Q5B). The respondents favored the 2000 date as an intermediate expectation (Q5C).

Respondents (75.5%) agreed or strongly agreed that in the absence of published hard copy, information viewable only on a computer screen with print-out available for permanent retention will be widely accepted as a readable format (Q6A). On desirability, some of the respondents shifted from very positive and positive to undecided (the shift was most noticeable among ARL directors and law librarians). Of the respondents, 39% selected the date 2000 as the more likely time for the occurrence (Q6C).

The question "On-line information will be priced so that most people could afford to use on-line service" produced a most divided response (Q7A). Scientists were divided as were ARL directors. Library science professors and law deans agreed with the assertion, and law librarians gave only slight support. ARL directors scored significantly differently from law deans who were more in agreement. On the other hand, all the respondent groups found the prospect to be desirable (Q7B) and felt that the event would happen after 2000 (Q7C).

The respondents agreed by a strong majority that use of on-line public catalogs will significantly increase demands for document delivery (Q8A). The most striking pattern among the respondents was that of the ARL directors who overwhelmingly agreed. Following in agreement were library science professors and network personnel. Law deans and law librarians agreed as well, with the law deans expressing more doubts. ARL directors in supporting the assertion scored significantly differently from scientists and law deans. Respondents found this proposition to be desirable as well (Q8B). Although some scientists and law deans had reservations, the overall response was that this is expected to be an early development.

By a strong majority (86.4%), the respondents agreed or strongly agreed that in the future, intelligent terminals, software, or other forms of computer technology will be used to analyze and channel queries to appropriate databases for information (Q9A). ARL directors in strongly agreeing scored significantly differently from law librarians in their support. Again, the respondents found the possibility to be desirable, but the same respondents split on the timing of the occurrence. The scientists expected the event to occur by 1990. ARL directors also had expectations of an early development, whereas law librarians and law deans expected a later development.

Question 10, "Distributed databases (computer storage, e.g., tapes acquired for local or in-house computers) will replace remote on-line information sources," received a mixed response by the respondents (Q10A). Some ARL directors voiced the most reservations, whereas other ARL directors supported the assertion. Law deans were more undecided than ARL directors. In like manner, respondents exhibited a similar pattern on desirability (Q10B). Only 169 respondents reacted to the question as to when the event would occur (Q10C). The scientists along with ARL directors expected an earlier occurrence, and law deans and law librarians expressed more reservations.

Question 11, "The technology of disks (compact, digital, laser, optical, video) combined with microcomputers will provide an information retrieval capability superior to dial-up databases," a slightly different version of question 10, received stronger agreement than the preceding question (Q11A). The strong agreement from the scientists was significant, as was the extreme similarity between ARL directors and law deans. On desirability, the respondents split. Scientists scored significantly differently from law deans in their support, with the scientists being more supportive. As to when the event would occur, the respondents split, with scientists expecting the earliest occurrence and the other respondent groups favoring later development.

Of the respondents, 49.8% (104) agreed that by the year 2000, disks (whether compact, digital, laser, optical, or video) will replace hard-copy information by less than 25% (Q12A). Eighty-three respondents chose 26% to 50%, 19 chose 51% to 75%, and 3 chose 76% to 90%. One hundred five respondents, in effect, said that at least up to 50% of the collection would be replaced by discs by 2000. Conversely, only 3 of 209 respondents felt that a substantial segment of the entire collection, that is, 76% to 100% of the collection, would be replaced by discs by 2000. The respondent groups reacted in a similar manner to the question, although the law deans favored the 26% to 50% category over the under 25% category. In like manner, the respondents (209) found the assertion to be desirable, but not very desirable. The scientists scored significantly differently from the law deans and law librarians, who chose a smaller percentage of hard-copy replacement.

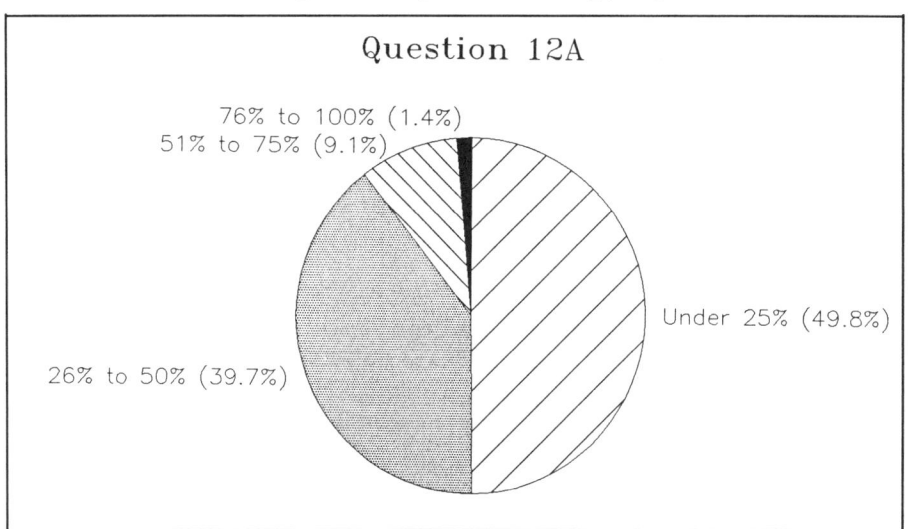

The respondents (81.3%) disagreed or strongly disagreed with the proposition "Interactive television, cable systems, or on-line systems like Viewtron or other videotex systems will replace the library as an information resource" (Q13A). Scientists strongly disagreed, whereas law deans, who scored in a significantly different manner from other respondent groups, were relatively less opposed to the development. On desirability, the respondents either considered the proposal undesirable or were undecided. The respondent groups were very similar in both agreement and desirability, although law deans were slightly more in agreement with the proposition than the other groups. On the question of timing, 97.1% of the respondents stated that it would never happen (Q13C).

Respondents strongly agreed that other technologies would be developed that would permit access to information even faster and cheaper than those described above (Q14A). Library science professors and networkers with higher expectations scored significantly differently from ARL directors in their expectations of new technology. On desirability, there was a shift among the respondents to a position of higher desirability (Q14B), particularly among law librarians and ARL directors. The respondents expected a late development. The scientists were split between 2000 and post-2000, and ARL directors, law deans, and law librarians favored a later development.

Respondents split on the question "By the year 2000, automated library technology will be characterized primarily by: A. Networks of personal computers or terminals; B. Access of full-text databases, such as LEXIS and WESTLAW; C. Video-disk technology; D. Laser-disk technology; E. Combination of above; identify; and F. Other." The respondents chose as follows: 24 A; 12 B; 3 C; 11 D; 69 A, B, C, D; 22 A, B, D; 15 A, D; 10 A, B; and 13 unspecified combination.

Question 16, "What role and function for libraries do you envision in the years beyond 1990? A. Continued role as general information resource; B. New role as computer-based information guide; C. A and B above; D. No role," posed little difficulty for the 219 respondents: 18 chose A, 8 chose B, and 193 chose C.

LIBRARY COLLECTIONS AND AUTOMATED INFORMATION ACCESS

By a wide majority, the respondents (75%) agreed or strongly agreed that increased automated information will slow the rate of growth in hard-copy acquisitions for the library (Q17A). Law librarians and law deans in strongly agreeing scored significantly differently from library science professors and ARL directors. Questioned on the desirability of this issue, the respondents shifted more to an undecided stance, although the majority still stated the development was desirable (Q17B). Library science professors scored significantly differently from law deans, law librarians, and scientists. On event time, respondents concluded that the development would happen fairly soon (Q17C), but ARL directors and library science professors were less supportive of an early occurrence than law deans and law librarians.

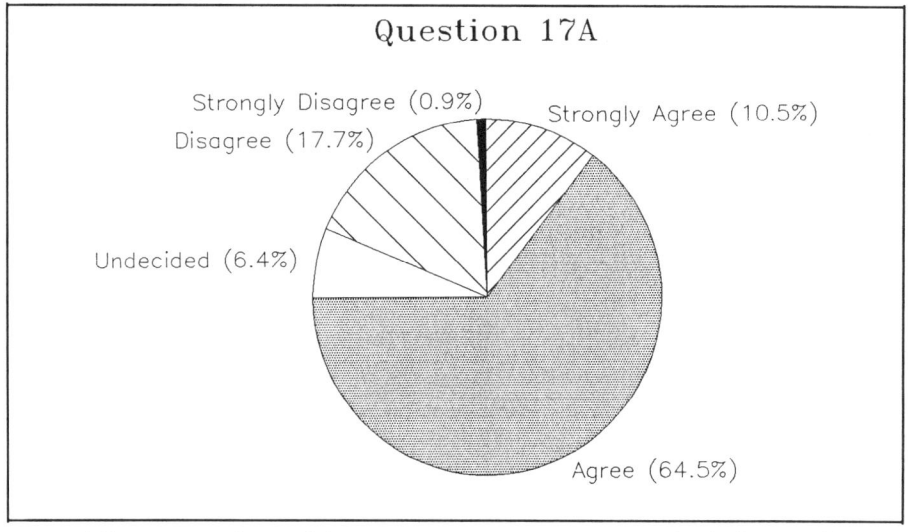

The question "As access to automated information increases, annual hard copy acquisitions of basic library materials will be reduced to one copy" split the respondents (Q18A), with law librarians and law deans agreeing, ARL directors and library science professors disagreeing and scientists equally split. ARL directors and library science professors in disagreeing more scored significantly differently from law librarians and law deans. On desirability, the respondents shifted toward the undesirable categories. The respondent groups split in the same margin as on the agreement question. On event time the respondents split, with law deans and law librarians seeing early developments and ARL directors and library science professors seeing later developments.

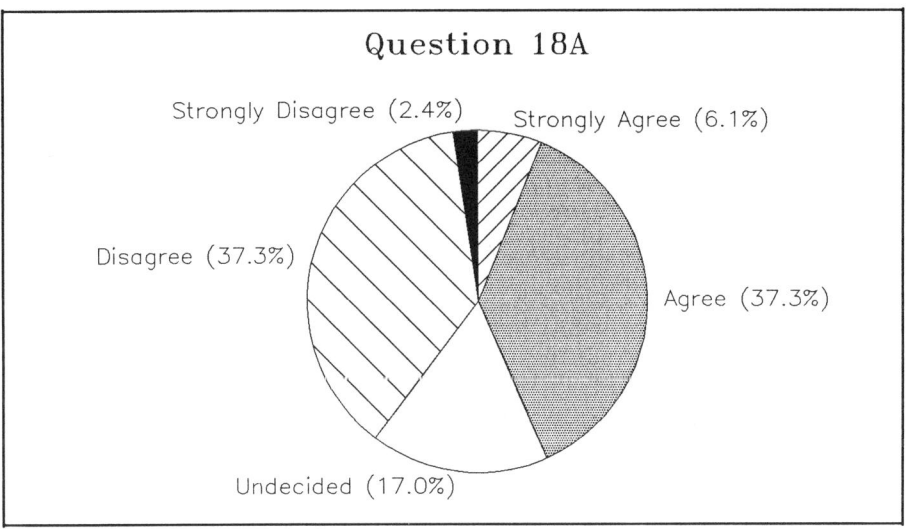

When asked what percentage of annual hard-copy *acquisitions* of basic library materials will be reduced to one copy by the year 2000, the respondents split widely (Q19A). Law deans expected greater changes, but ARL directors had the highest showing (45.2%) in the "Under 25%" response. Seventeen of the 24 scientists stated that under 50% will be reduced. Only 7 of the 24 scientists stated that over 50% of the acquisitions will be reduced. Law deans scored significantly differently from scientists and law librarians who expected greater reductions. On desirability, all the groups found the proposal desirable, although there was a significant number of undecided respondents. Law librarians in finding the trend most desirable scored significantly differently from ARL directors, law deans, and library science professors.

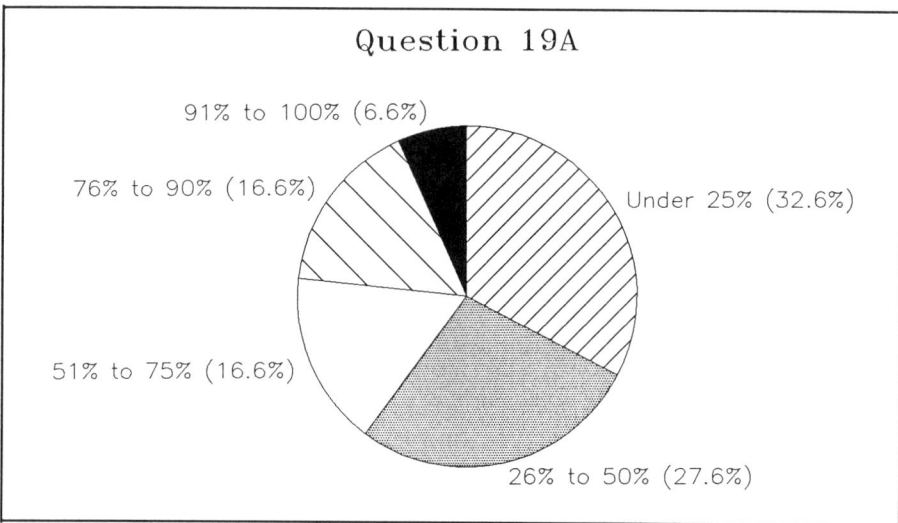

In contrast with acquisitions, the percentage of the hard-copy *collection* of basic library materials that will be reduced to one copy by the year 2000 was perceived as less by the respondents (Q20A). Law librarians displayed a similar attitude on acquisitions and collections, but law deans went to a higher percentage on collections. ARL directors shifted to a lower percentage on the collection question as did the scientists and library science professors. On desirability, law librarians expecting a smaller percentage of reduction scored significantly differently from law deans and library science professors.

When they were asked about the type of library materials they envision for the library in future years, once basic book materials are available in automated form, the respondents expressed no uniformity of opinion (Q21).

Findings of the Questionnaire

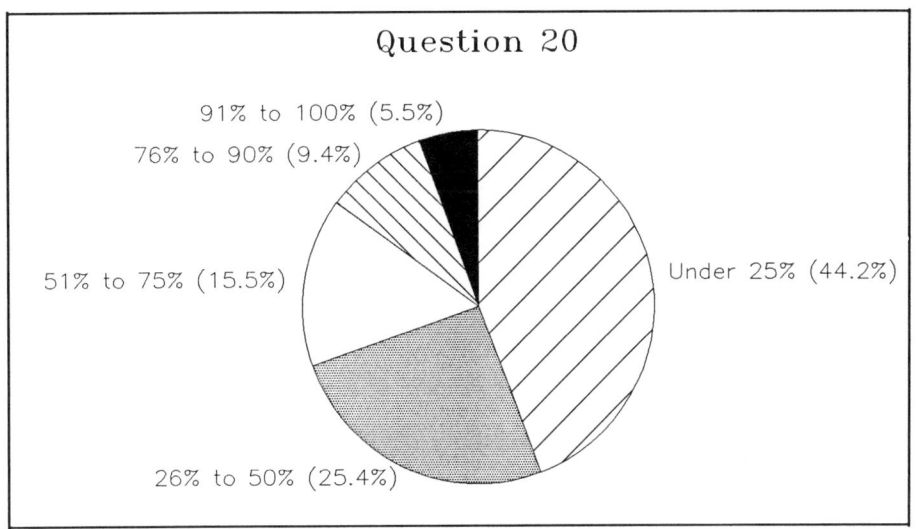

BUDGETING

The respondents (210) split widely on the issue of who would set policy for automated information budgeting (Q22). ARL directors favored librarian control, whereas law deans and law librarians split among the major alternatives. Respondents expected the development to occur by 1990. On the other hand, 189 of 212 respondents felt that automated information budgets will be administered and managed by the librarian (Q23).

The question of separating automated information budgets completely from budgets for library materials and binding received a divided but largely negative response (Q24A). Respondents scored in a similar manner on the desirability question. In regard to agreement and desirability, all groups scored significantly differently from the scientists who agreed with the idea of separating the budgets.

The question "Institutional fiscal officers will continue to allocate substantial funds for automated information though these expenditures generate no tangible hard copy additions to the library" did not seem to trouble the respondents (Q25A and B). Respondents expect this development by 1990.

Comparing the automated information budget with the library materials budget in the year 1990 and beyond, the respondents (206) felt that the automated information budget would be greater, but only by a narrow margin (Q26A). On the other hand, library science professors and scientists expected "more" by a larger margin.

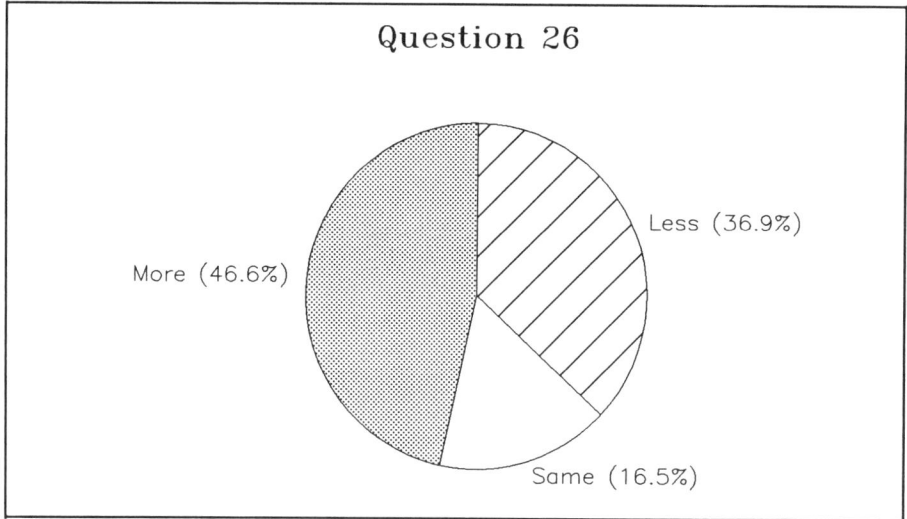

Of 217 respondents a significant majority (123) felt that in light of possible changes in book-collecting policies, there would be special difficulties in acquiring the funding to build a new library building or addition (Q27). Law librarians felt the problem was less acute than did ARL directors and law deans.

The question "In a year in which the allocations are reduced, the budget for automated information should be preserved at the present level; increased; or decreased" produced 87 "preserved" responses, 53 "increased" responses, and 47 "decreased" responses (187 respondents). The splits among the respondent groups proved to be most interesting. The law librarians took a very proautomation stance, whereas the law deans supported the status quo with a split of opinion on the two alternatives. The ARL directors revealed the least overall support for automation. Library science professors were like the law deans in favoring the status quo. The

Findings of the Questionnaire

scientists split with 8 "preserved" responses, 9 "increased" responses, and 8 "decreased" responses.

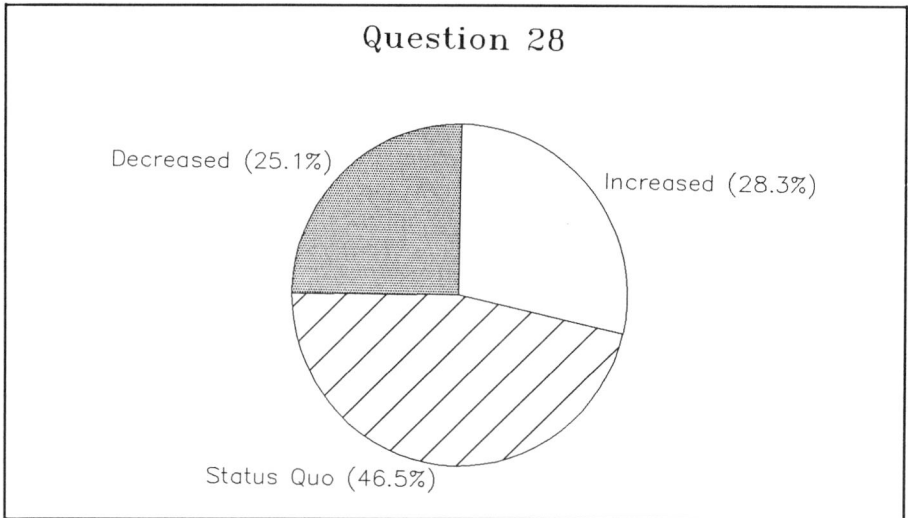

Of the respondents, 63.7% stated that in a year of budget reductions, when the information is available in computer databases, hard copy should be reduced or canceled first as opposed to canceling an information system when the hard copy is available or canceling other materials (Q29). In contrast to the prior question (Q28), the respondent groups were consistent among themselves in their responses. The number of respondents (179) was lower than in the previous questions (Q26 and Q28).

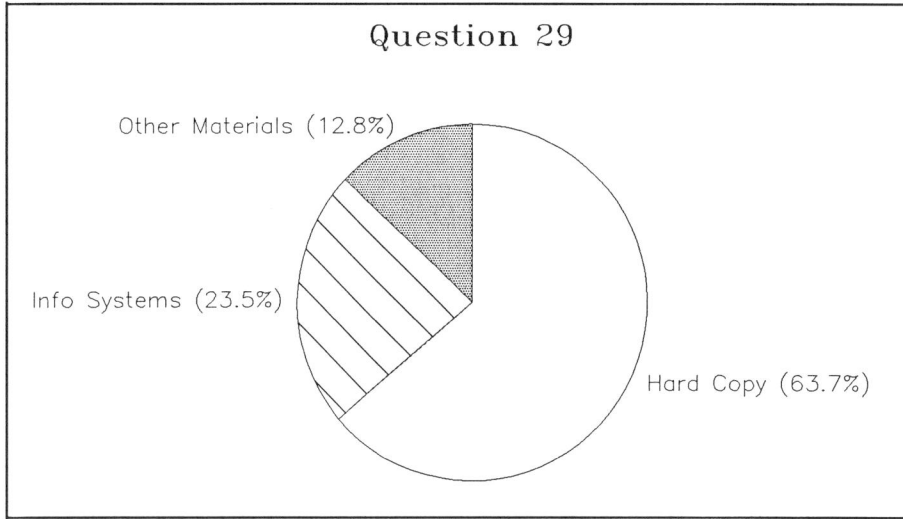

PAYMENT FOR AUTOMATED INFORMATION ACCESS

Faculty

The respondents (212) were widely split on the question of who will absorb the costs of faculty access to automated information (Q30).

It is significant to note that of the 212 respondents only 6 held the faculty alone accountable. Among the four largest groups of responses, there seemed to be agreement that the college or department and the library will carry the principal obligation to furnish faculty with computer access.

In law schools, 14 law deans favored the option of college or department, 12 favored a combination of library and college or department, and 9 favored the library. None of the law deans favored the faculty option. In contrast, 3 law librarians favored the faculty option, 18 favored the college or department, and 11 favored the combination of library and college or department. In sum, the positions of law deans and law librarians were similar.

The respondents generally supported the probability of a formula being devised to determine the amount of access, hardware, and service that should be provided free to faculty (Q31A). Law librarians, law deans, and library science professors gave the proposition strong agreement, but ARL directors tended to be less supportive. ARL directors scored significantly differently from the law deans and law librarians who were more supportive of the formula propositions. The respondents, when asked about the desirability of the proposition, shifted to an attitude of very desirable. Law deans and law librarians in supporting the desirability scored significantly differently from ARL directors and scientists. Respondents expected the development to occur in the 1990s.

The assertion that faculty will have to pay for some of the costs to access on-line information beyond a predetermined reasonable, limited amount received a mixed response (Q32A). Library science professors and networkers in agreeing with the proposition scored significantly differently from law deans, law librarians, and scientists. On the desirability issue, there was a significant shift, particularly among ARL directors and law deans, against the desirability of the development. At the same time there was a slight shift among some law librarians toward favoring the proposition. The majority of respondents felt that the development would occur in the 1990s.

Students

Whereas 122 of the respondents felt that it was desirable or very desirable for faculty members to pay for some of the costs to access on-line information, only 34 respondents felt that students should pay on a per-use basis (Q33B). On the issue of event time for student payment, 48 respondents said that it would never happen. There were no discernible differences among the respondent groups on the basic question of agreement as to the future of the issue (Q33A); in contrast, 155 respondents agreed or strongly agreed that faculty would pay some costs. Law librarians in disagreeing more scored significantly differently from library science professors and networkers, scientists, and ARL directors.

On the question "By 1990 most research university or law school student fees will cover the costs of automated information retrieval, word processing, and other related computer costs in the library" there was a split of opinion (Q34A). Law librarians were more in agreement and ARL directors less so. Law librarians scored significantly differently from ARL directors. On the issue of desirability the respondents shifted with a stronger showing of desirability (Q34B). A similar response in agreement was expressed for the proposition that "the library will provide to students a limited amount of access to automated information free of charge."

Library Patrons (Other than Faculty and Students)

A negative reaction was evoked on the issue of libraries providing free automated information to everyone (Q36A). But on desirability, the respondents were more supportive (Q36B). Law librarians, in being the least in agreement, scored significantly differently from library science professors, networkers, and scientists.

A question on providing of coin-operated machines to patrons received mixed results (Q37A). Generally supported, the proposition had its doubters. Law deans and law librarians followed the broader patterns noted.

PERSONNEL

The respondents of the five groups agreed that increased automation would change the number and/or composition of library staff, that these developments were desirable, and that the events would occur in the 1990s rather than the 2000s. On the issue of agreement, scientists who expressed the most agreement with the idea scored significantly differently from law librarians who were slightly less in agreement. On the issue of desirability, scientists who were most supportive scored significantly differently from law deans who were slightly less so.

The majority of respondents agreed that the number of administrative librarians would remain unchanged or possibly increase. Only the scientists disagreed in that the number would decrease (Q39).

On the other hand, there was a clear indication that respondents agreed that public service librarians would increase in number (Q40A). Only the scientists split differently. Thus, ARL directors, law deans, and law librarians expressed very similar agreement on the future of public service librarians. ARL directors, however, expected the increase to occur earlier than did the law deans, and the law librarians expected the changes even later.

Technical service librarians will decrease in number, according to the groups (Q41A); but the respondents were not as much in agreement with this prediction as with the prediction of the growth of public service librarians. Whereas 75.7% (159) of the respondents predicted an increase in public service staff, the percentages decreased to 59% (125) predicting a decrease in technical service librarians.

The future of support staff is viewed differently by law and nonlaw groups (Q42). Law deans, law librarians, and scientists agreed that support staff would decrease or remain unchanged, whereas ARL directors expected the support staff to increase. Again, ARL directors expected the changes to occur earlier than did the law groups.

The majority of the respondents agreed that the number of library-trained professionals working in library information science programs will increase and that the increase will occur in the 1990s (Q43).

The assertion that "Library-trained professionals should be paid more for expertise in computer use" received very mixed results. Law deans, law librarians, scientists, and library science professors gave limited agreement to the proposal (Q44A). On the other hand, ARL directors reacted with far less agreement, scoring significantly differently from scientists, law librarians, and law deans. When the respondents were queried concerning the desirability of the proposed payment scheme, there was a slight shift from the desirable categories to the undecided and undesirable categories. Respondents stated as well that the proposed events would occur in the 1990s rather than the 2000s.

The proposal that personnel without library training but with computer science training should be paid commensurately with those in the computer specialty received strong agreement (Q45A). Scientists, with higher support, scored significantly differently from law deans. The respondents also found the proposal to be desirable to the same extent (Q45B). These events, according to the respondents, will occur in the 1990s rather than the 2000s.

Respondents agreed that as a result of increased automation and changes in the library, the library will allocate funds for the training and reeducation of library personnel (Q46A). The respondents agreed also on the desirability question (Q46B). Library science professors and networkers, in agreeing the most with the proposal, scored significantly differently from law deans and law librarians. Again, the respondents expected the development to occur in the 1990s (Q46C).

COMPUTER EQUIPMENT

The final section of the questionnaire posed inquiries concerning the future probabilities of faculty members and students owning their own computers or using computers at their institutions. The general thrust of the respondents' answers to the five questions was a positive consensus that faculty and students at all types of institutions will have access to some type of computer terminal, that these developments would be most desirable, and that these events would happen in the mid-1990s. Only the assertion "By 1990 each student will be required to have a personal computer" evoked a more reserved response.

The question (Q48) "Each faculty member will own or be furnished a personal computer or a terminal for information access and word and data processing" received the agreement of the five groups. ARL directors, the least supportive, scored

Findings of the Questionnaire

significantly differently from law deans and law librarians who more strongly agreed.

The two questions (Q49 and Q50) as to whether students would own or be furnished personal computers again generated agreement but less so than the faculty question. On both questions, ARL directors and law librarians scored significantly differently (less agreement) than library science professors and scientists in agreement with the proposals. The third question (Question 51), whether students would be required to have a personal computer, evoked the least agreement. Law librarians, law deans and ARL directors scored significantly differently from scientists, library science professors, and networkers who were more in agreement with the proposal. Furthermore, in the progression from "ownership" to "furnished" to "required" the responses evidenced less agreement. The law librarians and law deans joined the ARL directors as the least supportive, leaving the scientists, library science professors, and networkers as the more supportive of the proposals. The law deans and librarians make a distinction between faculty and students on the issue of computer equipment.

Finally, the respondents' answers split on the question "By the year 1990 which department will be responsible for the computer operation, including budgets, personnel, and equipment?" The largest group (47 or 22.4%) of the total respondents (210) selected college or departmental library. Law deans and law librarians favored "College or departmental library," whereas ARL directors favored "Parent institution library" (10) or a combination of "Parent institution library" and "Computer center" (7) (Q47).

Notes

1. E. Babbie, *The Practice of Social Research,* 4th ed. (Belmont, Calif.: Wadsworth Publishing Co., 1986).
2. L. H. Kidder, Claire Selltiz, Lawrence S. Wrightsman, and Stuart W. Cook, *Research Methods in Social Relations,* 4th ed. (New York: Holt, Rinehart & Winston, 1981).
3. Computing was performed through the use of facilities of the Northeast Regional Data Center of the State University System of Florida, located on the campus of the University of Florida in Gainesville.
4. SPSSX, *User's Guide* (New York: McGraw Hill Co., 1983).

4
Conclusions

A review of the statistical findings of the six sections of the questionnaire reveals a vast array of issues and data susceptible to multiple and perhaps conflicting interpretations. Since each of the 51 questions consists of two or usually three parts, the researcher must reason through approximately 150 questions that relate to agreement, desirability, and time span, and that have been further subanalyzed as to the position that five critical groups have taken on these futuristic issues. There is great variety as well in the nature of questions found in the six sections: some questions are philosophical, some technical, and some managerial. The interpretations of these questions could focus on many aspects ranging from how law deans and law librarians vary from scientists on event time to the differences between ARL directors and law librarians on the future of the book.

The authors have viewed these issues with particular reference to the fundamental issue of what the future holds for libraries. This issue can be seen from a futuristic perspective of computerized information replacing or complementing book materials and from a budgetary perspective of the cost of computer services consuming the acquisitions book budget.

The futuristic studies on the direction of libraries and computers completed to date have focused on the former issue, that is, the future of libraries, as an abstract issue with the usual extremist claims that books will never die or that computerized information will replace all printed materials in short order. In contrast to personal opinions, F. W. Lancaster's fine study *The Impact of a Paperless Society on the Research Library of the Future*[1] represented a Delphic survey of the opinions of librarians, technologists, and publishers concerning the technological and economic feasibility and the actual occurrence and desirability of certain printed materials' being replaced by electronic transmissions. Lancaster's study deserves meritorious comment because it was empirically based and discussed many critical questions. Lancaster in his conclusions posited a possible future information system that resembled more recent descriptions of the electronic workstation and other scenarios descriptive of libraries of the future. Susan H. Crooks's "Libraries in the Year 2000"[2] consisted of creative and graphic scenarios of a printed text service without books (the Classics Reading Company), a public reference service (Reference Questions USA), a community culture center (Metropolis Public Library), a college/university information service (Redbrick University Library), and a research service (The Humanities Research Institute). These scenarios presented glimpses of the interactions between technology and book materials that it is theorized will exist in the year 2000. More recently Gary Kildall, in an interview in *PC Magazine*,[3] predicted that "within the next 15 years, the printed book may be replaced by notebook-style computers with optical disk readers. The reasons are mainly economic. It already costs less to produce a compact disk read-only memory (CD ROM) optical disk platter that holds 550 megabytes--the equivalent of about 200 printed books--than it does to print the same amount of information on paper." Taking a parallel but different perspective, Jack Simpson, president of Mead Data Central, has predicted that "a worldwide megalibrary of electronic information is emerging which will be composed of hundreds of massive, specialized online libraries, each focused on a specific area of knowledge."[4] The scenarios forecasted by Lancaster, Crooks, Kildall, and Simpson, whether based on survey information or the opinions of sophisticated observers,

Conclusions

did not center on many of the futuristic issues that interest us, however.

The three of us, with our primary interest in the future of the library with special concern for the replacement of books by computerized information, the consumption of the acquisitions book budget by automation service costs, and the impact of technology on the overall library or departmental budget, have focused on the opinions of five key groups in regard to the six subject areas set forth in the body of this report. This guaranteed that the opinions would be empirically based and constitute a cross-section of representative opinions.

The following two scenarios describing libraries by the year 2000, one for academic research libraries and one for law libraries, are based upon responses to the questionnaire and indicate the majority opinions of those within the various groups. Although the scenarios are similar in many respects, there are distinguishable characteristics in terms of technology's impact on the size of collections, decisions about acquisitions, electronic information expenditures under leaner budgets, interlibrary loans, numbers of support staff, and payment for faculty and student access to computing.

Scenario for the Academic Research Library by the Year 2000

(Based upon predictions by academic research library directors, library science professors, network directors, scientists, and publishers)

TECHNOLOGY

Books will continue to be published.
Less information will be published in book formats.
More information will be available in multimedia formats.
More information will be available in electronic formats.

Microform will be replaced by information in electronic formats.

Information available only through a computer will be acceptable copy.

Computer technologies will improve access to appropriate electronic information.

Distributed databases will replace on-line electronic information.

Disk technology will provide information retrieval capability superior to on-line systems.

Disk format will replace under 25% of hard copy.

Interactive television, cable, or videotext systems will not replace the library as an information resource.

Newer technology will provide faster, less expensive access to electronic information.

Automated library technology will consist of a combination of personal computers, on-line information systems, and disks.

LIBRARY POLICY

Book collections will not be reduced in size as more electronic information becomes available.

Interlibrary loans may not be affected by the increase in electronic information.

Library services will be a mix of the traditional type with instruction in accessing electronic information.

On-line catalog use will increase demand for document delivery.

Student fees may or may not cover costs for access and other related computer costs.

The role of libraries will continue as a general information resource of hard-copy materials combined with a new role of providing electronic information.

Conclusions

Increased automated information will slow the rate of growth of acquisitions.

Increase in electronic information will not necessarily reduce acquisitions to one hard copy.

Under 25% of annual acquisitions will be reduced to one hard copy.

Under 25% of hard-copy collections will be reduced to one copy.

Library collections, like present ones, will consist of a variety of materials: hard copy, disks, and software.

In a year of reduced budgets hard-copy materials should be reduced or canceled first.

The number of administrative librarians will remain unchanged.

The number of public service librarians will increase.

The number of technical service librarians will decrease.

The number of support staff will increase.

The number of professionals working in the libraries' information science programs will increase.

Librarians will be the beneficiaries of funds allocated for training and reeducation.

It is unclear which university unit will be responsible for the computer operations budget by 1990.

ECONOMICS

On-line information may not be affordable by most people.

The librarian will set electronic information budgeting policy.

The librarian will administer and manage the electronic information budget.

Electronic information budgets will be combined with library materials budgets.

Institutional fiscal officers will continue to allocate funds for electronic information access even though no tangible, permanent product is produced.

- Librarians are divided in opinion on the size of future budgets for electronic information as compared with library materials budgets. Nonlibrarians indicate that electronic information budgets will be larger.
- Library building funds will become more difficult to justify as emphasis on electronic information resources increases and hard-copy collections are reduced.
- In a year of reduced budgets, the automated information budget should be preserved. (The largest percentage of library directors, however, indicated a preference for decreased automated information budgets.)
- Costs of faculty access to automated information will be absorbed by a combination of library, college or department, and faculty funds.
- A formula will be devised to determine the amount of access, hardware, and services provided free to faculty, although library directors may disagree and consider this undesirable.
- Faculty will have to pay some costs of access to automated information that exceeds a reasonable amount; however, this is considered undesirable.
- Students may or may not pay per-use costs to access information. Students' paying the costs would be undesirable.
- Student fees to cover costs for access and other related computer costs probably will be determined on an institution-by-institution basis. No majority opinion was discernible.
- A limited amount of access will be provided free to students.

PUBLIC POLICY

- Patrons will accept information in computer formats when that is the only form available.

Libraries have no obligation to provide information to patrons free of charge even if the information is available only in electronic form.

The library will provide a mechanism for patrons to pay for access.

Each faculty member will own or be furnished a computer for information access and word processing.

Most students will own personal computers upon enrolling in college.

Each student who does not have a computer will be furnished one.

Students will not be required to have personal computers.

Scenario for the Law Library by the Year 2000

(Based upon predictions by law librarians and law deans)

TECHNOLOGY

Books will continue to be published.

Less information will be published in book formats.

More information will be available in multimedia formats.

More information will be available in electronic formats.

Microform will be replaced by information in electronic formats.

Computer technology will provide for analyzing queries and switching to appropriate databases.

Distributed databases will coexist with on-line information sources.

Disk technology will replace approximately 25% of hard copy.

Interactive television will not replace libraries as information sources.

Newer technology will provide information faster and cheaper.

Library technology will be characterized by a combination of networking personal computers, on-line databases, and disks.

Technology will have an impact upon numbers and composition of library personnel.

LIBRARY POLICY

Less borrowing from libraries will occur.

Librarians will provide traditional types of services along with guidance in computer use.

There will be more demand for document delivery because of on-line catalogs that are available to patrons.

Libraries will function in a dual capacity as general information resources and as computer-based information resources.

Rate of growth of hard-copy acquisitions will decline.

Basic library acquisitions will be reduced to one hard copy.

Approximately 25% of basic library acquisitions will be reduced to one hard copy.

Under 25% of the basic collections will be reduced to one hard copy.

After basic collections are available in electronic form, collections will consist of treatise-type hard copy and some software and computers.

The number of administrative librarians will remain unchanged.

Public service librarians will increase in numbers.

Technical service librarians will decrease in numbers.

Support staff will remain the same or decrease slightly.

The number of library-trained professionals will increase.

Librarians will be responsible for computer operation, budget, and equipment.

Conclusions

ECONOMICS AND FINANCES

Electronic information may not be priced low enough so that everyone can afford to access it.

Budget policy will be set by the librarian and dean.

Librarians will manage the library/computer budget.

Electronic information budgets will be a part of the library materials budget.

Institutional fiscal officers will continue to allocate funds for electronic information even though no hard copy results.

Electronic information funding as compared with library materials budget dollars is unpredictable. Both librarians and deans responded in nearly identical numbers to the "more" and "less" categories. The category "same" had a low response rate.

Changes in book collection policies resulting from new technologies will have a negative impact upon new-building funding requests.

Electronic information allocations will be preserved at present levels even if the library materials budget is reduced.

In a year of reduced budgets, hard-copy materials will be canceled first when information is available in electronic format.

Faculty access to electronic information probably will be paid by the college, although in some institutions the library or the faculty will pay.

Formulas will be developed for determining how much to allocate to each faculty for computer expenditures.

Faculty will have to pay some costs for access if they exceed a reasonable amount.

Students will not pay a per-use charge for information access.

Fees or tuition will cover the costs of student computer services.

A limited amount of free access will be provided to students.

Library-trained professionals with computer expertise will be paid higher salaries.

Computer-trained specialists will be paid on the same salary scale as their computer-trained colleagues.

Libraries will fund training programs for staff.

The library director will be responsible for the computer budget.

PUBLIC POLICY

Patrons will accept information in electronic formats when that is the only form available.

Libraries have no obligation to provide free legal information to patrons even if the information is available only in electronic format.

Libraries may provide coin-operated systems so patrons may pay.

Faculty will be furnished personal computers or terminals for information access and word processing.

Students enrolling in college will own personal computers or terminals.

A student who does not have a personal computer or terminal will be supplied with access to one.

Students will not be required to possess personal computers or terminals.

Scenario for Libraries beyond the Year 2000

A review of the respondents' opinions and personal comments on the questionnaire indicates a set of strong perceptions and predictions as to the future of libraries for the period of 1986 through 2000 and then greater uncertainty about the post-2000 period. Apparently, the respondents exemplify the commonly held view that one can readily predict over a five- or ten-year period but that beyond that time, the task of predicting becomes hazardous. At the same time, the

Conclusions

subject of the future of libraries is so fascinating and so important that we must direct our interest to this area.

We have already seen some of the respondents' speculations about the post-2000 period:

1. A large majority of the respondents agreed that the publication of printed books will continue to increase in the future despite the increase of publication of information in computerized formats (60.4% of respondents chose post-2000, 31.5% chose 2000, and 8.1% chose 1990; Q1A).
2. Of the respondents, 43.9% concluded that book collections of libraries of the future will be reduced in size as more information becomes available in computerized formats in the post-2000 era, and 43.5% forecast that this would occur by the year 2000 (43.9% chose post-2000, 29% chose 2000, 14.5% chose 1990, and 13.5% chose never; Q2A).
3. Only 29.8% of the respondents felt that in the post-2000 period more people will buy the information they want to read in a computer-generated format and will borrow less from a library. A larger percentage (54.5%) thought this would occur in this century (29.8% chose post-2000, 32.5% chose 2000, 22% chose 1990, and 15.7% chose never; Q3A).
4. Although the largest single group of respondents (39.8%) agreed that in the future, the services that librarians provide patrons will be predominantly guidance in retrieving information in the nonbook format, an almost equal number (38.7%) expect this to occur prior to post-2000 (39.8% chose post-2000, 28.2% chose 2000, 10.5% chose 1990, and 21.5% chose never; Q4A).
5. The majority of the respondents rejected the prediction that interactive television, cable systems, or on-line systems, like Viewtron or other videotex systems will replace the library as an information resource (25.9% chose post-2000, 10.2% chose 2000, 1.8% chose 1990, and 62% chose never; Q13A).

6. Comparing the automated information budget with the library materials budget in the year 1990 and beyond, respondents said that the automated budget will be more (46.6%), same (16.5%), or less (36.9%).
7. A large majority of the respondents chose a dual role for the libraries beyond 1990, consisting of: (A) a continued role as general information resource, and (B) a new role as computer-based information guide (8.2% chose A and 3.7% chose B. The C option combined A and B at 88.17%; Q16A).

Respondents' opinions on the future of the book indicate that library collections in the post-2000 period will be multimedia in nature with large book holdings coexisting with computer facilities. The next two questions, though, show that the respondents hesitated to set the exact mix of books and computer services that will be available. It is difficult to determine the reason for the hesitancy. The responses on questions 4 and 5 indicate that the same respondents rejected the opinions that computer services will totally displace paper information resources. Question 6 again indicates that the respondents were split on the future mixture of book and computer services, although they were aware of and sensitive to the growing importance of automation costs. Question 7 is most important in that the respondents overwhelmingly selected a combination role for future libraries and arguably rejected extremist views of the future of the library.

Thus, we are left with a view of the respondents consisting of strong enthusiasm for the new technologies but with some exceptions, combined with a middle-of-the-road acceptance of the probability of the growth of all media in the future decades. The respondents expect the new technology to make its greater effects in the post-2000 period, but anticipate many significant changes in the pre-2000 era.

Authors' Commentary

As cited in this report, respected authorities in the library profession predict dramatic changes in libraries by the turn of the century.[5] Some even venture that libraries will become paperless or disappear altogether.[6] Some respondents to the instant questionnaire agree with many of the forecasts; but the area of strongest concurrence is that books will continue to be published simultaneously with increased electronic information into the post-2000 era.

Electronic publication and communications might contribute to the declining influence of libraries. Although it is true that these two factors are escalating in quality and utilization, surprisingly the outcome is an increase in paper products. Both transmission of information and desktop publishing enhance the ability to accumulate better and more accurate data and publish faster and easier than ever before. More titles are available in hard copy each year, not less. The new capability of publishing a single title in several media suggests a creative approach to meeting the various expectations of readers and librarians. Thus, predictions of the decline or demise of books and libraries at least in the pre-2000 span are not substantiated by this report.

Except for a few institutions on the leading edge of the technology, there appears to be slow momentum toward changing the way academic research libraries will be operating by the year 2000. As predicted, the most evident changes are occurring in technical processes: in automating library procedures, not accessing substantive information. Thus, for a number of reasons, academic research libraries may not witness changes in the near future as rapidly as anticipated.

Size, diversity, and depth of subject content of academic library collections will continue to operate as barriers to total conversion to electronic information formats. When the new disk technology was first announced, tales of storing all the information in the Library of Congress on disks that would fit into one or several drawers in a filing cabinet abounded. A jukebox type of hardware would provide access to all that information either in a library or at an individual's workstation. Very little has been accomplished in the several years since these pronouncements were made, and few full-text databases have become available. Those databases that are on the market usually consist of access tools. This would tend to indicate that there is no real demand or the economy is not ripe for general, full-text electronic information now or in the near future. Also, it appears that many librarians cannot justify the cost or are reluctant to use the on-line or disk technology. Disks have not been widely accepted by librarians, and many are skeptical about introducing the technology in libraries. Disks require patrons to use disk readers in libraries, and multiple disks require multiple stations to spread that use. Some have expressed concern about CD ROM technology, indicating that it may not be the panacea once thought. Thus, it remains unclear if significant full-text information conversion either on disk or on-line will be available to academic libraries prior to the year 2000.

The commercial sector plays a major role in determining what information will be produced in a particular format. If conversion to an electronic format is not considered economically viable or marketable, the information probably will remain in existing hard-copy formats. Much of the retrospective collections of academic libraries will fall into this category, requiring patrons to visit libraries to utilize these collections. Librarians perhaps will band together and seek support from the scholars in the various disciplines to ensure that essential information is converted to electronic formats. Improved scanning devices may offer a solution to the stalemate before the end of the century, which could change the entire picture.

If the conversion to electronic formats continues at a slow pace, academic research library directors may not be faced with major fiscal decisions of budgeting for hard-copy acquisitions in competition with electronic information accessed in the library. Even when they are faced with this dilemma, more librarian respondents indicate that they would

Conclusions

resolve this problem in favor of hard copy. Access services of on-line databases such as on Dialog, disks, and other sources, along with documents on demand services, however, are becoming very popular with faculty and students. This factor will play a major role in fiscal planning in the future as more scholars desire access to these research tools and expect the institutions to absorb the costs of information retrieval. Librarians and administrators will have to face the more difficult challenge of allocating resources for individualized research at a workstation of choice, which may be in the library, office, or elsewhere, and consider the sacrifice of other acquisitions that could be more evenly spread over the university community.

In academic libraries in which costs of electronic information access are closely monitored and a few individuals are delegated the responsibility for searching, the opportunity for using the technology is very limited. Librarians who are restricted to the use of specific technology and are not permitted to experiment with computers beyond their assigned duties may find themselves in a type of environment that creates an inertia among the staff that is difficult or impossible to overcome. Much compartmentalization exists on library staffs today and impedes advancement into the new technology.

As professional staffs emerge as tomorrow's information specialists, they will play a prominent role in selecting, organizing, and retrieving information in the traditional sources and in the electronic formats. New skills in understanding, creating, and managing information, communications, systems, and planning will evolve. More individuals, calling themselves information specialists but lacking library training, will be offering information retrieval services. Librarians will recognize the importance of obtaining the necessary skills to become competitive and to function in the information age. Library and information science schools will design new models of library practice for the next generation of library scholars. New programs will shift emphasis to access of information from the traditional acquisitions functions. Proper training of professional library staff through formal education, institutes, seminars, and professionally sponsored meetings will be vital to give librarians the opportunity to participate in bringing technology into the libraries' future.

In spite of these barriers, librarians' interests and enthusiasm remain high, judging from the number of articles currently appearing in leading library journals and other publications. It is perceived at least by some of our respondents that major changes in academic libraries will be evident by the year 2000.

In contrast, many law school deans and librarians anticipate that new technology will have a major impact on legal libraries. The almost complete acceptance and adoption of computer technology in law schools will promote the continued acquisition of the latest technology for the law school community.

A principal advantage in producing electronic information for the legal profession is that law is a specific discipline with a field of basic legal titles well indexed and well known to the legal community. Legal scholars are familiar with the research tools and know how to conduct legal research; therefore, they welcome the improved rapid access to information through the electronic media.

Law is the only field in which vast quantities of full-text electronic information are available for research. That the legal community has accepted on-line information databases as reliable research resources is no longer questioned. Two major companies produce legal databases of electronic information that are contributing to the enormous success of technology in the legal field. At the beginning of this decade only a few subscriptions to Mead Data Central's LEXIS and West Publishing Company's WESTLAW were held by law schools. Today all law schools acknowledge these systems as an integral, mandatory aspect of the libraries' programs. In the future these two systems will contain full texts of all basic legal resources, obviating the necessity for law libraries to possess these materials in multiple hard copies. It is likely that by the turn of the century many law school libraries, except perhaps for a few spacious ones, will have made substantial reductions in their hard-copy serial acquisitions and collections.

Beyond these full-text programs, other databases are becoming available. The recent response to the information access offering of INFOTRAC and LEGALTRAC on laser disk at a cost far greater than hard copy serves as an extremely successful introduction of the disk technology to law school library patrons. Other databases of interest to law schools have been announced. These successful introductory legal products will spur interest in additional experimentation and production of data on disks.

The on-line and disk legal databases are very popular with the law school community primarily because they do not cost the faculty and students money directly and they are available for use at almost the same hours as the library is open. Faculty use of on-line databases can be extended beyond library confines and hours. Students, too, will be using on-line services outside the library before the year 2000. Undoubtedly, the enthusiastic acceptance of these systems will promote further developments. In the future readers may anticipate in-depth, full-text treatment of specific subject areas in the electronic format.

These different systems are accepted by law librarians, too, as they are offered on an annual subscription rate that simplifies budgeting and controls expenditures. Most frequently the costs are absorbed in the library materials budgets, but in other instances librarians seek special funds for database services to protect the book funds against depletion. Internal budgeting politics of each institution probably will continue to determine the source of funding for electronic information.

Again, many law libraries today are providing information access services other than LEXIS and WESTLAW to faculty and students. A direct charge may or may not accompany this service. The prime benefit for the law school community is access to a growing number of peripheral databases. In the future many more competitors will offer databases of keen interest. Charges for some of these will be based on an educational rate for law libraries, a unique advantage for law schools. Because of the proliferation of substantive law and related databases, expenditures for electronic information will increase more rapidly than for all other library materials, and in the post-2000 years these expenditures may equal or exceed all other library materials.

Accompanying our questionnaire was a request for figures for law library expenditures for bibliographic and information retrieval by computer. Since the returns did not represent all law school libraries, these estimates may not reflect the actual total expenditures for all accredited law schools. But in the earliest year for which figures are available, 1975-76, approximately $20,000 was reported as having been spent.

In the years that followed, the estimated sums expended by law libraries on information retrieval and bibliographic services increased:

1976-77	$103,000
1977-78	$295,700
1978-79	$755,000

In subsequent years, the expenditures were reported to and published by the American Bar Association:

1979-80	$1,812,523
1980-81	$2,478,964
1981-82	$3,236,515
1982-83	$4,343,704
1983-84	$5,582,944
1984-85	$6,665,770
1985-86	$7,335,056

Thus, law libraries are spending more dollars each year on electronic information. If this trend continues, law libraries will be spending three times as much on electronic information retrieval and bibliography by the year 2000.

An analysis of the figures for 1985-86 indicates that law libraries as a whole are not spending a large percentage of their budgets on information retrieval as yet. The 2 largest spenders are allocating 36.7% and 28.7% of their library materials budget to information retrieval, and the next 18 largest spenders are allocating between 18.9% and 11.4% of their budgets to this area. Of the remaining libraries, 154 are spending less than 11.4% of their budgets on information retrieval. But these figures are increasing and leave little doubt that in the future larger sums and proportions of the library materials budgets will be spent on electronic information. It appears that the expenditures for electronic information will continue to rise until eventually these amounts will be greater than expenditures for other library materials.

The law school library of the future will evolve out of the changing environment. Book collections will come under scrutiny as librarians reexamine collection policies, budgets, and space. As more information becomes available in electronic form, many of the original source materials, published serially, that are now prominently displayed for convenient intensive use will be relegated to remote locations as backup, and multiple copies will be removed. Today's law libraries look alike with long rows of serials occupying the majority of prime shelf space. Tomorrow's libraries will house large treatise-type collections in the most prominent areas, catering to the special interests of faculty and students of individual institutions. Treatises that are read from cover to cover will become the focal point of law library collections. In addition to book collections, law libraries will maintain extensive collections of information disks and manuals as well as software for use, circulation, or copying.

Scholars' workstations will occupy floor space now dedicated to tables and carrels. Faculty and students will use these for convenience in augmenting work begun at their residential workstations.

Undoubtedly, at the turn of the century, academic law library functions will be automated. Already a large number of law libraries are fully automated or contemplating the installation of an integrated library system. Again, the fact that law libraries are generally smaller than academic libraries may account for the significant progress they are making. Piggybacking on the parent institution's library system may reduce costs and hassles for law libraries. The popularity of automated library systems along with the capability of sharing resources, information, and messages will spur remaining law librarians to press for automated systems.

Training of professional law librarians as information specialists already is recognized as vital to the successful operation of law libraries. Library schools, professional associations, and electronic information providers will continue to sponsor programs regularly to benefit those who are most closely associated with information systems. Close ties among users, subscribers, providers, and compilers will continue so as to ensure proper use, training, and experience with information retrieval systems.

Obviously, librarians and administrators face many difficult issues in the next ten to fifteen years. Will the library exist without walls, as a paperless institution, as a less-paper entity? How will technology, library budgets, and space problems be resolved? There seems to be overwhelming agreement that technology already has had a major impact on libraries and library staffs and will play an even more significant role in years to come on information dimensions, budgeting, and library services. Forecasting for the future of a given library, or libraries generally, is challenging, for no one really knows what the future will bring. In 1980 few would have predicted the explosive interest, frenzied buying, and dramatic cost reduction of personal computers; yet these events, more than any other, have catapulted librarians into the technological era. The pressure to accelerate the automation of information and libraries arises in part out of the desire of

Conclusions

personal computer owners to exploit the potential of their workstations in the academic pursuit of knowledge.

Policies and budgets set for libraries and information centers today should reflect the known technological advancement of the past and retain the flexibility to incorporate the unknown, but anticipated, innovations of the future. This is not a profound revelation to librarians, for this is the way they have been implementing policy decisions for years. Rapidly changing technology, however, and its associated impact on academic institutions make reliable forecasting imperative. A broad perspective and vision for libraries must encompass things yet to come in order to accommodate them within the existing library environment. This is vital to the survival of libraries and library services.

Notes

1. F. W. Lancaster, *The Impact of a Paperless Society on the Research Library of the Future* (Springfield, Va.: NTIS, 1980), 99.
2. Susan H. Crooks, "Libraries in the Year 2000," in *Document Delivery--Background Papers Commissioned by the Network Advisory Committee*, Network Planning Paper, no. 7 (Washington, D.C.: Network Development Office, Library of Congress, 1982).
3. Ron Jeffries, "Goodbye, Gutenberg," *PC Magazine* 4, no. 95 (12 November 1985).
4. Jack Simpson, "Simpson Sees Emergence of Worldwide Electronic Megalibrary," *Advanced Technology/Libraries* 14, no. 3 (June 1985).
5. Barbara B. Moran, *Academic Libraries: The Changing Knowledge Centers of Colleges and Universities* (Washington, D.C.: ERIC) 1984), 4.
6. David A. Thomas, "The 'Paperless Law Library' in the United States," *Law Librarian: Bulletin of the British and Irish Association of Law Libraries* 17, nos. 13-17 (April 1986).

Selected Bibliography

The selected bibliography covers the years 1982-87. It builds on the references in the study *The Impact of a Paperless Society on the Research Library of the Future* by F. W. Lancaster, Laura Drasgow, and Ellen Macks published in 1979 and the 2,500-entry *Automation in Libraries LITA Bibliography 1978-1982* compiled by Anne G. Adler et al. published in 1983.

BIBLIOGRAPHIES

Adler, Anne G., Elizabeth A. Baker, Li Ai L. Lee, Rita M. Marsales, and Jean R. Swanson, comps. *Automation in Libraries: A LITA Bibliography, 1978-1982.* Ann Arbor, Mich.: Pierian, 1983.

Bewsey, Julia J. *Microcomputers and Libraries: An Annotated Bibliography.* CompuBibs, no. 8. New York: Vantage Information Consultants, 1985.

ARTICLES

"AAP Electronic Manuscript Project Moves Forward." *ASIS Bulletin* 10 (August 1984):6.

Abbott, G. L. "Video-based Information Systems in Academic Library Media Centers." *Library Trends* 34 (Summer 1985):151-59.

Adams, John, and Adams, Robin. "Videotex and Teletext: New Roles for Libraries." *Wilson Library Bulletin* 57 (November 1982):206-11.

Anderson, M. R. A. "A Telecommunications Primer for Microcomputer Users." *Show-Me Libraries* 36 (September 1985):12-16; 37 (October-November 1985):20-22.

Andrews, G. "Cable-and Fireless? This Time the Profession Must Overcome Its Technological Inertia." *Library Association Record* 84 (November 1982):387.

Artandi, Susan. "Computers and the Postindustrial Society: Symbiosis or Information Tyranny?" *Journal of the American Society for Information Science* 33 (September 1982):303-7.

Aveney, Brian. "Electronic Publishing and Library Technical Services." *Library Resources & Technical Services* 1 (January-March 1984):68-75.

Badertscher, D. G. "Examination of the Dynamics of Change in Information Technology as Viewed from Law Libraries and Information Centers." *Law Library Journal* 75 (Spring 1982):198-211.

Badler, Mitchell. "COM: A Records Medium for the '80s." *Information and Records Management* 16 (January 1982):23, 24, 26.

Bagnall, R. S., and Hench, J. B. "Are We Prepared for the Technological Revolution in Scholarly Research?" *Change* 15 (July-August 1983):38-42.

Banks, R. L. "COM vs. Optical Disk: Where's the Beef?" *Journal of Information and Image Management* 19 (February 1986):21-23.

Bardes, D. "Video Technology: Conveying Information Visually." *Wilson Library Bulletin* 59 (April 1985):523-26.

Borrell, J. "Developments in Electronic Publishing." *ASIS Bulletin* 8 (June 1982):11-15.

Boss, Richard. "Microcomputers in Libraries: The Quiet Revolution." *Wilson Library Journal* 59 (June 1985):653-60.

_____. "Technology and the Modern Library." *Library Journal* 109 (15 June 1984):1183-89.

Brisco, Peter; Bodtke-Roberts, Alice; Douglas, Nancy; Heinold, Michele; Koller, Nancy; and Peirce, Roberta. "Ashurbanipal's Enduring Archetype: Thoughts on the Library's Role in the Future." *College & Research Libraries* 47 (March 1986):121-26.

Brown, R. L. "Copyright and Computer Databases: The Case of Bibliographic Utility." *Rutgers Computer & Technology Law Journal* 11 (1985):17-49.

Brownrigg, E. B., and Lynch, C. A. "Electrons, Electronic Publishing, and Electronic Display." *Information Technology & Libraries* 4 (September 1985):201-7.

Brownrigg, Edwin; Lynch, Clifford; and Engle, Mary. "Technical Services in the Age of Electronic Publishing." *Library Resources and Technical Services* 28 (January-March 1984):59-67.

Butler, Brett. "Online Public Access: The Sleeping Beast Awakens." *ASIS Bulletin* 10 (December 1983):6-10.

Butler, M. A. "Electronic Publishing and Its Impact on Libraries: A Literature Review." *Library Resources and Technical Services* 28 (January 1984):41-58.

_____. "Publishers, Technological Change, and Copyright: Maintaining the Balance." *Drexel Library Quarterly* 20 (Summer 1984):28-41.

Campbell, N. A. "On Paperless-ness." *Canadian Library Journal* 41 (August 1984):181-86.

Cooke, E. D. "ALA Statement on Cable Communications Act of 1982." *Information Technology and Libraries* 1 (September 1982):291-94.

Corcoran, Mary; Hlava, Majorie; and Kelly, Jane, eds. "Special Issue: Online." *Special Libraries* 76 (Spring 1985):81-127.

Cornish, E. "Library of the Future." *Futurist* 19 (December 1985):2, 39.

Cortez, Edwin M. "Library Automation and Management Information Systems." *Journal of Library Administration* 4 (Fall 1983):21-33.

Costigan, K. "Memory Takes a Quantum Leap." *Science Digest* 93 (Fall 1985):24.

Couric, E. "Electronic Mail Means Instant Delivery." *ABA Journal* 71 (January 1985):96-99.

Dahlin, R. "Electronic Publishing Steps Forward and Back." *Publishers Weekly* 221 (4 June 1982):26-31.

Dale, J. "Libraries and Telecommunications." *Nebraska Library Association Quarterly* 14 (Winter 1983):12-13.

Dealy, John F. "Telecommunications: Policy Issues and Options for the 1980's." *Brookings Review* 1 (Winter 1982):30-33.

De Gennaro, R. "Libraries, Technology and the Information Marketplace." *Library Journal* 107 (1 June 1982):1045-54.

_____. "Into the Information Age: Report of the Director of Libraries, University of Pennsylvania, 1982-3." Philadelphia: University of Pennsylvania *Almanac* insert, 17 January 1983.

_____. "Shifting Gears: Information Technology and the Academic Library." *Library Journal* 109 (15 June 1984):1204-9.

Desroches, Richard A. and Rudd, Marie. "Shelf Space Management: A Microcomputer Application." *Information Technology and Libraries* 2 (June 1983):187-89.

Diebler, M. "Library Superstation: A Guide to Satellite Earth Stations." *Information Technology and Libraries* 1 (September 1982):231-37.

_____. "Video-teleconferencing for Libraries and Librarians." *American Libraries* 13 (October 1982):599-600.

Dougherty, R. "The Computer Revolution in Research Libraries." *UNESCO Courier* 38 (February 1985):26-27.

Dougherty, R. M., and Lougee, W. P. "As Electronic Publishing Evolves and Libraries Adapt to It, What Will Survive?" *Library Journal* 110 (February 1985):41-44.

Durance, C. J., and others. "iNet Canadian Libraries: New Telecommunications Facilities for Libraries and Information Services." *Canadian Journal of Information Science* 7 (June 1982):1-10.

Eastman, Ann H. "Books, Publishing, Libraries in the Information Age." *Library Trends* 33 (Fall 1984):121-47.

"Electronic Mail: A New Communications Alternative." *Management Information Service Report* 17 (October 1985):1-19.

"Electronic Publishing." *Publishers Weekly* 226 (23 November 1984):29-58.

Elmer-Dewitt, P. "Terminals among the Stacks." *Time*, 25 February 1985, 92.

Ertel, Monica M. "Microcomputers in Libraries." *Special Libraries* 75 (April 1984):95-101.

Farr, R. C. "The Local Area Network (LAN) and Library Automation." *Library Journal* 108 (15 November 1983):2130-32.

Farrington, J. W. "Video Disc: A Versatile New Storage Medium." *Serials Librarian* 7 (Winter 1982): 35-40.

Fersko-Weiss, H. "Electronic Mail: The Emerging Connection." *Personal Computer* 9 (January 1985):71-74+.

Fields, H. "Cooperation Urged for LC Disk Program." *Publishers Weekly* 228 (29 November 1985):15.

Gale, J. C. "Use of Optical Disks for Information Storage and Retrieval." *Information Technology and Libraries* 3 (December 1984):379-82.

Goldstein, Charles M. "Computer-Based Information Storage Technologies." In *Annual Review of Information Science and Technology*, edited by Martha E. Williams, 19:65-96. White Plains, N.Y.: Knowledge Industry Publications, 1984.

Green, W. "Information Revolution and the Future of Libraries: Toward a Paperless Future." *Kentucky Libraries* 48 (Fall 1984):14-20.

Gregory, G. "The Vital Connection." *World Press Review* 32 (January 1985):36-37.

Grieves, R. T. "Short Circuiting Reference Books." *Time*, 13 June 1983, 76.

Griffiths, Jose-Marie, and King, Donald. "Educating the Information Professional of the Future." In *1984 Challenges to an Information Society: Proceedings of the 47th ASIS Annual Meeting*, edited by Barbara Flood, Joanne Witiak, and Thomas H. Hogan, 21:68-73. White Plains, N.Y.: Knowledge Industry Publications, 1984.

Grimes, G. H., ed. "Electronic Library." *Media Spectrum* 9 (1982):3-15.

Grossman, David. "Electronic Publishing: Eight Trends of '84." In *ALA Yearbook*, edited by Robert Wedgeworth, 10:111-12. Chicago, Ill.: American Library Association, 1985.

"The Growth of Library Networks." *Special Libraries* 73 (January 1982):1-38.

Guskin, Alan E.; Stoffle, Carla J.; and Baruth, Barbara E. "Library Future Shock: The Microcomputer Revolution and the New Role of the Library." *College and Research Libraries* 45 (May 1984):177-83.

Haar, J. M. "The Policies of Information: Libraries and Online Retrieval Systems." *Library Journal* 111 (1 February 1986):40-43.

Haas, W. J. "Computing in Documentation and Scholarly Research." *Science* 215 (12 February 1982):857-61.

Hancock, P. M. C. "Computers-in-House Databases and Their Uses." *New Library Journal* 135 (18 October 1985):1042-44.

Hegarty, K. "Myths of Library Automation." *Library Journal* 110 (1 October 1985):43-49.

Helgerson, Linda W. "CD-ROM: A Revolution in the Making." *Library Hi Tech* 4 (Spring 1986):23-27.

Hernon, Peter. "Provision of Federal Government Publications in Electronic Format to Depository Libraries." *Government Information Quarterly* 2 (1985):231-34.

Herther, Nancy. "Access to Information: An Optical Disk Solution." *Wilson Library Bulletin* 60 (May 1986):19-21.

──────. "CD-ROM Technology: A New Era for Information Storage and Retrieval." *Online* 9 (November 1985):17-28.

Hickey, Thomas B., and Calabrese, Andrew M. "Electronic Document Delivery: OCLC's Prototype System." *Library Hi Tech* 4 (Spring 1986):65-71.

Hildreth, Charles R. "Online Public Access Catalogs." In *Annual Review of Information Science and Technology*, edited by Martha E. Williams, 20:233-85. White Plains, N.Y.: Knowledge Industry Publications, 1985.

Hills, P. J. "The Scholarly Communication Process." In *Annual Review of Information Science and Technology*, edited by Martha E. Williams, 18:99 125. White Plains, N.Y.: Knowledge Industry Publications, 1983.

Hunter, Karen A. "Electronic Delivery of Scientific Information." *Drexel Library Quarterly* 20 (Summer 1984):75-86.

Hurly, P. "The Promise and Perils of Videotex." *Futurist* 19 (April 1985):7-13.

Igwe, P. O. E. "The Electronic Age and Libraries: Present Problems and Future Prospects." *International Library Review* 18 (January 1986):75-84.

Information Systems Consultants, Inc. *Videodisc and Optical Digital Disk Technologies and Their Applications in Libraries: A Report to the Council on Library Resources*. Washington, D.C.: Council on Library Resources, 1985.

Jones, C. L. "Impact of Technology on User of Academic and Research Libraries." *IFLA Journal* 10 (1984):49-56.

──────. "Library Patrons in an Age of Discontinuity." *Journal of Academic Librarianship* 10 (July 1984):151-54.

Kauffman, S. B. "Automated Legislative Information Systems: A New Tool for Legal Research?" *Law Library Journal* 76 (Spring 1983):233-63.

Kellen, D. "Information Retrieval--The Present Future." *Australian Library Journal* 32 (May 1983):47-55.

Kilgour, Frederick G. "OCLC: Origins, Today, and Tomorrow." *Journal of Library and Information Science* 8 (April 1982):41-53.

Kochen, Manfred. "Information and Society." In *Annual Review of Information Science and Technology*, edited by Martha E. Williams, 18:277-304. White Plains, N.Y.: Knowledge Industry Publications, 1983.

Koenig, M. E. D. "Fiber Optics and Library Technology." *Library Hi Tech* 2 (1984):9-15.

Lacey, Paul A. "Views of a Luddite." *College and Research Libraries* 43 (March 1982):110-18.

Lancaster, F. W. "Evolving Paperless Society and Its Implications for Libraries." *International Forum on Information Documentation* 7 (October 1982):3-10.

_____. "The Paperless Society Revisited." *American Libraries* 16 (September 1985):553-55.

"Law Library Automation: A Symposium." *Law Library Journal* 77 (1984-85):3-156.

"Legal Issues in Electronic Publishing: A Symposium." *Federal Communications Law Journal* 36 (September 1984):149-224.

Lerner, Rita G.; Metaxas, Ted; Scott, John T.; Adams, Peter D.; and Judd, Peggy. "Primary Publication Systems and Scientific Text Processing." In *Annual Review of Information Science and Technology*, edited by Martha E. Williams, 18:127-49. White Plains, N.Y.: Knowledge Industry Publications, 1983.

Line, Maurice B. "National Planning and the Impact of Electronic Technology on Document Provision and Supply." *Libri* 35 (September 1985):181-90.

Lowenstein, F. "The Plastic Library." *Technology Review* 86 (August-September 1983):80-81.

Lunau, Carrol D. "The High Tech Revolution: A Canadian Library Perspective." *Special Libraries* 77 (Winter 1986):9-14.

Lundeen, Gerald W., and Davis, Charles H. "Library Automation." In *Annual Review of Information Science and Technology*, edited by Martha E. Williams, 17:161-86. White Plains, N.Y.: Knowledge Industry Publications, 1982.

Lunin, L. F., and Paris, J., eds. "Videodisc and Optical Disk: Technology, Research, and Applications." *American Society for Information Science Journal* 34 (November 1983):405-40.

Lynch, Clifford A., and Brownrigg, Edwin B. "Library Applications of Electronic Imaging Technology." *Information Technology and Libraries* 5 (June 1986):100-5.

Lytle, Susan S., and Hall, Hal W. "Software, Libraries and the Copyright Law." *Library Journal* 110 (July 1985):33-39.

McCoy, R. W. "The Electronic Scholar: Essential Tasks for the Scholarly Community." *Library Journal* 110 (1 October 1985):39-42.

McLean, Neil. "New Technology in Academic Libraries." In *Studies in Library Management*, edited by Anthony Vaughan, 7:146-66. London: Bingley, 1982.

Manburg, A., and Goldman, R. "Computer Technology for Information Retrieval: Tool for the Educator as Change Agent." *Educational Technology* 23 (June 1983):41-42.

Margrath, L. L. "Computers in the Library: The Human Element." *Information Technology and Libraries* 1 (September 1983):266-70.

Markoff, J. "Trends in Telecommunications." *Byte* 9 (July 1984):341-42.

Markoff, J., and Robinson, P. "A Laser Disk for Databases." *Byte* 10 (January 1985):418-21.

Martin, Susan K. "The New Technologies and the Library Networks." *Library Journal* 109 (15 June 1984):1194-96.

Mason, Robert M. "The Challenge of the Micro Revolution." *Library Journal* 109 (15 June 1984):1219-20.

Matthews, J. R., and Williams, J. F. "Telecommunication Technologies for Libraries: A Basic Guide." *Library Technology Reports* 19 (July-August 1983):335-94.

Matthews, Joseph R. "20 Q's & A's on Automated Integrated Library Systems." *American Libraries* 13 (June 1982):367-71.

"Microfilm: Symposium." *Law Library Journal* 76 (Spring 1983):299-393.

Molholt, P. A. "On Converging Paths: The Computing Center and the Library." *Journal of Academic Librarianship* 11 (November 1985):284-88.

Moore, C. D. "Ownership of Access Information: Exploring the Application of Copyright Law to Library Catalog Records." *Computer Law Journal* 4 (Fall 1983):305-72.

Morton, H. C., and Rutiman, H. "A Profile of Scholarly Journals: The MLA Findings." *Change* 15 (May-June 1983):54-55.

Murphy, Brower. "CD-ROM and Libraries." *Library Hi Tech* 3 (1985):21-26.

Nadeski, Karen, and Pontius, FairJack. "Developments in Micrographics, Video Technology, and Use." *Library Resources and Technical Services* 28 (July-September 1984):219-38.

Neavill, G. B. "Electronic Publishing, Libraries, and the Survival of Information." *Library Resources and Technical Services* 28 (January 1984):76-89.

Nielsen, Brian. "Teacher or Intermediary: Alternative Professional Models in the Information Age." *College and Research Libraries* 43 (May 1982):183-91.

Noel, D. G. "Prolegomena to a Golden Age: How Technology Could Make or Break Libraries in the Future." *LASIE* 13 (September-October 1982):2-12.

Parker, J. S. "Libraries and Archives for Tomorrow." *UNESCO Courier* 38 (February 1985):4-8.

Parkhurst, B. "Books and Satellites." *Publishers Weekly* 226 (26 October 1984):35-36.

"Patrons View Library's Catalog from Home." *Information Technology and Libraries* 1 (March 1982):73.

Pratt, Allan D. "Microcomputers in Libraries." In *Annual Review of Information Science and Technology*, edited by Martha E. Williams, 19:247-69. White Plains, N.Y.: Knowledge Industry Publications, 1984.

"Publishers Go Electronic." *Business Week*, 11 June 1984, 84-87+.

Raitt, David I. "Information Delivery Systems." In *Annual Review of Information Science and Technology*, edited by Martha E. Williams, 20:50-90. White Plains, N.Y.: Knowledge Industry Publications, 1985.

"Report of the Academic Computing Committee." Philadelphia: University of Pennsylvania *Almanac*, 29 November 1983.

Richards, Timothy F. "The Online Catalog: Issues in Planning and Development." *Journal of Academic Librarianship* 10 (March 1984):4-9.

Ridgway, J. "Compact Disc--A Revolution in the Making." *Canadian Library Journal* 43 (February 1986):23-29.

Rochell, C. C. "Designing Tomorrow's Libraries." *Architectural Record* 171 (August 1983):91.

Russel, Robert Arnold. "The High Tech Revolution." *Special Libraries* 77 (Winter 1986):1-8.

Sandler, C. "The Reader's Guide Goes Electronic." *Creative Computing* 11 (April 1985):28+.

Santosuosso, Joe. "The Library as a Gateway to Online Services." In *ASIS '85: Proceedings of the 48th ASIS Annual*

Meeting, edited by Carol A. Parkhurst, 22:106-10. White Plains, N.Y.: Knowledge Industry Publications, 1985.

Savage, N. "New Technology in Libraries: A Report." *Wilson Library Bulletin* 58 (February 1984):411-14.

Schaub, J. A. "CD-ROM for Public Access Catalogs." *Library Hi Tech* 3 (1985):7-13.

Schmidt, K. A. "Electronic Publishing and the Academic Library." In *Library and Information Association [US] National Conference*, no. 1, pp. 181-88. Chicago: American Library Association, 1984.

Segal, Jo An S. "Networking and Decentralization." In *Annual Review of Information Science and Technology*, edited by Martha E. Williams, 20:203-31. White Plains, N.Y.: Knowledge Industry Publications, 1985.

Shaughnessy, D. L., and Lynch, C. A. "Telecommunications for an Online Catalog." *Information Technology and Libraries* 2 (March 1983):73-86.

Shotwell, R. "What's New--and Promising--in Videotex." *Publishers Weekly* 225 (4 May 1984):26.

Shuford, R. S. "An Introduction to Fiber Optics: Connections Networks." *Byte* 10 (January 1985):197-98+.

Sievert, M. E. C. "Electronic Publishing: Some Ethical Questions for Librarians." *Show-Me Libraries* 36 (May 1985):21-23.

Sleeth, J., and LaRue J. "All-out Library: A Design for Computer-powered, Multidimensional Services." *American Libraries* 14 (October 1983):594-96.

Smith, Anthony. "Information Technology and the Myth of Abundance." In *Library Lit. 14--The Best of 1983*, edited by Bill Katz, 227-44. Metuchen, N.J.: Scarecrow Press, 1984. Reprinted from *Daedalus*, Fall 1982.

Sonnenmann, Sabine S. "The Videodisc as a Library Tool." *Special Libraries* 74 (January 1983):7-13.

Spain, T. "Grolier Encyclopedia to Bow in New Formats." *Publishers Weekly* 228 (16 August 1985):18.

Selected Bibliography

"Special Section: Optical Disks." *Information Technology and Libraries* 4 (June 1985):137-53.

Stirling, J. F. "Technological Developments in Information Transfer: Some Implications for Academic Libraries." *Journal of Librarianship* 14 (October 1982):235-46.

Stirling, Keith, ed. "Microcomputer Applications in Library and Information Services." *Drexel Library Quarterly* 20 (Fall 1984):1-97.

Strauss, Diane. "A Checklist of Issues to Be Considered Regarding the Addition of Microcomputer Data Disks to Academic Libraries." *Information Technology and Libraries* 5 (June 1986):129-32.

Surprenant, T. T. "Future Libraries: The Electronic Environment." *Wilson Library Bulletin* 56 (January 1982):336-41.

_____. "Future Libraries [Artificial Intelligence]." *Wilson Library Bulletin* 57 (February 1983):499-500+.

_____. "Future Libraries [Means by which Information Is Transmitted]." *Wilson Library Bulletin* 57 (December 1982):328-29; Discussion, 57 (March 1983):551.

_____. "Future of Libraries: Optical Disks!" *Wilson Library Bulletin* 59 (October 1984):120-21.

Surprenant, T. T., and Zande, J. "Developing Crisis in Information: A Librarian's Perspective." *IFLA Journal* 9 (1983):222-29.

Swanson, Don R. "Miracles, Microcomputers and Librarians." *Library Journal* 107 (1 June 1982):1055-59.

Technology Assessment Report: Speech Pattern Recognition, Optical Character Recognition, Digital Raster Scanning. Washington, D.C.: National Archives and Record Service, General Services Administration, 1984.

"Technology in Libraries." *Catholic Library World* 55 (February 1984):290-304.

"Telecommunicating and Libraries: The Next Challenge." *Technicalities* 4 (May 1984):1+.

Thoma, George R. "Premastering: A Critical Step in Videodisc Development." In *Productivity in the Information Age: Proceedings of the 46th ASIS Annual Meeting*, 20:41-47. White Plains, N.Y.: Knowledge Industry Publications, 1983.

Trautman, Rodes, and Gothberg, Helen M. "A Reference Tools Database: A Proposed Application for a Microcomputer at the Reference Desk." *Reference Librarian* 5-6 (Fall-Winter 1982):195-98.

Turlock, B. J. "Technology and the Post-Industrial Society: The Academic Library in the 1980's and Beyond." *Catholic Library World* 55 (February 1984):298-304.

Turner, J. A. "Computerized Data-based Services for Research Bringing Era of 'Free' Library Service to End." *Chronicle of Higher Education* 29 (19 September 1984):23+.

Veith, Richard H. "Videotex and Teletext." In *Annual Review of Information Science and Technology*, edited by Martha E. Williams, 18:3-28. White Plains, N.Y.: Knowledge Industry Publications, 1983.

Wagschal, P. H. "Interactive Technologies in Academic Library." *Library Trends* 34 (Summer 1985):141-50.

Ward, David V. "Applying the First Amendment to Electronic Information Media." In *1984 Challenges to an Information Society: Proceedings of the 47th ASIS Annual Meeting*, edited by Barbara Flood, Joanne Witiak, and Thomas H. Hogan, 21:48-51. White Plains, N.Y.: Knowledge Industry Publications, 1984.

Weinberg, S. "New Library Tool: Optical Disc and Micro." *American School and University* 57 (July 1985):10.

White, H. S. "Academic Libraries, Online Searching and Information Technology." *Journal of Academic Librarianship* 11 (November 1985):268-74.

Williams, J. F., and Matthews, J. R. "Planning for Telecommunications Service." *Library Technology Reports* 19 (November-December 1983):603-41.

Williams, Martha. "Databases, Computer Readable." In *The ALA Yearbook*, edited by Robert Wedgeworth, 8:103-8. Chicago: American Library Association, 1983.

Williamson, R. "Public Online Access to Library Material." *LASIE* 14 (September-October 1983):9-13.

Woods, Lawrence A. "Applications of Microcomputers in Libraries." *Bulletin of the Florida Chapter, Special Libraries Association* 14 (April 1982):64-79.

BOOKS

Armstrong, Chris, and Keenan, Stella, eds. *Information Technology in the Library/Information School Curriculum: An International Conference*. Aldershot, Hants, England: Gower, 1985.

Association of Research Libraries, Systems and Procedures Exchange Center. *Telecommunications*. SPEC Kit and Flyer Series, no. 98. Washington, D.C.: Association of Research Libraries, 1983.

Aveney, Brian, and Butler, Brett, eds. *Online Catalogs, Online Reference: Converging Trends*. Library and Information Technology Series, no. 2. Chicago: American Library Association, 1984.

Baughcum, Alan, and Faulhaber, Gerald R., eds. *Telecommunications Access and Public Policy: Proceedings of the Workshop on Local Access, September 1982, St. Louis, Missouri*. Norwood, N.J.: Ablex, 1984.

Beaumont, Jane, and Krueger, Donald. *Microcomputers for Libraries: How Useful Are They?* Ottawa, Canada: Canadian Library Association, 1983.

Binder, Michael B. *Videotex and Teletext: New Online Resources for Libraries*. Foundations in Library and Information Science, vol. 21. Greenwich, Conn.: JAI Press, 1985.

Boss, Richard. *Telecommunications for Library Management*. White Plains, N.Y.: Knowledge Industry Publications, 1985.

_____. *Automating Library Acquisitions*. White Plains, N.Y.: Knowledge Industry Publications, 1982.

Burton, Paul F. *Microcomputer Applications in Academic Libraries*. Library and Information Research Report, no. 16. London: British Library, 1983.

Chen, Mrs. C. C., and Bressler, S. E. *Microcomputers in Libraries*. New York: Neal-Schuman, 1982.

Clark, Philip M. *Microcomputer Spreadsheet Models for Libraries*. Chicago: American Library Association, 1985.

Cline, Hugh F., and Sinnot, Lorraine T. *The Electronic Library: The Impact of Automation on Academic Libraries*. Lexington, Mass.: Lexington Books, 1983.

Clinic on Library Applications of Data Processing. *Library Automation as a Source of Management Information*, edited by F. W. Lancaster. Urbana-Champaign: University of Illinois, Graduate School of Library and Information Science, 1982.

Clinic on Library Applications of Data Processing. *Professional Competencies--Technology and the Librarian*, edited by Linda C. Smith. Urbana-Champaign: University of Illinois, Graduate School of Library and Information Science, 1983.

Clinic on Library Applications of Data Processing. *Telecommunications--Making Sense out of New Technology and New Legislation*, edited by J. L. Divilbiss. Urbana-Champaign: University of Illinois, Graduate School of Library and Information Science, 1985.

Cohen, E., and Cohen, A. *Automation, Space Management, and Productivity: A Guide for Libraries*. New York: R. R. Bowker, 1982.

Collier, Mel. *Local Area Networks: The Implications for Library and Information Science*. London: British Library, 1984.

Compaine, Benjamin M., ed. *Understanding New Media: Trends and Issues in Electronic Distribution of Information*. Cambridge, Mass.: Ballinger Publishing, 1984.

Selected Bibliography

Conference on Fee-Based Research in College and University Libraries. *Fee-Based Research in College and University Libraries, June 17-18, 1982.* Greenvale, N.Y.: Center for Business Research, B. Davis Schwartz Memorial Library, C. W. Post Center, Long Island University, 1983.

Corbin, John. *Managing the Library Automation Project.* Phoenix, Ariz.: Oryx Press, 1985.

Davis, George R. *The Local Network Handbook.* New York: McGraw Hill, 1982.

Dizard, Wilson P., Jr. *The Coming Information Age: An Overview of Technology, Economics and Politics.* 2d ed. Chicago: Longman, 1985.

Dowlin, Kenneth E. *The Electronic Library: The Promise and the Process.* New York: Neal-Schuman, 1984.

Edelman, Hendrik, ed. *Libraries and Information Science in the Electronic Age.* Philadelphia: Institute for Scientific Information Press, 1986.

Forester, Tom, ed. *The Information Technology Revolution.* Cambridge, Mass.: MIT Press, 1985.

Foster, Constance L. *The Shattered Stereotype: The Academic Library in Technological Transition.* 1983. ERIC Reproduction Service: ED 237-107.

Future of Libraries: Panel Discussion by Librarians, Administrators, Faculty, and Students. Papers from the Millionth Volume Celebration. Albany, N.Y.: SUNY-Albany, 1982.

The Future of Library Automation: A Symposium. West Newton, Mass.: CL System, 1984.

Greenberg, Martin, ed. *Electronic Publishing Plus: Media for a Technological Future.* White Plains, N.Y.: Knowledge Industry Publications, 1985.

Grosch, Audrey. *Distributed Computing and the Electronic Library: Micros to Superminis.* White Plains, N.Y.: Knowledge Industry Publications, 1985.

Hayes, Robert M. *University, Information Technology and Academic Libraries.* Norwood, N.J.: Ablex, 1986.

International Association of Technological University Libraries. *The Future of Information Resources for Science and Technology and the Role of Libraries*, edited by Nancy Fjallbrant. Gothenburg, Sweden: International Association of Technological Libraries, 1985.

International Association of Technological University Libraries. *The Future of Serials: Publication, Automation and Management*, edited by Nancy Fjallbrant. Gothenburg, Sweden: International Association of Technological Libraries, 1983.

Jacob, Mary Ellen, ed. *Telecommunications Networks: Issues and Trends.* White Plains, N.Y.: Knowledge Industry Publications, 1986.

Jones, Kevin P., ed. *Intelligent Information Retrieval.* London: Aslib, 1984.

Katz, W. A., and Fraley, R. A. *Video to Online: Reference Service and the New Technology.* Binghamton, N.Y.: Haworth Press, 1983.

Kenney, B. L., ed. *Cable for Information Delivery: A Guide for Librarians, Educators and Cable Professionals.* White Plains, N.Y.: Knowledge Industry Publications, 1984.

Kent, Allen, and Galvin, Thomas J. *Information Technology: Critical Choices for Library Decision-Makers.* Books in Library and Information Science, vol. 40. New York: Marcel Dekker, 1982.

Keren, Carl, and Perlmutter, Linda, eds. *International Conference on the Application of Mini- and Micro-Computers in Information, Documentation, and Libraries.* Amsterdam: North Holland, 1983.

Kerr, Donald M.; Braithwaite, Karl; Metropolis, N.; Sharp, David H.; and Rota, Gian-Carlo; eds. *Science, Computer, and the Information Onslaught: A Collection of Essays.* New York: Academic Press, 1984.

Kibirige, Harry M. *The Information Dilemma: A Critical Analysis of Information Pricing and the Fees Controversy.* New Directions in Librarianship, no. 4. Westport, Conn.: Greenwood, 1983.

Knowledge Industry Publications. *Libraries in the Age of Automation: A Reader for the Professional Librarian.* White Plains, N.Y.: Knowledge Industry Publications, 1986.

Koenig, M. E. D., ed. *Managing the Electronic Library: Papers of the 1982 Conference of the Library Management Division of SLA.* New York: Special Libraries Association, 1984.

Lancaster, F. W. *Libraries and Librarians in an Age of Electronics.* Arlington, Va.: Information Resources Press, 1982.

Library Government Documents and Information Conference. *New Technology and Documents Librarianship*, edited by Peter Hernon. Westport, Conn.: Meckler Publishers, 1983.

Liebaers, H.; Haas, W. J.; and Biervliet, W. E.; eds. *New Information Technologies and Libraries.* Dordrecht, Holland: D. Reidel, 1985.

Linking Today's Libraries, Tomorrow's Technologies: Report of the Bibliographic and Communication Network Pilot Project. Canadian Network Papers, no. 7. Ottawa: National Library of Canada, 1984.

Lovacy, Ian. *Automating Library Procedures: A Survivor's Handbook.* Phoenix, Ariz.: Oryx Press, 1984.

Martin, Susan K., ed. *Advances in Library Automation and Networking.* Greenwich, Conn.: JAI Press, 1984.

Matthews, Joseph R., ed. *A Reader on Choosing an Automated Library System.* Chicago: American Library Association, 1983.

National Conference of Library and Information Technology Association. *Crossroads*, edited by M. Gorman. Chicago: American Library Association, 1984.

Neustadt, Richard M. *The Birth of Electronic Publishing.* White Plains, N.Y.: Knowledge Industry Publications, 1982.

Norman, Adrian. *Electronic Document Delivery: The Artemis Concept.* White Plains, N.Y.: Knowledge Industry Publications, 1982.

Reynolds, Dennis. *Library Automation: Issues and Applications.* New York: R. R. Bowker, 1985.

Rice, James. *Introduction to Library Automation.* Littleton, Colo.: Libraries Unlimited, 1984.

Roth, Judith Paris, ed. *Essential Guide to CD-ROM.* Westport, Conn.: Meckler Publishing, 1986.

Saffady, W. *Introduction to Automation for Librarians.* Chicago: American Library Association, 1983.

_____. *Micrographics.* 2d ed. Littleton, Colo.: Libraries Unlimited, 1985.

_____. *Video-based Information Systems: A Guide for Educational, Business, Library and Home Use.* Chicago: American Library Association, 1985.

Sigel, Efrem, Joseph Roizen, Colin McIntyre, and Max Wilkinson. *The Future of Videotext: The Coming Revolution in Home/Office Information Retrieval.* White Plains, N.Y.: Knowledge Industry Publications, 1983.

Silverstein, Jeffrey, and Elwell, Chris. *Database/Electronic Publishing: Review and Forecast, 1985.* White Plains, N.Y.: Knowledge Industry Publications, 1985.

Spigai, Frances, and Sommer, Peter. *Guide to Electronic Publishing.* White Plains, N.Y.: Knowledge Industry Publications, 1982.

Spyers-Duran, Peter, and Mann, Thomas W., Jr., eds. *Financing Information Services: Problems, Changing Approaches, and New Opportunities for Academic and Research Libraries.* New Directions in Librarianship, no. 6. Westport, Conn.: Greenwood Press, 1985.

Stuart-Stubbs, Basil, ed. *Changing Technology and Education for Librarianship and Information Science.* Foundations in Library and Information Science, vol. 20. Greenwich, Conn.: JAI Press, 1985.

Thompson, James. *The End of Libraries*. London: Clive Bingley, 1982.

U.S. Congress. Joint Committee on the Library. *Books in Our Future: A Report from the Librarian of Congress to Congress*. Washington, D.C.: U.S. Government Printing Office, 1984.

U.S. Congress. Joint Committee on Printing. Ad Hoc Committee on Depository Library Access to Federal Automated Data Bases. *Provision of Federal Government Publications in Electronic Format to Depository Libraries: Report, 1984*. 98th Cong., 2d sess., 1984. Senate Print 98260.

Varleji, Jana, ed. *Communication/Information/Libraries: A New Alliance*. Jefferson, N.C.: McFarland and Co., 1985.

Viggiano, Nancy M., ed. *Readings in Technology*. New York: Special Libraries Association, 1984.

Walton, Robert A. *Microcomputers: A Planning and Implementation Guide for Librarians and Information Professionals*. Phoenix, Ariz.: Orynx, 1983.

Williams, H. L., ed. *Computerised Systems in Library and Information Services*. London: Aslib, 1983.

Woods, Lawrence A., and Pope, Nolan F. *The Librarians Guide to Microcomputer Technology and Applications*. White Plains, N.Y.: Knowledge Industry Publications, 1983.

Zorkoczy, Peter. *Information Technology: An Introduction*. White Plains, N.Y.: Knowledge Industry Publications, 1983.

Appendixes

Appendix A

QUESTIONNAIRE WITH FREQUENCIES OF RESPONDENTS' OPINIONS

Name: _____ Title: _____

Institution or Organization: _____

Address: _____

IMPACT OF TECHNOLOGY ON INFORMATION PUBLICATION

Please circle one response in each column on each question. Unmarked responses to questions will be considered a "don't know" response and so interpreted. Write comments in spaces provided; feel free to write additional comments on separate sheets.

EVENT	How Strongly Do You Agree That the Event Will Occur? A	How Desirable Is the Event? B	When Will The Event Happen? C
1. Publication of printed books will continue to increase in the future despite the increase of publication of information in computerized and multi-media formats. Comments:	Strongly Agree 74 33.2% Agree 126 56.5% Undecided 8 3.6% Disagree 14 6.3% Strongly Disagree 1 .4%	Very Desirable 58 26.5% Desirable 108 49.3% Undecided 34 15.5% Undesirable 19 8.7% Very Undesirable 0	To 1990 16 8.1% To 2000 62 31.5% Post-2000 119 60.4%
2. Book collections of the libraries of the future will be reduced in size as more information becomes available in computerized and multi-media formats. Comments:	Strongly Agree 27 12.2% Agree 99 44.6% Undecided 11 5.0% Disagree 77 34.7% Strongly Disagree 8 3.6%	Very Desirable 29 13.6% Desirable 95 44.6% Undecided 34 16.0% Undesirable 50 23+% Very Undesirable 5 2.3%	1990 29 14.5% 2000 58 29.0% Post-2000 86 43.0% Never 27 13.5%

The Twenty-First Century

3. In the future more people will buy the information they want to read in a computer-based or computer-generated format and will borrow less from a library. Comments:	Strongly Agree 16 7.3% Agree 111 50.5% Undecided 23 10.5% Disagree 65 29.5% Strongly Disagree 5 2.3%	Very Desirable 13 6.1% Desirable 79 37.1% Undecided 59 27.7% Undesirable 56 26.3% Very Undesirable 6 2.8%	1990 42 22.0% 2000 62 32.5% Post-2000 57 29.8% Never 30 15.7%
4. In the future the services libraries provide patrons will be predominantly guidance in retrieving information in the non-book format. Comments:	Strongly Agree 15 6.8% Agree 62 27.9% Undecided 26 11.7% Disagree 105 47.3% Strongly Disagree 14 6.3%	Very Desirable 13 6.3% Desirable 57 27.4% Undecided 64 30.8% Undesirable 64 30.8% Very Undesirable 10 4.8%	1990 19 10.5% 2000 51 28.2% Post-2000 72 39.8% Never 39 21.5%
5. Microform will be replaced by a form of computer-based or computer-generated technology. Comments:	Strongly Agree 62 28.2% Agree 106 48.2% Undecided 15 6.8% Disagree 35 15.9% Strongly Disagree 2 .9%	Very Desirable 69 32.1% Desirable 93 43.3% Undecided 26 12.1% Undesirable 26 12.1% Very Undesirable 1 .5%	1990 36 18.2% 2000 91 46.0% Post-2000 56 28.3% Never 15 7.6%
6. In the absence of published hard copy, automated information viewable only on a computer screen (with print-out available for permanent retention) will be widely accepted as a readable format. Comments:	Strongly Agree 32 14.5% Agree 135 61.1% Undecided 11 5.0% Disagree 33 14.9% Strongly Disagree 10 4.5%	Very Desirable 21 9.8% Desirable 109 50.9% Undecided 43 20.1% Undesirable 31 14.5% Very Undesirable 10 4.7%	1990 47 24.5% 2000 75 39.1% Post-2000 55 28.6% Never 15 7.8%

Questionnaire

7. Online information will be priced so that most people could afford to use online services. Comments:	Strongly Agree 22 9.9% Agree 88 39.6% Undecided 37 16.7% Disagree 64 28.8% Strongly Disagree 11 5.0%	Very Desirable 104 48.6% Desirable 86 40.2% Undecided 16 7.5% Undesirable 6 2.8% Very Undesirable 2 .9%	1990 45 23.2% 2000 66 34.0% Post-2000 60 30.9% Never 23 11.9%
8. Use of online public catalogs will significantly increase demands for document delivery. Comments:	Strongly Agree 71 32.0% Agree 109 49.1% Undecided 25 11.3% Disagree 17 7.7% Strongly Disagree	Very Desirable 52 24.4% Desirable 124 58.2% Undecided 31 14.6% Undesirable 5 2.3% Very Undesirable 1 .5%	1990 121 62.7% 2000 48 24.9% Post-2000 18 9.3% Never 6 3.1%
9. In the future intelligent terminals, software, or other form of computer technology will be used to analyze and channel queries to appropriate databases for information. Comments:	Strongly Agree 61 27.5% Agree 131 59.0% Undecided 22 9.9% Disagree 7 3.2% Strongly Disagree 1 .5%	Very Desirable 71 33.3% Desirable 115 54.0% Undecided 20 9.4% Undesirable 5 2.3% Very Undesirable 2 .9%	1990 67 33.0% 2000 76 37.4% Post-2000 53 26.1% Never 7 3.4%
10. Distributed databases (computer storage, e.g. tapes acquired for local or in-house computers) will replace remote online information sources. Comments:	Strongly Agree 37 16.9% Agree 91 41.6% Undecided 47 21.5% Disagree 41 18.7% Strongly Disagree 3 1.4%	Very Desirable 52 25.0% Desirable 82 39.4% Undecided 48 23.1% Undesirable 22 10.6% Very Undesirable 4 1.9%	1990 52 30.8% 2000 67 39.6% Post-2000 35 20.7% Never 15 8.9%

The Twenty-First Century

11. The technology of disks (compact, digital, laser, optical, video) combined with microcomputers will provide an information retrieval capability superior to dial-up databases. Comments:	Strongly Agree 72 33.2% Agree 95 43.8% Undecided 32 14.7% Disagree 18 8.3% Strongly Disagree 0	Very Desirable 84 40.4% Desirable 88 42.3% Undecided 31 14.9% Undesirable 5 2.4% Very Undesirable 0	1990 66 34.2% 2000 83 43.0% Post-2000 35 18.1% Never 9 4.7%
12. By the year 2000 disks (compact, digital, laser, optical, video) will replace hard copy information to the following extent:	Under 25% 104 49.8% 26% to 50% 83 39.7% 51% to 75% 19 9.1% 76% to 90% 3 1.4% 91% to 100% 0	Very Desirable 44 21.1% Desirable 111 53.1% Undecided 45 21.5% Undesirable 9 4.3 Very Undesirable 0	
13. Interactive television, cable systems, or online systems like Viewtron or other videotex systems will replace the library as an information resource. Comments:	Strongly Agree 0 Agree 17 7.7% Undecided 24 10% Disagree 137 62.3% Strongly Disagree 42 19.1%	Very Desirable 1 .5% Desirable 8 3.9% Undecided 46 22.5% Undesirable 112 54.9% Very Undesirable 37 18.1%	1990 3 1.8% 2000 17 10.2% Post-2000 43 25.9% Never 103 62.0%
14. Other technologies will be developed that will permit access to information even faster and cheaper than those described above. Comments:	Strongly Agree 35 16.3% Agree 140 65.1% Undecided 33 15.3% Disagree 4 1.9% Strongly Disagree 3 1.4%	Very Desirable 58 28.3% Desirable 115 56.1% Undecided 30 14.6% Undesirable 2 1.0% Very Undesirable 0	1990 9 5.0% 2000 50 27.9% Post-2000 118 65.9% Never 2 1.1%

Questionnaire

	(Check only one response):		
15. By the year 2000 auto- mated library technology will be characterized primarily by: Comments:	A. Networks of personal computers or terminals	24	11.4%
	B. Access of full-text databases, such as LEXIS and WESTLAW	12	5.7%
	C. Video-disk technology	3	1.4%
	D. Laser-disk technology	11	5.2%
	E. Combination of above; identify	160	76.3%
	F. Other (See Appendix C for details)		

	(Check only one response):		
16. What role and function for libraries do you envi- sion in the years beyond 1990? Comments:	A. Continued role as general information resource	18	8.2%
	B. New role as computer-based informa- tion guide	8	3.7%
	C. A and B above	193	88.1%
	D. No role	0	

GENERAL COMMENTS ON ABOVE SECTION:

LIBRARY COLLECTIONS AND AUTOMATED INFORMATION

17. Increased automated infor- mation will slow the rate of growth in hard copy acquisi- tions for the library. Comments:	Strongly Agree 23 10.5% Agree 142 64.5% Undecided 14 6.4% Disagree 39 17.7% Strongly Disagree 2 .9%	Very Desirable 25 12.0% Desirable 109 52.4% Undecided 43 20.7% Undesirable 30 14.4% Very Undesirable 1 .5%	1990 82 42.3% 2000 64 33.0% Post-2000 40 20.6% Never 8 4.1%

The Twenty-First Century

18. As access to automated information increases, annual hard copy acquisitions of basic library materials will be reduced to one copy. Comments:	Strongly Agree 13 6.1% Agree 79 37.3% Undecided 36 17.0% Disagree 79 37.3% Strongly Disagree 5 2.4%	Very Desirable 11 5.5% Desirable 69 34.7% Undecided 48 24.1% Undesirable 67 33.7% Very Undesirable 4 2.0%	1990 36 22.8% 2000 56 35.4% Post-2000 32 20.3% Never 34 21.5%
19. What percentage of the annual hard copy acquisitions of basic library materials will be reduced to one copy by the year 2000? Comments:	Under 25% 59 32.6% 26% to 50% 50 27.6% 51% to 75% 30 16.6% 76% to 90% 30 16.6% 91% to 100% 12 6.6%	Very Desirable 21 11.6% Desirable 93 51.4% Undecided 41 22.7% Undesirable 22 12.2% Very Undesirable 4 2.2%	
20. What percentage of the hard copy collection of basic library materials will be reduced to one copy by the year 2000? Comments:	Under 25% 80 44.2% 26% to 50% 46 25.4% 51% to 75% 28 15.5% 76% to 90% 17 9.4% 91% to 100% 10 5.5%	Very Desirable 23 13.0% Desirable 94 53.1% Undecided 39 22.0% Undesirable 19 10.7% Very Undesirable 2 1.1%	

	Same As Now	Hard Copy	Laser Disk	Reporters	Software
21. What type of library materials do you envision for the library in future years once the basic book materials are available in automated form? Comments:	(a) 14 10.6% (b) 1 1.0% (c) 2 3.1%	32 24.1% 13 13.0% 10 15.4%	14 10.5% 18 18.0% 5 7.7%	19 14.3% 14 14.% 9 13.9%	25 18.8% 14 14% 18 27.7%

114

Questionnaire

GENERAL COMMENTS ON ABOVE SECTION:

BUDGETING

			1990	
22. Policy for automated information budgeting will be set by: Comments:	49	A. Librarian 23.3%	137	80.6%
		B. Dean	2000	
	8	3.8%	24	14.1%
		C. Faculty Committee	Post-2000	
	10	4.8%	9	5.3%
		D. Combination of above; identify	Never	
	113	53.8% (See Appendix C)	0	

				1990	
23. Automated information budgets will be administered and managed by the librarian. Comments:	189	A. Yes 89.2%	130	78.8%	
		B. No		2000	
	5	2.4%	26	15.8%	
		C. If no, by whom?		Post-2000	
		Various (See Appendix C) 8		4.8%	
				Never	
				1	.6%

					1990	
24. Automated information budgets will be separated completely from budgets for library materials and binding. Comments:	Strongly Agree 19 8.8%		Very Desirable 19 9.3%		89	54.3%
	Agree		Desirable		2000	
	58 27.9%		45 22.0%		21	12.8%
	Undecided		Undecided		Post-2000	
	17 7.9%		33 16.1%		10	6.1%
	Disagree		Undesirable		Never	
	99 46.0%		84 41.0%		44	26.8%
	Strongly Disagree		Very Undesirable			
	22 10.2%		24 11.7%			

115

The Twenty-First Century

25. Institutional fiscal officers will continue to allocate substantial funds for automated information even though these expenditures generate no tangible hard copy additions to the library. Comments:	Strongly Agree 32 15.0% Agree 152 71.0% Undecided 20 9.3% Disagree 8 3.7% Strongly Disagree 2 .9%	Very Desirable 49 23.7% Desirable 136 65.7% Undecided 20 9.7% Undesirable 1 .5% Very Undesirable 1 .5%	1990 120 68.6% 2000 42 24.0% Post-2000 11 6.3% Never 2 1.1%

26. Comparing the automated information budget with the library materials budget in the year 1990 and beyond, the automated information budget will be: Comments:	____ A. Less 76 36.9% ____ B. The same 34 16.5% ____ C. More 96 45.6%

27. In light of the possible changes in book collecting policies, would you anticipate any special difficulty in acquiring the funding to build a new library building or addition? Comments:	____ A. Yes 123 56.7% ____ B. No 52 24.0% ____ C. Don't know 42 19.4%

28. In a year in which the allocations are reduced, the budget for automated information should be:
Comments:
	____ A. Preserved at the present level
	              87 46.5%
	____ B. Increased
	              53 28.3%
	____ C. Decreased
	              47 25.1%

29. In a year of reduced budgets, what types of materials should be reduced or cancelled first?
Comments:
	____ A. Hard copy when information available in computer databases
	              114 63.7%
	____ B. Information system when hard copy available
	              42 23.5%
	____ C. Others materials
	              23 12.8%

Questionnaire

GENERAL COMMENTS ON ABOVE SECTION:

PAYMENT FOR AUTOMATED INFORMATION ACCESS

I. Faculty

30. Who will absorb the costs of faculty access to automated information?

Comments:

____A. Library   34   16.0%
____B. College or Department   48   22.6%
____C. Faculty   6   2.8%
____D. Combination of above; specify: 124   58.6%

31. A formula will be devised to determine the amount of access, hardware, and service that should be provided free to faculty.
Comments:

Strongly Agree	Very Desirable	1990
31 14.8%	49 24.4%	115 69.3%
Agree	Desirable	2000
103 49.0%	87 43.3%	24 14.5%
Undecided	Undecided	Post-2000
36 17.1%	31 15.4%	6 3.6%
Disagree	Undesirable	Never
35 16.7%	27 13.4%	21 12.7%
Strongly Disagree	Very Undesirable	
5 2.4%	7 3.5%	

32. Faculty will have to pay for some of the costs to access online information beyond a pre-determined, reasonable, limited amount.
Comments:

Strongly Agree	Very Desirable	1990
37 17.1%	39 19.0%	131 75.3%
Agree	Desirable	2000
118 54.4%	83 40.5%	18 10.3%
Undecided	Undecided	Post-2000
28 12.9%	32 15.6%	6 3.4%
Disagree	Undesirable	Never
32 14.7%	44 21.5%	19 10.9%
Strongly Disagree	Very Undesirable	
2 .9%	7 3.4%	

The Twenty-First Century

II. Students

33. Students will pay on a per use basis for the costs of information retrieval services. Comments:	Strongly Agree 8 3.8% Agree 52 24.6% Undecided 37 17.5% Disagree 95 45.0% Strongly Disagree 19 9.0%	Very Desirable 5 2.5% Desirable 29 14.3% Undecided 30 14.8% Undesirable 106 52.2% Very Undesirable 33 16.3%	1990 77 49.7% 2000 17 11.0% Post-2000 13 8.4% Never 48 31.0%

34. By 1990 most research university or law school student fees will cover the costs of automated information retrieval, word processing, and other related computer costs in the library. Comments:	Strongly Agree 18 8.2% Agree 95 43.4% Undecided 36 16.4% Disagree 62 28.3% Strongly Disagree 8 3.7%	Very Desirable 35 17.2% Desirable 107 52.5% Undecided 29 14.2% Undesirable 26 12.7% Very Undesirable 7 3.4%	

35. The library will provide to students a limited amount of access to automated information free of charge. Comments:	Strongly Agree 48 22.1% Agree 135 62.2% Undecided 17 7.8% Disagree 14 6.5% Strongly Disagree 3 1.4%	Very Desirable 70 34.5% Desirable 107 52.7% Undecided 12 5.9% Undesirable 10 4.9% Very Undesirable 4 2.0%	1990 148 85.1% 2000 9 5.2% Post-2000 8 4.6% Never 9 5.2%

Questionnaire

III. Library Patrons (Other than Faculty and Students)

36. The library will pay for the costs to access automated information for everyone when that information is available only online. Comments:	Strongly Agree 8 3.7% Agree 38 17.5% Undecided 36 16.6% Disagree 109 50.2% Strongly Disagree 26 12.0%	Very Desirable 19 9.4% Desirable 56 27.7% Undecided 43 21.3% Undesirable 66 32.7% Very Undesirable 18 8.9%	1990 72 47.1% 2000 21 13.7% Post-2000 13 8.5% Never 47 30.7%
37. The library will furnish computers/terminals to patrons to access information and will collect the costs through coin or card operated machines or legal tender. Comments:	Strongly Agree 17 7.8% Agree 113 51.8% Undecided 46 21.1% Disagree 37 17.0% Strongly Disagree 5 2.3%	Very Desirable 18 8.8% Desirable 88 43.1% Undecided 48 23.5% Undesirable 43 21.1% Very Undesirable 7 3.4%	1990 95 60.9% 2000 31 19.9% Post-2000 9 5.8% Never 21 13.5%

GENERAL COMMENTS ON ABOVE SECTION:

PERSONNEL

38. In the future as there are changes in the library collection format and increased automation, the number and/or composition of library staff will change. Comments:	Strongly Agree 42 19.0% Agree 155 70.1% Undecided 14 6.3% Disagree 9 4.1% Strongly Disagree 1 .5%	Very Desirable 40 19.2% Desirable 139 66.8% Undecided 24 11.5% Undesirable 4 1.9% Very Undesirable 1 .5%	1990 122 65.6% 2000 54 29.0% Post-2000 8 4.3% Never 2 1.1%

THE TWENTY-FIRST CENTURY

39. The number of administrative librarians will: Comments:	___A. Increase ___B. Decrease ___C. Remain unchanged	52 24.9% 35 16.7% 122 58.4%	1990 98 61.6% 2000 58 33.3% Post-2000 8 5.0%	
40. The number of public service librarians will: Comments:	___A. Increase ___B. Decrease ___C. Remain unchanged	159 75.7% 20 9.5% 31 14.8%	1990 123 70.7% 2000 48 27.6% Post-2000 3 1.7%	
41. The number of technical service librarians will: Comments:	___A. Increase ___B. Decrease ___C. Remain unchanged	48 22.6% 125 59.0% 39 18.4%	1990 110 64.0% 2000 55 32.0% Post-2000 7 4.1%	
42. The number of support staff will: Comments:	___A. Increase ___B. Decrease ___C. Remain unchanged	70 33.0% 80 37.7% 62 29.2%	1990 112 65.1% 2000 52 30.2% Post-2000 8 4.7%	
43. The number of library trained professionals working in the libraries' information science program will: Comments:	___A. Increase ___B. Decrease ___C. Remain unchanged	143 80.3% 13 7.3% 22 12.4%	1990 98 68.1% 2000 43 29.9% Post-2000 3 2.1%	
44. Library-trained professionals should be paid more for expertise in computer use. Comments:	___A. Yes ___B. No			

Questionnaire

45. Personnel without library but with computer science training should be paid commensurate with salaries in the computer specialty. Comments:	Strongly Agree 15 7.3% Agree 109 53.2% Undecided 39 19.0% Disagree 39 19.0% Strongly Disagree 3 1.5%	Very Desirable 16 8.4% Desirable 99 51.8% Undecided 42 22.0% Undesirable 31 16.2% Very Undesirable 3 1.6%	1990 102 71.8% 2000 26 18.3% Post-2000 6 4.2% Never 8 5.6%	
46. As a result of increased automation and changes in the library, the library will allocate funds for the training and re-education of library personnel. Comments:	Strongly Agree 48 22.1% Agree 130 59.9% Undecided 25 11.5 Disagree 12 5.5%3 Strongly Disagree 2 .9%	Very Desirable 78 37.5% Desirable 113 54.3% Undecided 13 6.3% Undesirable 3 1.4% Very Undesirable 1 .5%	1990 138 77.1% 2000 29 16.2% Post-2000 4 2.2% Never 8 4.5%	

GENERAL COMMENTS ON ABOVE SECTION:

COMPUTER EQUIPMENT

47. By the year 1990 which department will be responsible for the computer operation, including budgets, personnel, and equipment? Comments:	A. College or Dept. Library B. College or Department C. Computer Center D. Parent institution library E. Combination of above; identify (See Appendix C) F. Other	47 14 15 22 112 1	22.4% 6.7% 7.1% 10.5% 53.5% .5%

The Twenty-First Century

48. Each faculty member will own or be furnished a personal computer or a terminal for information access and word and data processing. Comments:	Strongly Agree 69 31.1% Agree 135 60.8% Undecided 6 2.7% Disagree 11 5.0% Strongly Disagree 1 .5%	Very Desirable 93 43.9% Desirable 102 48.1% Undecided 10 4.7% Undesirable 6 2.8% Very Undesirable 1 .5%	1990 117 59.1% 2000 60 30.3% Post-2000 18 9.1% Never 3 1.5%
49. Most students enrolling in college will own personal computers. Comments:	Strongly Agree 47 21.1% Agree 137 61.4% Undecided 14 6.3% Disagree 24 10.8% Strongly Disagree 1 .4%	Very Desirable 70 33.2% Desirable 119 56.4% Undecided 16 7.6% Undesirable 5 2.4% Very Undesirable 1 .5%	1990 95 48.2% 2000 78 39.6% Post-2000 20 10.2% Never 4 2.0%
50. Each student who does not have a personal computer or a terminal will be furnished one for information access and word and data processing for individual use or in labs. Comments:	Strongly Agree 36 16.3% Agree 114 51.6% Undecided 34 15.4% Disagree 35 15.8% Strongly Disagree 2 .9%	Very Desirable 59 27.7% Desirable 110 51.6% Undecided 30 14.1% Undesirable 13 6.1% Very Undesirable 1 .5%	1990 91 52.6% 2000 50 28.9% Post-2000 23 13.3% Never 9 5.2%
51. By 1990 each student will be required to have a personal computer. Comments:	Strongly Agree 9 4.1% Agree 40 18.3% Undecided 50 22.8% Disagree 106 48.4% Strongly Disagree 14 6.4%	Very Desirable 21 10.3% Desirable 56 27.5% Undecided 53 26.0% Undesirable 65 31.9% Very Undesirable 9 4.4%	1990 2000 Post-2000 Never

GENERAL COMMENTS ON ABOVE SECTION:

Appendix B

RESPONDENTS' OPINIONS EXPRESSED IN CROSS-TABLES

QUESTIONNAIRE RESPONSES

QUESTION	LIB SCI PROFS	SCIENTIFIC TECHNICAL	LIBRARY NETWORK	PUBLISHERS	RESEARCH LIBRARIANS	LAW DEANS	LAW LIBRARIANS	ROW TOTALS
Q1A								
STRONGLY AGREE	9	8	2	0	16	16	23	74
AGREE	6	21	6	3	22	23	45	126
UNDECIDED	1	1	0	0	2	2	2	8
DISAGREE	2	3	0	0	4	1	4	14
STRONGLY DISAGREE	0	0	0	0	0	1	0	1
TOTALS	18	33	8	3	44	43	74	223
Q1B								
VERY DESIRABLE	10	10	3	0	11	9	15	58
DESIRABLE	4	15	5	3	22	19	40	108
UNDECIDED	3	4	0	0	6	9	12	34
UNDESIRABLE	1	3	0	0	3	6	6	19
TOTALS	18	32	8	3	42	43	73	219
Q1C								
1990	2	3	0	1	2	4	4	16
2000	4	10	3	2	13	11	19	62
POST-2000	11	17	5	0	23	24	39	119
TOTALS	17	30	8	3	38	39	62	197

The Twenty-First Century

QUESTIONNAIRE RESPONSES

QUESTION	LIB SCI PROFS	SCIENTIFIC TECHNICAL	LIBRARY NETWORK	PUBLISH- ERS	RESEARCH LIBRARIANS	LAW DEANS	LAW LIBRARIANS	ROW TOTALS
Q2A								
STRONGLY AGREE	0	4	0	1	3	8	11	27
AGREE	12	15	3	2	13	21	33	99
UNDECIDED	0	1	0	0	3	1	6	11
DISAGREE	5	12	4	0	21	13	22	77
STRONGLY DISAGREE	1	0	1	0	3	0	3	8
TOTALS	18	32	8	3	43	43	75	222
Q2B								
VERY DESIRABLE	1	5	0	1	3	11	8	29
DESIRABLE	9	15	4	1	18	14	34	95
UNDECIDED	4	3	2	0	5	6	14	34
UNDESIRABLE	3	5	1	1	14	12	14	50
VERY UNDESIRABLE	1	0	1	0	1	0	2	5
TOTALS	18	28	8	3	41	43	72	213
Q2C								
1990	1	5	0	2	3	7	11	29
2000	6	12	1	1	9	13	16	58
POST-2000	7	11	5	0	20	14	29	86
NEVER	2	1	2	0	8	5	9	27
TOTALS	16	29	8	3	40	39	65	200

Respondents' Opinions

QUESTIONNAIRE RESPONSES

QUESTION	LIB SCI PROFS	SCIENTIFIC TECHNICAL	LIBRARY NETWORK	PUBLISH- ERS	RESEARCH LIBRARIANS	LAW DEANS	LAW LIBRARIANS	ROW TOTALS
Q3A								
STRONGLY AGREE	0	3	1	1	3	3	5	16
AGREE	7	19	3	1	15	24	42	111
UNDECIDED	3	5	2	0	4	4	5	23
DISAGREE	6	4	2	1	21	12	19	65
STRONGLY DISAGREE	1	2	0	0	0	0	2	5
TOTALS	17	33	8	3	43	43	73	220
Q3B								
VERY DESIRABLE	1	6	0	0	1	3	2	13
DESIRABLE	4	12	0	1	11	17	34	79
UNDECIDED	2	7	6	1	13	11	19	59
UNDESIRABLE	9	4	2	1	16	10	14	56
VERY UNDESIRABLE	1	2	0	0	0	0	3	6
TOTALS	17	31	8	3	41	41	72	213
Q3C								
1990	1	10	1	2	6	11	11	42
2000	4	11	3	0	15	8	21	62
POST-2000	7	5	0	0	10	13	22	57
NEVER	4	4	2	0	6	4	10	30
TOTALS	16	30	6	2	37	36	64	191

The Twenty-First Century

QUESTIONNAIRE RESPONSES

QUESTION	LIB SCI PROFS	SCIENTIFIC TECHNICAL	LIBRARY NETWORK	PUBLISH-ERS	RESEARCH LIBRARIANS	LAW DEANS	LAW LIBRARIANS	ROW TOTALS
Q4A								
STRONGLY AGREE	0	3	1	1	1	5	4	15
AGREE	4	9	2	2	8	11	26	62
UNDECIDED	0	4	1	0	3	11	7	26
DISAGREE	13	16	4	0	25	15	32	105
STRONGLY DISAGREE	1	1	0	0	7	1	4	14
TOTALS	18	33	8	3	44	43	73	222
Q4B								
VERY DESIRABLE	0	3	1	1	2	5	1	13
DESIRABLE	2	12	2	1	8	11	21	57
UNDECIDED	3	7	2	1	12	13	26	64
UNDESIRABLE	10	7	3	0	15	11	18	64
VERY UNDESIRABLE	2	1	0	0	4	0	3	10
TOTALS	17	30	8	3	41	40	69	208
Q4C								
1990	0	4	0	0	1	6	8	19
2000	3	10	4	2	10	5	17	51
POST-2000	5	9	1	0	16	15	26	72
NEVER	5	5	2	0	10	5	12	39
TOTALS	13	28	7	2	37	31	63	181

Respondents' Opinions

QUESTIONNAIRE RESPONSES

QUESTION	LIB SCI PROFS	SCIENTIFIC TECHNICAL	LIBRARY NETWORK	PUBLISH-ERS	RESEARCH LIBRARIANS	LAW DEANS	LAW LIBRARIANS	ROW TOTALS
Q5A								
STRONGLY AGREE	4	14	4	2	9	13	16	62
AGREE	12	11	3	1	23	19	37	106
UNDECIDED	1	1	0	0	3	5	5	15
DISAGREE	1	4	1	0	8	5	16	35
STRONGLY DISAGREE	0	1	0	0	1	0	0	2
TOTALS	18	31	8	3	44	42	74	220
Q5B								
VERY DESIRABLE	5	14	3	2	11	17	17	69
DESIRABLE	11	9	5	1	19	15	33	93
UNDECIDED	1	4	0	0	6	5	10	26
UNDESIRABLE	1	3	0	0	5	4	13	26
VERY UNDESIRABLE	0	0	0	0	1	0	0	1
TOTALS	18	30	8	3	42	41	73	215
Q5C								
1990	4	9	3	2	5	5	8	36
2000	9	14	4	1	19	20	24	91
POST-2000	2	6	1	0	13	10	24	56
NEVER	1	1	0	0	3	0	10	15
TOTALS	16	30	8	3	40	35	66	198

THE TWENTY-FIRST CENTURY

QUESTIONNAIRE RESPONSES

QUESTION	LIB SCI PROFS	SCIENTIFIC TECHNICAL	LIBRARY NETWORK	PUBLISH-ERS	RESEARCH LIBRARIANS	LAW DEANS	LAW LIBRARIANS	ROW TOTALS
Q6A								
STRONGLY AGREE	1	6	2	2	4	5	12	32
AGREE	9	19	5	1	28	26	47	135
UNDECIDED	0	1	0	0	2	4	4	11
DISAGREE	5	4	0	0	9	7	8	33
STRONGLY DISAGREE	2	3	0	0	1	1	3	10
TOTALS	17	33	7	3	44	43	74	221
Q6B								
VERY DESIRABLE	1	5	0	1	3	4	7	21
DESIRABLE	6	16	7	2	20	21	37	109
UNDECIDED	2	4	0	0	11	9	17	43
UNDESIRABLE	5	3	0	0	9	7	7	31
VERY UNDESIRABLE	3	3	0	0	0	1	3	10
TOTALS	17	31	7	3	43	42	71	214
Q6C								
1990	3	12	2	3	9	8	10	47
2000	5	11	4	0	16	16	23	75
POST-2000	4	5	1	0	11	10	24	55
NEVER	4	3	0	0	4	0	4	15
TOTALS	16	31	7	3	40	34	61	192

QUESTIONNAIRE RESPONSES

QUESTION	LIB SCI PROFS	SCIENTIFIC TECHNICAL	LIBRARY NETWORK	PUBLISH-ERS	RESEARCH LIBRARIANS	LAW DEANS	LAW LIBRARIANS	ROW TOTALS
Q7A								
STRONGLY AGREE	2	6	1	1	2	4	6	22
AGREE	11	10	2	2	16	22	25	88
UNDECIDED	0	2	1	0	8	9	17	37
DISAGREE	2	11	4	0	17	8	22	64
STRONGLY DISAGREE	3	3	0	0	1	0	4	11
TOTALS	18	32	8	3	44	43	74	222
Q7B								
VERY DESIRABLE	9	15	5	1	17	19	38	104
DESIRABLE	9	11	3	2	19	17	25	86
UNDECIDED	0	2	0	0	4	5	5	16
UNDESIRABLE	0	1	0	0	3	0	2	6
VERY UNDESIRABLE	0	1	0	0	0	0	1	2
TOTALS	18	30	8	3	43	41	71	214
Q7C								
1990	5	8	3	2	9	5	13	45
2000	6	9	3	1	19	11	17	66
POST-2000	3	6	0	0	9	14	28	60
NEVER	3	7	1	0	3	4	5	23
TOTALS	17	30	7	3	40	34	63	194

The Twenty-First Century

QUESTIONNAIRE RESPONSES

QUESTION	LIB SCI PROFS	SCIENTIFIC TECHNICAL	LIBRARY NETWORK	PUBLISH-ERS	RESEARCH LIBRARIANS	LAW DEANS	LAW LIBRARIANS	ROW TOTALS
Q8A								
STRONGLY AGREE	6	7	4	1	24	5	24	71
AGREE	9	16	3	1	19	23	38	109
UNDECIDED	1	6	1	1	0	7	9	25
DISAGREE	2	4	0	0	1	6	4	17
TOTALS	18	33	8	3	44	41	75	222
Q8B								
VERY DESIRABLE	5	8	3	0	13	5	18	52
DESIRABLE	12	14	4	2	25	24	43	124
UNDECIDED	1	7	1	1	3	9	9	31
UNDESIRABLE	0	2	0	0	1	1	1	5
VERY UNDESIRABLE	0	0	0	0	0	1	0	1
TOTALS	18	31	8	3	42	40	71	213
Q8C								
1990	13	19	7	1	29	19	33	121
2000	1	6	0	1	11	7	22	48
POST-2000	2	1	0	0	2	5	8	18
NEVER	1	0	0	0	0	3	2	6
TOTALS	17	26	7	2	42	34	65	193

Respondents' Opinions

QUESTIONNAIRE RESPONSES

QUESTION	LIB SCI PROFS	SCIENTIFIC TECHNICAL	LIBRARY NETWORK	PUBLISH- ERS	RESEARCH LIBRARIANS	LAW DEANS	LAW LIBRARIANS	ROW TOTALS
Q9A								
STRONGLY AGREE	1	13	7	1	13	11	15	61
AGREE	15	16	1	1	30	24	44	131
UNDECIDED	1	2	0	1	0	8	10	22
DISAGREE	1	2	0	0	0	0	4	7
STRONGLY DISAGREE	0	0	0	0	0	0	1	1
TOTALS	18	33	8	3	43	43	74	222
Q9B								
VERY DESIRABLE	4	14	5	0	16	12	20	71
DESIRABLE	12	11	3	2	24	22	41	115
UNDECIDED	1	4	0	0	1	8	6	20
UNDESIRABLE	1	0	0	0	1	0	3	5
VERY UNDESIRABLE	0	1	0	0	0	0	1	2
TOTALS	18	30	8	2	42	42	71	213
Q9C								
1990	2	20	5	1	16	11	12	67
2000	11	10	2	1	18	12	22	76
POST-2000	4	1	1	0	6	13	28	53
NEVER	1	1	0	0	0	0	5	7
TOTALS	18	32	8	2	40	36	67	201

The Twenty-First Century

QUESTIONNAIRE RESPONSES

QUESTION	LIB SCI PROFS	SCIENTIFIC TECHNICAL	LIBRARY NETWORK	PUBLISH-ERS	RESEARCH LIBRARIANS	LAW DEANS	LAW LIBRARIANS	ROW TOTALS
Q10A								
STRONGLY AGREE	1	8	3	1	4	4	16	37
AGREE	10	13	2	2	21	15	28	91
UNDECIDED	4	3	1	0	6	17	16	47
DISAGREE	3	6	1	0	12	5	14	41
STRONGLY DISAGREE	0	2	0	0	0	1	0	3
TOTALS	18	32	7	3	43	42	74	219
Q10B								
VERY DESIRABLE	2	10	2	1	12	7	18	52
DESIRABLE	10	10	1	2	14	14	31	82
UNDECIDED	2	3	3	0	7	16	17	48
UNDESIRABLE	3	5	1	0	8	2	3	22
VERY UNDESIRABLE	0	2	0	0	1	1	0	4
TOTALS	17	30	7	3	42	40	69	208
Q10C								
1990	5	11	2	1	12	9	12	52
2000	3	12	2	2	17	8	23	67
POST-2000	4	1	1	0	4	9	16	35
NEVER	2	3	0	0	3	2	5	15
TOTALS	14	27	5	3	36	28	56	169

QUESTIONNAIRE RESPONSES

QUESTION	LIB SCI PROFS	SCIENTIFIC TECHNICAL	LIBRARY NETWORK	PUBLISH-ERS	RESEARCH LIBRARIANS	LAW DEANS	LAW LIBRARIANS	ROW TOTALS
Q11A								
STRONGLY AGREE	4	16	4	1	11	12	24	72
AGREE	12	9	3	0	22	19	30	95
UNDECIDED	1	3	0	1	6	6	15	32
DISAGREE	1	3	1	1	3	4	5	18
TOTALS	18	31	8	3	42	41	74	217
Q11B								
VERY DESIRABLE	7	16	4	1	15	13	28	84
DESIRABLE	10	11	2	0	17	17	31	88
UNDECIDED	1	3	2	1	6	7	11	31
UNDESIRABLE	0	0	0	0	2	2	1	5
TOTALS	18	30	8	2	40	39	71	208
Q11C								
1990	7	19	3	1	12	10	14	66
2000	8	9	4	1	21	14	26	83
POST-2000	1	2	0	1	4	8	19	35
NEVER	1	2	1	0	1	0	4	9
TOTALS	17	32	8	3	38	32	63	193

QUESTIONNAIRE RESPONSES

QUESTION	LIB SCI PROFS	SCIENTIFIC TECHNICAL	LIBRARY NETWORK	PUBLISH-ERS	RESEARCH LIBRARIANS	LAW DEANS	LAW LIBRARIANS	ROW TOTALS
Q12A								
UNDER 25 %	8	15	2	2	24	15	38	104
26% TO 50%	9	12	5	1	15	20	21	83
51% TO 75%	1	5	1	0	2	3	7	19
76% TO 90%	0	1	0	0	0	1	1	3
TOTALS	18	33	8	3	41	39	67	209
Q12B								
VERY DESIRABLE	3	11	0	2	10	8	10	44
DESIRABLE	12	16	7	1	20	16	39	111
UNDECIDED	1	4	1	0	7	12	20	45
UNDESIRABLE	2	1	0	0	3	2	1	9
TOTALS	18	32	8	3	40	38	70	209

THE TWENTY-FIRST CENTURY

QUESTIONNAIRE RESPONSES

QUESTION	LIB SCI PROFS	SCIENTIFIC TECHNICAL	LIBRARY NETWORK	PUBLISH-ERS	RESEARCH LIBRARIANS	LAW DEANS	LAW LIBRARIANS	ROW TOTALS
Q13A								
AGREE	0	1	0	2	3	7	4	17
UNDECIDED	0	3	0	1	2	8	10	24
DISAGREE	16	21	5	0	28	23	44	137
STRONGLY DISAGREE	2	7	3	0	10	4	16	42
TOTALS	18	32	8	3	43	42	74	220
Q13B								
VERY DESIRABLE	0	1	0	0	0	0	0	1
DESIRABLE	0	1	0	0	2	4	1	8
UNDECIDED	1	8	2	2	4	11	18	46
UNDESIRABLE	14	12	5	1	22	21	37	112
VERY UNDESIRABLE	3	6	1	0	11	3	13	37
TOTALS	18	28	8	3	39	39	69	204
Q13C								
1990	0	0	1	0	1	1	0	3
2000	0	5	0	2	4	2	4	17
POST-2000	3	5	0	0	5	11	19	43
NEVER	15	13	6	0	26	13	30	103
TOTALS	18	23	7	2	36	27	53	166

Respondents' Opinions

QUESTIONNAIRE RESPONSES

QUESTION	LIB SCI PROFS	SCIENTIFIC TECHNICAL	LIBRARY NETWORK	PUBLISH-ERS	RESEARCH LIBRARIANS	LAW DEANS	LAW LIBRARIANS	ROW TOTALS
Q14A								
STRONGLY AGREE	3	9	3	1	4	4	11	35
AGREE	13	20	4	2	27	29	45	140
UNDECIDED	2	0	1	0	8	8	14	33
DISAGREE	0	2	0	0	2	0	0	4
STRONGLY DISAGREE	0	1	0	0	1	0	1	3
TOTALS	18	32	8	3	42	41	71	215
Q14B								
VERY DESIRABLE	6	12	2	2	10	7	19	58
DESIRABLE	9	19	5	1	24	24	33	115
UNDECIDED	3	0	1	0	4	8	14	30
UNDESIRABLE	0	0	0	0	1	0	1	2
TOTALS	18	31	8	3	39	39	67	205
Q14C								
1990	0	3	1	0	3	0	2	9
2000	4	14	2	2	9	4	15	50
POST-2000	13	13	4	1	22	24	41	118
NEVER	0	1	0	0	0	0	1	2
TOTALS	17	31	7	3	34	28	59	179

THE TWENTY-FIRST CENTURY

QUESTIONNAIRE RESPONSES

QUESTION		LIB SCI PROFS	SCIENTIFIC TECHNICAL	LIBRARY NETWORK	PUBLISH-ERS	RESEARCH LIBRARIANS	LAW DEANS	LAW LIBRARIANS	ROW TOTALS
Q15									
	UNSPECIFIED COMB	0	1	2	0	4	5	1	13
A.	NETWORKS	2	3	1	1	7	6	4	24
B.	DATABASES	1	0	0	0	2	3	6	12
C.	VIDEO-DISK	0	1	0	0	0	2	0	3
D.	LASER-DISK	1	2	0	0	2	3	3	11
	A, B, C, D	6	14	2	1	11	10	25	69
	A, B, C	0	0	0	0	1	1	0	2
	A, B	1	1	0	0	0	2	6	10
	A, C, D	0	2	0	0	0	1	0	3
	A, C	0	0	0	0	0	0	1	1
	A, B, D	3	3	1	0	4	4	7	22
	A, D	0	1	1	0	5	1	7	15
	B, C, D	2	0	0	0	2	1	0	5
	B, C	0	0	0	0	0	1	0	1
	B, D	2	0	0	0	0	0	3	5
	C, D	0	0	0	0	0	0	2	2
	A, B, D, F---PERI	0	1	0	0	0	0	0	1
	GREATER MULTIPLI	0	0	0	0	1	0	0	1
	ALL & MORE DATAB	0	0	0	0	1	0	0	1
	NONE AS PRIME SO	0	2	0	0	0	0	0	2
	OTHER---UNSPECIFI	0	2	1	0	0	0	0	3
	UNSPECI. COMB. &	0	0	0	1	0	0	0	1
	ALL ABOVE & COMB	0	0	0	0	0	0	1	1
	A, B, D & OTHER	0	0	0	0	0	0	1	1
	B, C, D & BIB. S	0	0	0	0	0	0	1	1
	TOTALS	18	33	8	3	40	40	68	210

QUESTIONNAIRE RESPONSES

QUESTION		LIB SCI PROFS	SCIENTIFIC TECHNICAL	LIBRARY NETWORK	PUBLISH-ERS	RESEARCH LIBRARIANS	LAW DEANS	LAW LIBRARIANS	ROW TOTALS
Q16									
A.	CONTINUED POL	2	6	1	0	2	2	5	18
B.	NEW ROLE	0	1	0	0	1	5	1	8
C.	A & B	16	25	7	3	40	34	68	193
	TOTALS	18	32	8	3	43	41	74	219

Respondents' Opinions

QUESTIONNAIRE RESPONSES

QUESTION	LIB SCI PROFS	SCIENTIFIC TECHNICAL	LIBRARY NETWORK	PUBLISH-ERS	RESEARCH LIBRARIANS	LAW DEANS	LAW LIBRARIANS	ROW TOTALS
Q17A								
STRONGLY AGREE	1	3	1	2	1	5	10	23
AGREE	6	19	5	1	28	29	54	142
UNDECIDED	5	1	0	0	3	2	3	14
DISAGREE	6	7	2	0	11	6	7	39
STRONGLY DISAGREE	0	1	0	0	0	0	1	2
TOTALS	18	31	8	3	43	42	75	220
Q17B								
VERY DESIRABLE	1	2	2	1	5	6	8	25
DESIRABLE	3	18	5	1	17	20	45	109
UNDECIDED	5	7	0	0	8	10	13	43
UNDESIRABLE	9	3	1	1	7	5	4	30
VERY UNDESIRABLE	0	0	0	0	0	0	1	1
TOTALS	18	30	8	3	37	41	71	208
Q17C								
1990	4	14	2	1	10	19	32	82
2000	4	8	4	1	16	9	22	64
POST-2000	4	4	0	1	9	9	13	40
NEVER	2	1	1	0	2	0	2	8
TOTALS	14	27	7	3	37	37	69	194

The Twenty-First Century

QUESTIONNAIRE RESPONSES

QUESTION	LIB SCI PROFS	SCIENTIFIC TECHNICAL	LIBRARY NETWORK	PUBLISH- ERS	RESEARCH LIBRARIANS	LAW DEANS	LAW LIBRARIANS	ROW TOTALS
Q18A								
STRONGLY AGREE	0	2	0	1	2	5	3	13
AGREE	4	11	1	1	8	19	35	79
UNDECIDED	3	5	0	0	11	7	10	36
DISAGREE	8	11	5	0	20	10	25	79
STRONGLY DISAGREE	1	0	0	0	1	1	2	5
TOTALS	16	29	6	2	42	42	75	212
Q18B								
VERY DESIRABLE	0	2	0	1	1	3	4	11
DESIRABLE	3	9	0	0	9	17	31	69
UNDECIDED	3	8	1	0	11	10	15	48
UNDESIRABLE	8	8	5	1	14	11	20	67
VERY UNDESIRABLE	2	0	0	0	0	1	1	4
TOTALS	16	27	6	2	35	42	71	199
Q18C								
1990	1	9	0	1	2	12	11	36
2000	1	9	1	0	11	9	25	56
POST-2000	6	1	0	1	5	8	11	32
NEVER	5	2	5	0	8	4	10	34
TOTALS	13	21	6	2	26	33	57	158

Respondents' Opinions

QUESTIONNAIRE RESPONSES

QUESTION	LIB SCI PROFS	SCIENTIFIC TECHNICAL	LIBRARY NETWORK	PUBLISH-ERS	RESEARCH LIBRARIANS	LAW DEANS	LAW LIBRARIANS	ROW TOTALS
Q19A								
UNDER 25%	5	7	1	1	14	7	24	59
26% TO 50%	3	10	2	1	4	10	20	50
51% TO 75%	1	4	0	0	4	10	11	30
76% TO 90%	4	3	0	0	6	9	8	30
91% to 100%	1	0	1	0	3	3	4	12
TOTALS	14	24	4	2	31	39	67	181
Q19B								
VERY DESIRABLE	0	4	0	1	5	2	9	21
DESIRABLE	7	12	2	0	11	18	43	93
UNDECIDED	2	7	0	1	8	13	10	41
UNDESIRABLE	4	2	1	0	4	6	5	22
VERY UNDESIRABLE	1	0	1	0	2	0	0	4
TOTALS	14	25	4	2	30	39	67	181

QUESTIONNAIRE RESPONSES

QUESTION	LIB SCI PROFS	SCIENTIFIC TECHNICAL	LIBRARY NETWORK	PUBLISH-ERS	RESEARCH LIBRARIANS	LAW DEANS	LAW LIBRARIANS	ROW TOTALS
Q20A								
UNDER 25%	8	12	2	0	18	17	23	80
26% TO 50%	3	7	0	1	5	6	24	46
51% TO 75%	0	6	1	0	1	9	11	28
76% TO 90%	3	0	0	0	6	4	4	17
91% TO 100%	1	0	1	0	2	2	4	10
TOTALS	15	25	4	1	32	38	66	181
Q20B								
VERY DESIRABLE	0	3	1	1	5	4	9	23
DESIRABLE	9	12	2	0	15	16	40	94
UNDECIDED	2	6	0	1	6	11	13	39
UNDESIRABLE	2	4	1	0	4	6	2	19
VERY UNDESIRABLE	1	0	0	0	1	0	0	2
TOTALS	14	25	4	2	31	37	64	177

The Twenty-First Century

QUESTIONNAIRE RESPONSES

QUESTION	LIB SCI PROFS	SCIENTIFIC TECHNICAL	LIBRARY NETWORK	PUBLISH-ERS	RESEARCH LIBRARIANS	LAW DEANS	LAW LIBRARIANS	ROW TOTALS
Q21A								
A-V MATERIALS	0	2	0	1	1	0	5	9
SAME AS NOW	4	0	1	0	7	0	2	14
REPORTERS, ETC.	2	1	1	0	3	5	7	19
MISC. HARD-COPY	1	2	2	0	8	7	12	32
SOFTWARE & COMPU	1	3	0	2	3	3	13	25
LASER DISKS, ETC.	4	2	2	0	2	1	3	14
SPECIFIC BOOK TY	0	3	0	0	4	2	1	10
MICROFORM & ARCH	0	2	0	0	2	0	2	6
STUDY AIDS, ETC.	0	1	0	0	0	1	2	4
TOTALS	12	16	6	3	30	19	47	133
Q21B								
A-V MATERIALS	0	1	2	0	2	1	5	11
SAME AS NOW	0	0	0	0	0	0	1	1
REPORTERS, ETC.	0	0	0	0	6	3	5	14
MISC. HARD-COPY	2	0	0	1	1	3	6	13
SOFTWARE & COMPU	0	2	2	1	1	1	7	14
LASER DISKS, ETC.	2	3	0	0	5	2	6	18
SPECIFIC BOOK TY	1	5	0	0	6	3	2	17
MICROFORM & ARCH	0	1	0	0	2	2	3	8
STUDY AIDS, ETC.	0	2	0	0	1	0	1	4
TOTALS	5	14	4	2	24	15	36	100

QUESTIONNAIRE RESPONSES

QUESTION	LIB SCI PROFS	SCIENTIFIC TECHNICAL	LIBRARY NETWORK	PUBLISH-ERS	RESEARCH LIBRARIANS	LAW DEANS	LAW LIBRARIANS	ROW TOTALS
Q21C (CONTINUED)								
A-V MATERIALS	0	0	1	0	3	0	1	5
SAME AS NOW	1	0	0	0	0	0	1	2
REPORTERS, ETC.	0	0	1	2	2	1	3	9
MISC, HARD-COPY	0	0	1	0	3	1	5	10
SOFTWARE & COMPU	0	2	1	0	5	3	7	18
LASER DISKS, ETC.	0	0	0	0	1	1	3	5
SPECIFIC BOOK TY	0	4	0	0	4	1	1	10
MICROFORM & ARCH	0	0	0	0	0	0	5	5
STUDY AIDS, ETC.	0	0	0	0	0	0	1	1
TOTALS	1	6	4	2	18	7	27	65

Respondents' Opinions

QUESTIONNAIRE RESPONSES

QUESTION	LIB SCI PROFS	SCIENTIFIC TECHNICAL	LIBRARY NETWORK	PUBLISH-ERS	RESEARCH LIBRARIANS	LAW DEANS	LAW LIBRARIANS	ROW TOTALS
Q22A								
UNSPECIFIED COMB	2	7	1	0	7	4	9	30
A. LIBRARIAN	2	7	1	1	15	6	17	49
B. DEAN	1	1	1	0	1	2	2	8
C. FACULTY COMMI	1	5	0	0	1	2	1	10
A, B, C	3	6	2	0	5	11	20	47
A, B	3	1	1	1	3	17	21	47
A, C	3	1	0	0	9	0	3	16
IT DEPENDS	1	1	0	1	0	0	0	3
TOTALS	16	29	6	3	41	42	73	210
Q22B								
1990	7	13	4	1	32	32	48	137
2000	6	5	2	1	4	3	3	24
POST-2000	0	3	0	0	0	0	6	9
TOTALS	13	21	6	2	36	35	57	170

QUESTIONNAIRE RESPONSES

QUESTION	LIB SCI PROFS	SCIENTIFIC TECHNICAL	LIBRARY NETWORK	PUBLISH-ERS	RESEARCH LIBRARIANS	LAW DEANS	LAW LIBRARIANS	ROW TOTALS
Q23A								
CAMPUS-WIDE OFFI	0	0	1	0	1	0	0	2
YES	14	24	4	1	38	39	69	189
NO--UNSPEC.	0	2	0	0	1	1	1	5
IT DEPENDS	0	1	0	1	0	0	0	2
LIBRARIAN'S EMPL	0	1	0	0	0	0	1	2
COMMITTEE	1	1	0	0	0	1	2	5
ACCOUNTABLE DEPT	0	0	0	0	1	0	0	1
AUTOMATION OFFIC	0	1	0	1	2	1	0	5
CHANCELLOR LEVEL	1	0	0	0	0	0	0	1
TOTALS	16	30	5	3	43	42	73	212
Q23B								
1990	10	14	2	1	27	33	43	130
2000	2	6	3	1	6	2	6	26
POST-2000	0	2	0	0	0	0	6	8
NEVER	0	1	0	0	0	0	0	1
TOTALS	12	23	5	2	33	35	55	165

The Twenty-First Century

QUESTIONNAIRE RESPONSES

QUESTION	LIB SCI PROFS	SCIENTIFIC TECHNICAL	LIBRARY NETWORK	PUBLISH-ERS	RESEARCH LIBRARIANS	LAW DEANS	LAW LIBRARIANS	ROW TOTALS
Q24A								
STRONGLY AGREE	0	6	0	0	2	5	6	19
AGREE	5	10	2	1	10	10	20	58
UNDECIDED	1	2	0	0	5	2	7	17
DISAGREE	7	11	3	0	24	21	33	99
STRONGLY DISAGREE	3	1	1	1	3	5	8	22
TOTALS	16	30	6	2	44	43	74	215
Q24B								
VERY DESIRABLE	0	7	0	0	3	3	6	19
DESIRABLE	4	8	1	0	6	10	16	45
UNDECIDED	2	5	1	1	7	5	12	33
UNDESIRABLE	7	9	3	0	20	19	26	84
VERY UNDESIRABLE	3	1	1	1	4	4	10	24
TOTALS	16	30	6	2	40	41	70	205
Q24C								
1990	3	12	4	0	21	19	30	89
2000	4	4	1	0	3	5	4	21
POST-2000	1	1	0	1	0	0	7	10
NEVER	7	5	1	0	11	8	12	44
TOTALS	15	22	6	1	35	32	53	164

Respondents' Opinions

QUESTIONNAIRE RESPONSES

QUESTION	LIB SCI PROFS	SCIENTIFIC TECHNICAL	LIBRARY NETWORK	PUBLISH-ERS	RESEARCH LIBRARIANS	LAW DEANS	LAW LIBRARIANS	ROW TOTALS
Q25A								
STRONGLY AGREE	3	5	0	1	2	8	13	32
AGREE	9	20	5	1	36	28	53	152
UNDECIDED	1	3	0	1	4	6	5	20
DISAGREE	3	1	0	0	0	0	4	8
STRONGLY DISAGREE	1	0	0	0	0	1	0	2
TOTALS	17	29	5	3	42	43	75	214
Q25B								
VERY DESIRABLE	6	4	0	2	7	12	18	49
DESIRABLE	9	21	5	0	30	26	45	136
UNDECIDED	1	2	0	1	3	4	9	20
UNDESIRABLE	0	0	0	0	1	0	0	1
VERY UNDESIRABLE	1	0	0	0	0	0	0	1
TOTALS	17	27	5	3	41	42	72	207
Q25C								
1990	10	16	4	1	27	23	39	120
2000	3	10	1	0	7	10	11	42
POST-2000	1	1	0	0	1	0	8	11
NEVER	2	0	0	0	0	0	0	2
TOTALS	16	27	5	1	35	33	58	175

The Twenty-First Century

QUESTIONNAIRE RESPONSES

QUESTION	LIB SCI PROFS	SCIENTIFIC TECHNICAL	LIBRARY NETWORK	PUBLISHERS	RESEARCH LIBRARIANS	LAW DEANS	LAW LIBRARIANS	ROW TOTALS
Q26								
LESS	3	7	2	0	17	18	29	76
THE SAME	2	9	1	0	4	5	13	34
MORE	13	13	3	2	19	17	29	96
TOTALS	18	29	6	2	40	40	71	206

QUESTION	LIB SCI PROFS	SCIENTIFIC TECHNICAL	LIBRARY NETWORK	PUBLISHERS	RESEARCH LIBRARIANS	LAW DEANS	LAW LIBRARIANS	ROW TOTALS
Q27								
YES	12	16	5	1	26	26	37	123
NO	4	7	1	1	13	10	16	52
DON'T KNOW	2	6	2	0	4	7	21	42
TOTALS	18	29	8	2	43	43	74	217

QUESTION	LIB SCI PROFS	SCIENTIFIC TECHNICAL	LIBRARY NETWORK	PUBLISHERS	RESEARCH LIBRARIANS	LAW DEANS	LAW LIBRARIANS	ROW TOTALS
Q28								
PRESERVED	10	8	2	0	13	17	37	87
INCREASED	3	9	3	1	8	9	20	53
DECREASED	4	8	0	0	15	9	11	47
TOTALS	17	25	5	1	36	35	68	187

Respondents' Opinions

QUESTIONNAIRE RESPONSES

QUESTION	LIB SCI PROFS	SCIENTIFIC TECHNICAL	LIBRARY NETWORK	PUBLISH-ERS	RESEARCH LIBRARIANS	LAW DEANS	LAW LIBRARIANS	ROW TOTALS
Q29								
HARD COPY	7	16	4	1	20	24	42	114
INFO SYSTEM	7	4	2	1	9	6	13	42
OTHER	2	4	0	0	5	4	8	23
TOTALS	16	24	6	2	34	34	63	179

QUESTION	LIB SCI PROFS	SCIENTIFIC TECHNICAL	LIBRARY NETWORK	PUBLISH-ERS	RESEARCH LIBRARIANS	LAW DEANS	LAW LIBRARIANS	ROW TOTALS
Q30								
UNSPEC. COMB.	2	6	1	0	7	1	6	23
A. LIBRARY	1	3	0	0	5	9	16	34
B. COLLEGE OR DEPT.	4	8	1	0	3	14	18	48
C. FACULTY	0	1	0	0	2	0	3	6
A, B, C	5	4	2	1	18	4	8	42
A, B	2	4	2	0	6	12	11	37
A, C	2	0	1	0	1	1	5	10
B, C	1	2	0	0	2	2	5	12
TOTALS	17	28	7	1	44	43	72	212

The Twenty-First Century

QUESTIONNAIRE RESULTS

QUESTION	LIB SCI PROFS	SCIENTIFIC TECHNICAL	LIBRARY NETWORK	RESEARCH LIBRARIANS	LAW DEANS	LAW LIBRARIANS	ROW TOTALS
Q31A							
STRONGLY AGREE	3	4	0	2	10	12	31
AGREE	10	14	6	18	19	36	103
UNDECIDED	2	3	1	8	8	14	36
DISAGREE	1	4	0	14	5	11	35
STRONGLY DISAGREE	1	2	1	0	0	1	5
TOTALS	17	27	8	42	42	74	210
Q31B							
VERY DESIRABLE	3	5	0	6	17	18	49
DESIRABLE	10	10	6	14	15	32	87
UNDECIDED	2	4	0	8	6	11	31
UNDESIRABLE	1	4	1	12	4	5	27
VERY UNDESIRABLE	1	2	1	0	0	3	7
TOTALS	17	25	8	40	42	69	201
Q31C							
1990	9	13	5	19	26	43	115
2000	4	4	1	4	4	7	24
POST-2000	0	1	0	2	1	2	6
NEVER	2	2	1	7	4	5	21
TOTALS	15	20	7	32	35	57	166

Respondents' Opinions

QUESTIONNAIRE RESPONSES

QUESTION	LIB SCI PROFS	SCIENTIFIC TECHNICAL	LIBRARY NETWORK	PUBLISH-ERS	RESEARCH LIBRARIANS	LAW DEANS	LAW LIBRARIANS	ROW TOTALS
Q32A								
STRONGLY AGREE	4	6	1	0	9	7	10	37
AGREE	12	12	6	1	27	22	38	118
UNDECIDED	0	5	1	1	2	4	15	28
DISAGREE	1	7	0	0	5	10	9	32
STRONGLY DISAGREE	0	0	0	0	0	0	2	2
TOTALS	17	30	8	2	43	43	74	217
Q32B								
VERY DESIRABLE	5	6	1	0	5	7	15	39
DESIRABLE	6	11	5	0	18	16	27	83
UNDECIDED	2	1	1	1	6	5	16	32
UNDESIRABLE	3	8	1	0	10	15	7	44
VERY UNDESIRABLE	1	1	0	1	2	0	2	7
TOTALS	17	27	8	2	41	43	67	205
Q32C								
1990	11	13	6	1	32	26	42	131
2000	5	4	1	0	1	1	6	18
POST-2000	0	1	0	0	1	1	3	6
NEVER	1	4	0	0	2	5	7	19
TOTALS	17	22	7	1	36	33	58	174

THE TWENTY-FIRST CENTURY

QUESTIONNAIRE RESPONSES

QUESTION	LIB SCI PROFS	SCIENTIFIC TECHNICAL	LIBRARY NETWORK	PUBLISH-ERS	RESEARCH LIBRARIANS	LAW DEANS	LAW LIBRARIANS	ROW TOTALS
Q33A								
STRONGLY AGREE	1	1	0	0	3	2	1	8
AGREE	8	10	4	1	9	7	13	52
UNDECIDED	2	4	0	0	10	11	10	37
DISAGREE	5	12	3	1	17	20	37	95
STRONGLY DISAGREE	1	0	1	0	3	3	11	19
TOTALS	17	27	8	2	42	43	72	211
Q33B								
VERY DESIRABLE	0	1	0	0	1	2	1	5
DESIRABLE	3	7	0	0	6	6	7	29
UNDECIDED	2	3	1	1	6	7	10	30
UNDESIRABLE	8	13	5	1	20	21	38	106
VERY UNDESIRABLE	4	2	1	0	8	5	13	33
TOTALS	17	26	7	2	41	41	69	203
Q33C								
1990	10	11	3	2	16	15	20	77
2000	2	5	1	0	4	1	4	17
POST-2000	1	1	0	0	5	3	3	13
NEVER	1	5	1	0	7	5	29	48
TOTALS	14	22	5	2	32	24	56	155

QUESTIONNAIRE RESPONSES

QUESTION	LIB SCI PROFS	SCIENTIFIC TECHNICAL	LIBRARY NETWORK	PUBLISH-ERS	RESEARCH LIBRARIANS	LAW DEANS	LAW LIBRARIANS	ROW TOTALS
Q34A								
STRONGLY AGREE	0	3	0	1	2	1	11	18
AGREE	8	13	4	1	14	22	33	95
UNDECIDED	2	4	2	0	8	9	11	36
DISAGREE	7	12	2	0	17	9	15	62
STRONGLY DISAGREE	1	0	0	0	1	2	4	8
TOTALS	18	32	8	2	42	43	74	219
Q34B								
VERY DESIRABLE	3	9	0	2	2	5	14	35
DESIRABLE	11	7	6	0	18	24	41	107
UNDECIDED	1	4	1	0	9	7	7	29
UNDESIRABLE	2	8	0	0	10	2	4	26
VERY UNDESIRABLE	1	0	0	0	1	2	3	7
TOTALS	18	28	7	2	40	40	69	204

Respondents' Opinions

QUESTIONNAIRE RESPONSES

QUESTION	LIB SCI PROFS	SCIENTIFIC TECHNICAL	LIBRARY NETWORK	PUBLISH-ERS	RESEARCH LIBRARIANS	LAW DEANS	LAW LIBRARIANS	ROW TOTALS
Q35A								
STRONGLY AGREE	3	7	1	1	5	13	18	48
AGREE	13	15	6	1	32	24	44	135
UNDECIDED	1	4	0	0	5	4	3	17
DISAGREE	0	3	1	0	2	1	7	14
STRONGLY DISAGREE	1	1	0	0	0	0	1	3
TOTALS	18	30	8	2	44	42	73	217
Q35B								
VERY DESIRABLE	9	9	2	1	12	15	22	70
DESIRABLE	8	14	5	0	23	21	36	107
UNDECIDED	0	1	0	0	3	4	4	12
UNDESIRABLE	0	2	1	0	3	1	3	10
VERY UNDESIRABLE	1	1	0	1	0	0	1	4
TOTALS	18	27	8	2	41	41	66	203
Q35C								
1990	13	16	3	2	35	30	49	148
2000	3	1	0	0	0	3	2	9
POST-2000	1	2	1	0	1	0	3	8
NEVER	0	1	1	0	2	1	4	9
TOTALS	17	20	5	2	38	34	58	174

THE TWENTY-FIRST CENTURY

QUESTIONNAIRE RESPONSES

QUESTION	LIB SCI PROFS	SCIENTIFIC TECHNICAL	LIBRARY NETWORK	PUBLISH-ERS	RESEARCH LIBRARIANS	LAW DEANS	LAW LIBRARIANS	ROW TOTALS
Q36A								
STRONGLY AGREE	1	0	0	0	3	1	3	8
AGREE	3	9	2	0	6	6	12	38
UNDECIDED	0	5	1	1	7	10	12	36
DISAGREE	14	15	4	0	23	19	34	109
STRONGLY DISAGREE	0	4	0	0	4	6	12	26
TOTALS	18	33	7	1	43	42	73	217
Q36B								
VERY DESIRABLE	3	4	0	0	4	3	5	19
DESIRABLE	5	10	5	0	14	10	12	56
UNDECIDED	5	5	1	1	5	12	14	43
UNDESIRABLE	5	9	0	0	13	13	26	66
VERY UNDESIRABLE	0	2	0	0	4	3	9	18
TOTALS	18	30	6	1	40	41	66	202
Q36C								
1990	6	10	2		16	16	22	72
2000	3	4	0		6	3	5	21
POST-2000	1	3	0		3	3	3	13
NEVER	6	6	1		9	5	20	47
TOTALS	16	23	3		34	27	50	153

Respondents' Opinions

QUESTIONNAIRE RESPONSES

QUESTION	LIB SCI PROFS	SCIENTIFIC TECHNICAL	LIBRARY NETWORK	PUBLISH-ERS	RESEARCH LIBRARIANS	LAW DEANS	LAW LIBRARIANS	ROW TOTALS
Q37A								
STRONGLY AGREE	0	4	0	1	2	2	8	17
AGREE	11	14	5	1	25	24	33	113
UNDECIDED	2	9	1	0	10	8	16	46
DISAGREE	5	5	2	0	7	6	12	37
STRONGLY DISAGREE	0	1	0	0	0	1	3	5
TOTALS	18	33	8	2	44	41	72	218
Q37B								
VERY DESIRABLE	1	5	0	1	2	2	7	18
DESIRABLE	7	12	1	0	17	24	27	88
UNDECIDED	3	4	3	0	14	7	17	48
UNDESIRABLE	6	8	3	0	8	7	11	43
VERY UNDESIRABLE	1	0	0	1	0	1	4	7
TOTALS	18	29	7	2	41	41	66	204
Q37C								
1990	10	14	2	2	25	15	27	95
2000	4	4	0	0	5	4	14	31
POST-2000	0	1	0	0	0	6	2	9
NEVER	2	3	1	0	3	3	9	21
TOTALS	16	22	3	2	33	28	52	156

THE TWENTY-FIRST CENTURY

QUESTIONNAIRE RESPONSES

QUESTION	LIB SCI PROFS	SCIENTIFIC TECHNICAL	LIBRARY NETWORK	PUBLISH-ERS	RESEARCH LIBRARIANS	LAW DEANS	LAW LIBRARIANS	ROW TOTALS
Q38A								
STRONGLY AGREE	4	9	1	1	9	6	12	42
AGREE	12	21	6	1	34	31	50	155
UNDECIDED	1	0	1	0	0	4	8	14
DISAGREE	1	1	0	0	1	1	5	9
STRONGLY DISAGREE	0	0	0	0	0	1	0	1
TOTALS	18	31	8	2	44	43	75	221
Q38B								
VERY DESIRABLE	3	8	1	1	9	5	13	40
DESIRABLE	13	20	5	0	28	28	45	139
UNDECIDED	1	0	1	0	1	7	14	24
UNDESIRABLE	1	1	0	0	1	0	1	4
VERY UNDESIRABLE	0	0	0	0	0	1	0	1
TOTALS	18	29	7	1	39	41	73	208
Q38C								
1990	11	16	4	1	26	23	41	122
2000	5	11	2	0	12	7	17	54
POST-2000	1	1	0	0	1	2	3	8
NEVER	0	0	0	0	0	1	1	2
TOTALS	17	28	6	1	39	33	62	186

QUESTIONNAIRE RESPONSES

QUESTION	LIB SCI PROFS	SCIENTIFIC TECHNICAL	LIBRARY NETWORK	PUBLISH-ERS	RESEARCH LIBRARIANS	LAW DEANS	LAW LIBRARIANS	ROW TOTALS
Q39A								
INCREASE	6	8	2	0	7	15	14	52
DECREASE	3	13	1	0	8	3	7	35
REMAIN UNCHANGED	8	9	4	1	28	20	52	122
TOTALS	17	30	7	1	43	38	73	209
Q39B								
1990	8	15	3		22	20	30	98
2000	8	8	1		9	7	20	53
POST-2000	0	1	1		0	1	5	8
TOTALS	16	24	5		31	28	55	159

Respondents' Opinions

QUESTIONNAIRE RESPONSES

QUESTION	LIB SCI PROFS	SCIENTIFIC TECHNICAL	LIBRARY NETWORK	PUBLISHERS	RESEARCH LIBRARIANS	LAW DEANS	LAW LIBRARIANS	ROW TOTALS
Q40A								
INCREASE	13	14	5	1	36	29	61	159
DECREASE	1	12	0	0	2	3	2	20
REMAIN UNCHANGED	3	4	2	0	5	7	10	31
TOTALS	17	30	7	1	43	39	73	210
Q40B								
1990	10	15	4	1	29	25	39	123
2000	6	8	2	0	5	6	21	48
POST-2000	1	1	0	0	0	0	1	3
TOTALS	17	24	6	1	34	31	61	174

QUESTIONNAIRE RESULTS

QUESTION	LIB SCI PROFS	SCIENTIFIC TECHNICAL	LIBRARY NETWORK	RESEARCH LIBRARIANS	LAW DEANS	LAW LIBRARIANS	ROW TOTALS
Q41A							
INCREASE	1	12	0	5	14	16	48
DECREASE	13	16	6	33	22	35	125
REMAIN UNCHANGED	3	2	1	5	5	23	39
TOTALS	17	30	7	43	41	74	212
Q41B							
1990	10	18	4	26	20	32	110
2000	6	6	2	7	10	24	55
POST-2000	1	2	0	0	1	3	7
TOTALS	17	26	6	33	31	59	172

THE TWENTY-FIRST CENTURY

QUESTIONNAIRE RESPONSES

QUESTION	LIB SCI PROFS	SCIENTIFIC TECHNICAL	LIBRARY NETWORK	PUBLISH-ERS	RESEARCH LIBRARIANS	LAW DEANS	LAW LIBRARIANS	ROW TOTALS
Q42A								
INCREASE	11	9	3	0	20	7	20	70
DECREASE	4	18	0	1	13	15	29	80
REMAIN UNCHANGED	2	5	4	1	11	16	23	62
TOTALS	17	32	7	2	44	38	72	212
Q42B								
1990	10	17	4		27	22	32	112
2000	6	8	1		6	7	24	52
POST-2000	0	2	0		0	1	5	8
TOTALS	16	27	5		33	30	61	172

QUESTIONNAIRE RESULTS

QUESTION	LIB SCI PROFS	SCIENTIFIC TECHNICAL	LIBRARY NETWORK	RESEARCH LIBRARIANS	LAW DEANS	LAW LIBRARIANS	ROW TOTALS
Q43A							
INCREASE	12	21	3	32	27	48	143
DECREASE	0	6	0	2	3	2	13
REMAIN UNCHANGED	0	3	1	4	6	8	22
TOTALS	12	30	4	38	36	58	178
Q43B							
1990	7	18	3	21	22	27	98
2000	4	6	1	9	4	19	43
POST-2000	0	1	0	0	1	1	3
TOTALS	11	25	4	30	27	47	144

Respondents' Opinions

QUESTIONNAIRE RESPONSES

QUESTION	LIB SCI PROFS	SCIENTIFIC TECHNICAL	LIBRARY NETWORK	PUBLISH- ERS	RESEARCH LIBRARIANS	LAW DEANS	LAW LIBRARIANS	ROW TOTALS
Q44A								
STRONGLY AGREE	0	4	1	1	1	4	13	24
AGREE	9	14	3	0	15	19	27	87
UNDECIDED	0	5	0	0	6	10	12	33
DISAGREE	7	5	2	0	16	10	16	56
STRONGLY DISAGREE	0	1	0	0	3	0	2	6
TOTALS	16	29	6	1	41	43	70	206
Q44B								
VERY DESIRABLE	0	5	1	1	1	6	14	28
DESIRABLE	9	13	3	0	12	18	23	78
UNDECIDED	1	5	0	0	6	9	14	35
INDESIRABLE	5	4	2	0	14	6	12	43
VERY UNDESIRABLE	1	2	0	0	4	0	2	9
TOTALS	16	29	6	1	37	39	65	193
Q44C								
1990	9	15	4	0	20	21	34	103
2000	4	5	1	1	4	5	11	31
POST-2000	0	2	0	0	2	1	1	6
TOTALS	13	22	5	1	26	27	46	140

The Twenty-First Century

QUESTIONNAIRE RESPONSES

QUESTION	LIB SCI PROFS	SCIENTIFIC TECHNICAL	LIBRARY NETWORK	PUBLISH-ERS	RESEARCH LIBRARIANS	LAW DEANS	LAW LIBRARIANS	ROW TOTALS
Q45A								
STRONGLY AGREE	0	3	2	1	3	3	3	15
AGREE	10	20	4	0	22	15	38	109
UNDECIDED	4	2	1	0	5	10	17	39
DISAGREE	3	4	1	0	10	11	10	39
STRONGLY DISAGREE	0	0	0	0	1	1	1	3
TOTALS	17	29	8	1	41	40	69	205
Q45B								
VERY DESIRABLE	0	3	2	1	3	3	4	16
DESIRABLE	9	17	4	0	22	16	31	99
UNDECIDED	5	5	0	0	6	9	17	42
UNDESIRABLE	3	4	1	0	5	9	9	31
VERY UNDESIRABLE	0	0	0	0	2	0	1	3
TOTALS	17	29	7	1	38	37	62	191
Q45C								
1990	9	18	5	1	27	14	28	102
2000	2	3	0	0	5	5	11	26
POST-2000	1	1	0	0	2	1	1	6
NEVER	0	0	0	0	2	1	5	8
TOTALS	12	22	5	1	36	21	45	142

Respondents' Opinions

QUESTIONNAIRE RESPONSES

QUESTION	LIB SCI PROFS	SCIENTIFIC TECHNICAL	LIBRARY NETWORK	PUBLISH-ERS	RESEARCH LIBRARIANS	LAW DEANS	LAW LIBRARIANS	ROW TOTALS
Q46A								
STRONGLY AGREE	3	11	1	2	11	6	14	48
AGREE	12	10	5	0	25	30	48	130
UNDECIDED	2	6	1	0	4	4	8	25
DISAGREE	1	2	0	0	4	2	3	12
STRONGLY DISAGREE	0	0	0	0	0	1	1	2
TOTALS	18	29	7	2	44	43	74	217
Q46B								
VERY DESIRABLE	10	14	5	2	15	10	22	78
DESIRABLE	8	9	2	0	23	30	41	113
UNDECIDED	0	3	0	0	2	2	6	13
UNDESIRABLE	0	2	0	0	1	0	0	3
VERY UNDESIRABLE	0	0	0	0	0	0	1	1
TOTALS	18	28	7	2	41	42	70	208
Q46C								
1990	13	18	5	2	31	24	45	138
2000	2	5	0	0	5	6	11	29
POST-2000	0	0	0	0	0	2	2	4
NEVER	1	2	0	0	1	2	2	8
TOTALS	16	25	5	2	37	34	60	179

QUESTIONNAIRE RESPONSES

QUESTION	LIB SCI PROFS	SCIENTIFIC TECHNICAL	LIBRARY NETWORK	PUBLISH-ERS	RESEARCH LIBRARIANS	LAW DEANS	LAW LIBRARIANS	ROW TOTALS
Q47								
A. COLLEGE LIBRARY	2	2	0	0	1	16	26	47
B. COLLEGE OR DEPT	1	5	1	0	0	3	4	14
C. COMPUTER CENTER	0	4	0	0	4	2	5	15
D. PARENT LIBRARY	3	5	1	0	10	2	1	22
A, B, C, D	4	1	0	0	3	1	5	14
A, B, C	1	0	0	0	0	0	5	6
A, B	0	2	0	0	0	4	10	16
C, D	0	2	0	0	1	0	2	5
C	1	1	0	0	1	4	5	12
B, D	0	0	0	0	0	3	0	3
D	0	1	0	0	1	1	1	4
C, D	0	1	0	0	5	1	0	7
C	0	0	0	0	1	1	0	2
D	0	0	0	0	0	0	1	1
D	3	1	2	0	7	0	3	16
UNSPECIFIED COMBINATION	1	2	2	0	6	0	1	12
DEPT. FOR STUDENT	0	0	0	0	0	1	0	1
VICE CHANCELLOR	1	0	0	0	0	0	0	1
DEPENDS ON INSTITUTION	1	2	2	1	1	0	1	8
WHOEVER USES	0	1	0	0	0	0	0	1
VARIES	0	0	0	0	0	0	1	1
B & UNSPEC. OTHER	0	1	0	0	0	0	0	1
TOTALLY DECENTRALIZED	0	1	0	0	0	0	0	1
TOTALS	18	32	8	1	41	39	71	210

Respondents' Opinions

QUESTIONNAIRE RESPONSES

QUESTION	LIB SCI PROFS	SCIENTIFIC TECHNICAL	LIBRARY NETWORK	PUBLISHERS	RESEARCH LIBRARIANS	LAW DEANS	LAW LIBRARIANS	ROW TOTALS
Q48A								
STRONGLY AGREE	4	10	2	2	7	19	25	69
AGREE	12	19	6	0	31	22	45	135
UNDECIDED	1	2	0	0	1	0	2	6
DISAGREE	1	1	0	0	5	2	2	11
STRONGLY DISAGREE	0	0	0	0	0	0	1	1
TOTALS	18	32	8	2	44	43	75	222
Q48B								
VERY DESIRABLE	9	15	2	2	14	20	31	93
DESIRABLE	8	14	5	0	24	19	32	102
UNDECIDED	1	0	1	0	0	2	6	10
UNDESIRABLE	0	1	0	0	3	1	1	6
VERY UNDESIRABLE	0	0	0	0	0	0	1	1
TOTALS	18	30	8	2	41	42	71	212
Q48C								
1990	10	19	3	2	22	26	35	117
2000	6	8	2	0	13	8	23	60
POST-2000	1	1	2	0	4	5	5	18
NEVER	0	1	0	0	1	0	1	3
TOTALS	17	29	7	2	40	39	64	198

THE TWENTY-FIRST CENTURY

QUESTIONNAIRE RESPONSES

QUESTION	LIB SCI PROFS	SCIENTIFIC TECHNICAL	LIBRARY NETWORK	PUBLISH-ERS	RESEARCH LIBRARIANS	LAW DEANS	LAW LIBRARIANS	ROW TOTALS
Q49A								
STRONGLY AGREE	5	11	3	1	4	10	13	47
AGREE	10	17	5	0	31	27	47	137
UNDECIDED	0	2	0	1	3	2	6	14
DISAGREE	3	3	0	0	6	4	8	24
STRONGLY DISAGREE	0	0	0	0	0	0	1	1
TOTALS	18	33	8	2	44	43	75	223
Q49B								
VERY DESIRABLE	9	15	5	2	7	15	17	70
DESIRABLE	7	13	3	0	30	22	44	119
UNDECIDED	1	3	0	0	3	2	7	16
UNDESIRABLE	1	1	0	0	1	1	1	5
VERY UNDESIRABLE	0	0	0	0	0	0	1	1
TOTALS	18	32	8	2	41	40	70	211
Q49C								
1990	11	17	4	1	22	18	22	95
2000	6	10	3	0	16	11	32	78
POST-2000	0	3	0	0	2	7	8	20
NEVER	0	1	0	0	0	1	2	4
TOTALS	17	31	7	1	40	37	64	197

Respondents' Opinions

QUESTIONNAIRE RESPONSES

QUESTION	LIB SCI PROFS	SCIENTIFIC TECHNICAL	LIBRARY NETWORK	PUBLISH-ERS	RESEARCH LIBRARIANS	LAW DEANS	LAW LIBRARIANS	ROW TOTALS
Q50A								
STRONGLY AGREE	3	12	1	1	3	4	12	36
AGREE	10	12	5	1	28	25	33	114
UNDECIDED	2	4	1	0	5	7	15	34
DISAGREE	3	5	1	0	6	6	14	35
STRONGLY DISAGREE	0	0	0	0	0	1	1	2
TOTALS	18	33	8	2	42	43	75	221
Q50B								
VERY DESIRABLE	5	17	4	2	8	9	14	59
DESIRABLE	9	10	3	0	24	27	37	110
UNDECIDED	3	4	0	0	4	3	16	30
UNDESIRABLE	1	1	0	0	4	3	4	13
VERY UNDESIRABLE	0	0	0	0	0	0	1	1
TOTALS	18	32	7	2	40	42	72	213
Q50C								
1990	7	19	5	1	24	15	20	91
2000	6	5	2	0	9	6	22	50
POST-2000	0	3	0	0	3	8	9	23
NEVER	2	1	0	0	1	1	4	9
TOTALS	15	28	7	1	37	30	55	173

QUESTIONNAIRE RESPONSES

QUESTION	LIB SCI PROFS	SCIENTIFIC TECHNICAL	LIBRARY NETWORK	PUBLISH-ERS	RESEARCH LIBRARIANS	LAW DEANS	LAW LIBRARIANS	ROW TOTALS
Q51A								
STRONGLY AGREE	1	6	0	0	2	0	0	9
AGREE	4	8	2	0	7	10	9	40
UNDECIDED	5	6	2	0	8	13	16	50
DISAGREE	8	12	3	1	25	14	43	106
STRONGLY DISAGREE	0	1	0	0	1	6	6	14
TOTALS	18	33	7	1	43	43	74	219
Q51B								
VERY DESIRABLE	1	11	0	1	4	1	3	21
DESIRABLE	7	7	2	0	13	15	12	56
UNDECIDED	4	5	3	0	9	14	18	53
UNDESIRABLE	4	7	2	0	13	9	30	65
VERY UNDESIRABLE	2	1	0	0	0	2	4	9
TOTALS	18	31	7	1	39	41	67	204

Appendix C

STATISTICALLY SIGNIFICANT DIFFERENCES IN RESPONDENTS' OPINIONS

QUESTION	REVIEW GROUP	MEAN	AGREE GRP DIFF LSD	GRP DIFF SCHEFFE	MEAN	DESIRABLE GRP DIFF LSD	GRP DIFF SCHEFFE	MEAN	EVENT TIME GRP DIFF LSD	GRP DIFF SCHEFFE
Q1A-Publication of printed books will continue to increase in the future despite the increase of publication of information in computerized and multi-media formats.	Qp1 Lib.Sci.Prof. & Network	1.77	N/D	N/D						
	Qp2 Sci. Tech.	1.97	N/D	N/D						
	Qp5 R. Lib. (ARL)	1.86	N/D	N/D						
	Qp7 Dir. AALL	1.79	N/D	N/D						
	Qp6 Law Deans AALS	1.82	N/D	N/D						
Q1B	Qp1 Lib.Sci.Prof. & Network				1.69		N/D			
	Qp2 Sci. Tech.				2.00		N/D			
	Qp5 R. Lib. (ARL)				2.02		N/D			
	Qp7 Dir. AALL				2.12	7*1	N/D			
	Qp6 Law Deans AALS				2.28	6*1	N/D			
Q1C	Qp1 Lib.Sci.Prof. & Network							2.56	N/D	N/D
	Qp2 Sci. Tech.							2.47	N/D	N/D
	Qp5 R. Lib. (ARL)							2.55	N/D	N/D
	Qp7 Dir. AALL							2.51	N/D	N/D
	Qp6 Law Deans AALS							2.56	N/D	N/D
Q2A-Book collections of the libraries of the future will be reduced in size as more information becomes available in computerized and multi-media formats.	Qp6 Law Deans AALS	2.44	N/D	N/D						
	Qp7 Dir. AALL	2.64	N/D	N/D						
	Qp2 Sci. Tech	2.66	N/D	N/D						
	Qp1 Lib.Sci.Prof. & Network	2.92	N/D	N/D						
	Qp5 R. Lib. (ARL)	3.19	5*6,7,2	N/D						

THE TWENTY-FIRST CENTURY

QUESTION	REVIEW GROUP	MEAN	AGREE GRP DIFF LSD	GRP DIFF SCHEFFE	MEAN	DESIRABLE GRP DIFF LSD	GRP DIFF SCHEFFE	MEAN	EVENT TIME GRP DIFF LSD	GRP DIFF SCHEFFE
Q2B	Gp2 Sci. Tech.				2.29		N/D			
	Gp6 Law Deans AALS				2.44		N/D			
	Gp7 Dir. AALL				2.56		N/D			
	Gp1 Lib.Sci.Prof. & Network				2.73		N/D			
	Gp5 R. Lib. (ARL)				2.80	5*2	N/D			
Q2C	Gp2 Sci. Tech.							2.28		N/D
	Gp6 Law Deans AALS							2.44		N/D
	Gp7 Dir. AALL							2.55	1*2	N/D
	Gp1 Lib.Sci.Prof. & Network							2.79		N/D
	Gp5 R. Lib. (ARL)							2.83	5*2	N/D
Q3A-In the future more people will buy the information they want to read in a computer-based or computer generated format and will borrow less from a library.	Gp2 Sci. Tech.	2.48		N/D						
	Gp6 Law Deans AALS	2.58		N/D						
	Gp7 Dir. AALL	2.60		N/D						
	Gp1 Lib.Sci.Prof. & Network	2.92		N/D						
	Gp5 R. Lib. (ARL)	3.00	5*2,7	N/D						
Q3B	Gp2 Sci. Tech.				2.48		N/D			
	Gp6 Law Deans AALS				2.68		N/D			
	Gp7 Dir. AALL				2.75		N/D			
	Gp5 R. Lib. (ARL)				3.07	5*2	N/D			
	Gp1 Lib.Sci.Prof. & Network				3.28	1*2,6,7	N/D			

Statistically Significant Differences

QUESTION	REVIEW GROUP	MEAN	AGREE GRP DIFF LSD	AGREE GRP DIFF SCHEFFE	MEAN	DESIRABLE GRP DIFF LSD	DESIRABLE GRP DIFF SCHEFFE	MEAN	EVENT TIME GRP DIFF LSD	EVENT TIME GRP DIFF SCHEFFE
Q3C	Gp2 Sci. Tech.							2.10		N/D
	Gp6 Law Deans AALS							2.28		N/D
	Gp5 R. Lib. (ARL)							2.43		N/D
	Gp7 Dir. AALL							2.48	1*2	N/D
	Gp1 Lib.Sci.Prof. & Network							2.77		N/D
Q4A-In the future the services libraries provide patrons will be predominantly guidance in retrieving information in the non-book format.	Gp6 Law Deans AALS	2.91								
	Gp7 Dir. AALL	3.08								
	Gp2 Sci. Tech.	3.09								
	Gp1 Lib.Sci.Prof. & Network	3.42								
	Gp5 R. Lib. (ARL)	3.66	5*2,6,7	5*6						
Q4B & Q4C	Gp2 Sci. Tech.				2.70		N/D	N/A	N/A	N/A
	Gp6 Law Deans AALS				2.75		N/D	N/A	N/A	N/A
	Gp7 Dir. AALL				2.01		N/D	N/A	N/A	N/A
	Gp5 R. Lib. (ARL)				3.27	5*2,6	N/D	N/A	N/A	N/A
	Gp1 Lib.Sci.Prof. & Network				3.44	1*2,6	N/D	N/A	N/A	N/A
Q5A & Q5B-Microform will be replaced by a form of computer-based or computer-generated technology.	Gp1 Lib.Sci.Prof. & Network	1.88	N/D	N/D	1.81		N/D			
	Gp2 Sci. Tech.	1.93	N/D	N/D	1.87		N/D			
	Gp6 Law Deans AALS	2.05	N/D	N/D	1.90		N/D			
	Gp5 R. Lib. (ARL)	2.30	N/D	N/D	2.19		N/D			
	Gp7 Dir. AALL	2.28	N/D	N/D	2.26	7*1	N/D			

THE TWENTY-FIRST CENTURY

QUESTION	REVIEW GROUP	MEAN	AGREE GRP DIFF LSD	AGREE GRP DIFF SCHEFFE	MEAN	DESIRABLE GRP DIFF LSD	DESIRABLE GRP DIFF SCHEFFE	MEAN	EVENT TIME GRP DIFF LSD	EVENT TIME GRP DIFF SCHEFFE
Q5C	Gp1 Lib.Sci.Prof. & Network							1.92		
	Gp2 Sci. Tech.							1.97		
	Gp6 Law Deans AALS							2.14		
	Gp5 R. Lib. (ARL)							2.35	5*1	7*1,2
	Gp7 Dir. AALL							2.55	7*1,2,6	
Q6A,B,C.-In the absence of published hard copy, automated information viewable only on a computer screen (with print-out available for permanent retention will be widely accepted as a readable format.	Gp2 Sci. Tech.	2.36	N/D	N/D	2.45	N/D	N/D	1.97	N/D	N/D
	Gp6 Law Deans AALS	2.37	N/D	N/D	2.52	N/D	N/D	2.06	N/D	N/D
	Gp5 R. Lib. (ARL)	2.43	N/D	N/D	2.60	N/D	N/D	2.25	N/D	N/D
	Gp1 Lib.Sci.Prof. & Network	2.54	N/D	N/D	2.83	N/D	N/D	2.35	N/D	N/D
	Gp7 Dir. AALL	2.23	N/D	N/D	2.46	N/D	N/D	2.36	7*1	N/D
Q7A,B,C.-Online information will be priced so that most people could afford to use online services.	Gp6 Law Deans AALS	2.49			1.66	N/D	N/D	2.50	N/D	N/D
	Gp1 Lib.Sci.Prof. & Network	2.73			1.46	N/D	N/D	2.13	N/D	N/D
	Gp2 Sci. Tech.	2.84	N/D	N/D	1.73	N/D	N/D	2.40	N/D	N/D
	Gp7 Dir. AALL	2.91	N/D	N/D	1.63	N/D	N/D	2.40	N/D	N/D
	Gp5 R. Lib. (ARL)	2.98	5*6		1.84	N/D	N/D	2.15	N/D	N/D
Q8A-Use of online public catalogs will significantly increase demands for document delivery.	Gp5 R. Lib. (ARL)	1.50								
	Gp1 Lib.Sci.Prof. & Network	1.85								
	Gp7 Dir. AALL	1.91	7*5							
	Gp2 Sci. Tech.	2.21	2*5	2*5						
	Gp6 Law Deans AALS	2.34	6*5,1,7	6*5						

Statistically Significant Differences

QUESTION	REVIEW GROUP	MEAN	AGREE GRP DIFF LSD	GRP DIFF SCHEFFE	MEAN	DESIRABLE GRP DIFF LSD	GRP DIFF SCHEFFE	MEAN	EVENT TIME GRP DIFF LSD	GRP DIFF SCHEFFE
Q8B	Gp1 Lib.Sci.Prof. & Network				1.77		N/D			
	Gp5 R. Lib. (ARL)				1.81		N/D			
	Gp7 Dir. AALL				1.90		N/D			
	Gp2 Sci. Tech.				2.10		N/D			
	Gp6 Law Deans AALS				2.23	6*1,5,7	N/D			
Q8C	Gp2 Sci. Tech.							1.31		N/D
	Gp1 Lib.Sci.Prof. & Network							1.33		N/D
	Gp5 R. Lib. (ARL)							1.36		N/D
	Gp7 Dir. AALL							1.68	7*2,5	N/D
	Gp6 Law Deans AALS							1.76	6*2,1,5	N/D
Q9A,B–In the future intelligent terminals, software, or other form of computer technology will be used to analyze and channel queries to appropriate databases for information.	Gp5 R. Lib. (ARL)	1.70		N/D	1.70	N/D	N/D			
	Gp2 Sci. Tech.	1.79		N/D	1.77	N/D	N/D			
	Gp1 Lib.Sci.Prof. & Network	1.81		N/D	1.77	N/D	N/D			
	Gp6 Law Deans AALS	1.93		N/D	1.90	N/D	N/D			
	Gp7 Dir. AALL	2.08	7*5	N/D	1.93	N/D	N/D			
Q9C	Gp2 Sci. Tech.							1.47		
	Gp5 R. Lib. (ARL)							1.75		
	Gp1 Lib.Sci.Prof. & Network							2.00	1*2	
	Gp6 Law Deans AALS							2.06	6*2	
	Gp7 Dir. AALL							2.39	7*2,5,1,6	7*2,5

THE TWENTY-FIRST CENTURY

QUESTION	REVIEW GROUP	MEAN	AGREE GRP DIFF LSD	GRP DIFF SCHEFFE	MEAN	DESIRABLE GRP DIFF LSD	GRP DIFF SCHEFFE	MEAN	EVENT TIME GRP DIFF LSD	GRP DIFF SCHEFFE
Q10A,B,C-Distributed databases (computer storage, e.g. tapes acquired for local or in-house computers) will replace remote online information sources.	Gp1 Lib.Sci.Prof. & Network	2.36	N/D	N/D	2.38	N/D	N/D	2.11	N/D	N/D
	Gp2 Sci. Tech.	2.41	N/D	N/D	2.30	N/D	N/D	1.85	N/D	N/D
	Gp5 R. Lib. (ARL)	2.60	N/D	N/D	2.33	N/D	N/D	1.94	N/D	N/D
	Gp6 Law Deans AALS	2.62	N/D	N/D	2.40	N/D	N/D	2.14	N/D	N/D
	Gp7 Dir. AALL	2.38	N/D	N/D	2.07	N/D	N/D	2.25	N/D	N/D
Q11A&B-The technology of disks compact, digital, laser, optical, video) combined with micro-computers will provide an information retrieval capability superior to dial-up databases.	Gp2 Sci. Tech.	1.77	N/D	N/D	1.57	N/D	N/D			
	Gp1 Lib.Sci.Prof. & Network	1.88	N/D	N/D	1.69	N/D	N/D			
	Gp7 Dir. AALL	2.01	N/D	N/D	1.79					
	Gp5 R. Lib. (ARL)	2.02	N/D	N/D	1.88	N/D	N/D			
	Gp6 Law Deans AALS	2.05	N/D	N/D	1.95	6*2	N/D			
Q11C	Gp2 Sci. Tech.							1.59		
	Gp1 Lib.Sci.Prof. & Network							1.80		
	Gp5 R. Lib. (ARL)							1.84		
	Gp6 Law Deans AALS							1.94	7*2,1,5	7*2
	Gp7 Dir. AALL							2.21		
Q12A&B-By the year 2000 disks compact, digital, laser, optical, video) will replace hard copy information to the following extent:	Gp2 Sci. Tech.	1.76	N/D	N/D	1.84		N/D			
	Gp5 R. Lib. (ARL)	1.46	N/D	N/D	2.08		N/D			
	Gp1 Lib.Sci.Prof. & Network	1.69	N/D	N/D	2.12		N/D			
	Gp7 Dir. AALL	1.57	N/D	N/D	2.17	7*2	N/D			
	Gp6 Law Deans AALS	1.74	N/D	N/D	2.21	6*2	N/D			

Statistically Significant Differences

QUESTION	REVIEW GROUP	MEAN	AGREE GRP DIFF LSD	GRP DIFF SCHEFFE	MEAN	DESIRABLE GRP DIFF LSD	GRP DIFF SCHEFFE	MEAN	EVENT TIME GRP DIFF LSD	GRP DIFF SCHEFFE
Q13A—Interactive television, cable systems, or online systems like Viewtron or other videotex systems will replace the library as an information resource.	Gp6 Law Deans AALS Gp7 Dir. AALL Gp5 R. Lib. (ARL) Gp2 Sci. Tech. Gp1 Lib.Sci.Prof. & Network	3.57 3.97 4.05 4.06 4.19	7*6 5*6 2*6 1*6	1*6						
Q13B	Gp6 Law Deans AALS Gp2 Sci. Tech. Gp7 Dir. AALL Gp1 Lib.Sci.Prof. & Network Gp5 R. Lib. (ARL)				3.59 3.75 3.90 4.04 4.08	7*6 1*6 5*6	N/D N/D N/D N/D N/D			
Q13C	Gp6 Law Deans AALS Gp2 Sci. Tech. Gp7 Dir. AALL Gp5 R. Lib. (ARL) Gp1 Lib.Sci.Prof. & Network							3.33 3.35 3.50 3.56 3.76	1*6	N/D N/D N/D N/D N/D
Q14A—Other technologies will be developed that will permit access to information even faster and cheaper than those described above.	Gp1 Lib.Sci.Prof. & Network Gp2 Sci. Tech. Gp7 Dir. AALL Gp6 Law Deans AALS Gp5 R. Lib. (ARL)	1.88 1.94 2.08 2.10 2.26	5*1	N/D N/D N/D N/D N/D						

THE TWENTY-FIRST CENTURY

QUESTION	REVIEW GROUP	MEAN	AGREE GRP DIFF LSD	GRP DIFF SCHEFFE	MEAN	DESIRABLE GRP DIFF LSD	GRP DIFF SCHEFFE	MEAN	EVENT TIME GRP DIFF LSD	GRP DIFF SCHEFFE
Q14B	Gp2 Sci. Tech.				1.61		N/D			
	Gp1 Lib.Sci.Prof. & Network				1.85		N/D			
	Gp5 R. Lib. (ARL)				1.92	7*2	N/D			
	Gp7 Dir. AALL				1.97	6*2	N/D			
	Gp6 Law Deans AALS				2.03		N/D			
Q14C	Gp2 Sci. Tech.							2.39		N/D
	Gp5 R. Lib. (ARL)							2.56		N/D
	Gp1 Lib.Sci.Prof. & Network							2.67		N/D
	Gp7 Dir. AALL							2.69	7*2	N/D
	Gp6 Law Deans AALS							2.86	6*2,5	N/D
Q15-By the year 2000 automated library technology will be characterized primarily by: (CHECK ONLY ONE RESPONSE)										
A. Networks of personal computers or terminals		N/D	N/D	N/D	N/D	N/D	N/D	N/D	N/D	N/D
B. Access of full-tex databases, such as LEXIS and WESTLAW		N/D	N/D	N/D	N/D	N/D	N/D	N/D	N/D	N/D
C. Video-disk technology		N/D	N/D	N/D	N/D	N/D	N/D	N/D	N/D	N/D
D. Laser-disk technology		N/D	N/D	N/D	N/D	N/D	N/D	N/D	N/D	N/D
E. Combination of above; identify		N/D	N/D	N/D	N/D	N/D	N/D	N/D	N/D	N/D
F. Other:		N/D	N/D	N/D	N/D	N/D	N/D	N/D	N/D	N/D

Statistically Significant Differences

QUESTION	REVIEW GROUP	MEAN	AGREE GRP DIFF LSD	GRP DIFF SCHEFFE	MEAN	DESIRABLE GRP DIFF LSD	GRP DIFF SCHEFFE	MEAN	EVENT TIME GRP DIFF LSD	GRP DIFF SCHEFFE
Q16-What role and function for libraries do you envision in the years beyond 1990?										
A. Continued role as general information resource		N/D	N/D	N/D	N/D	N/D	N/D	N/D	N/D	N/D
B. New role as computer-based information guide		N/D	N/D	N/D	N/D	N/D	N/D	N/D	N/D	N/D
C. A and B above		N/D	N/D	N/D	N/D	N/D	N/D	N/D	N/D	N/D
D. No role		N/D	N/D	N/D	N/D	N/D	N/D	N/D	N/D	N/D
Q17A-Increased automated information will slow the rate of growth in hard copy acquisitions for the library.	Gp7 Dir. AALL	2.13		N/D						
	Gp6 Law Deans AALS	2.21		N/D						
	Gp2 Sci. Tech.	2.48		N/D						
	Gp5 R. Lib. (ARL)	2.56	5*7	N/D						
	Gp1 Lib.Sci.Prof. & Network	2.73	1*7,6	N/D						
Q17B&C	Gp7 Dir. AALL				2.23		N/D	1.78	N/D	N/D
	Gp6 Law Deans AALS				2.34		N/D	1.73	N/D	N/D
	Gp2 Sci. Tech.				2.37		N/D	1.70	N/D	N/D
	Gp5 R. Lib. (ARL)				2.46		N/D	2.08	N/D	N/D
	Gp1 Lib.Sci.Prof. & Network				2.85	1*7,6,2	N/D	2.19	N/D	N/D
Q18A-As access to automated information increases, annual hard copy acquisitions of basic library materials will be reduced to one copy.	Gp6 Law Deans AALS	2.60								
	Gp7 Dir. AALL	2.84								
	Gp2 Sci. Tech.	2.86								
	Gp5 R. Lib. (ARL)	3.24	5*6,7							
	Gp1 Lib.Sci.Prof. & Network	3.45	1*6,7,2	1*6						

The Twenty-First Century

QUESTION	REVIEW GROUP	MEAN	AGREE GRP DIFF LSD	AGREE GRP DIFF SCHEFFE	MEAN	DESIRABLE GRP DIFF LSD	DESIRABLE GRP DIFF SCHEFFE	MEAN	EVENT TIME GRP DIFF LSD	EVENT TIME GRP DIFF SCHEFFE
Q18B	Gp7 Dir. AALL				2.76					
	Gp6 Law Deans AALS				2.75					
	Gp2 Sci. Tech.				2.81					
	Gp5 R. Lib. (ARL)				3.09	1*7,6,2,5	1*7,6			
	Gp1 Lib.Sci.Prof. & Network				3.64					
Q18C	Gp2 Sci. Tech.							1.81		
	Gp6 Law Deans AALS							2.12		
	Gp7 Dir. AALL							2.35	7*2	
	Gp5 R. Lib. (ARL)							2.73	5*2,6	5*2
	Gp1 Lib.Sci.Prof. & Network							3.32	1*2,6,7	1*2,6,7
Q19A—What percentage of the annual hard copy acquisitions of basic library materials will be reduced to one copy by the year 2000?	Gp2 Sci. Tech.	2.13		N/D						
	Gp7 Dir. AALL	2.22		N/D						
	Gp5 R. Lib. (ARL)	2.35		N/D						
	Gp1 Lib.Sci.Prof. & Network	2.50		N/D						
	Gp6 Law Deans AALS	2.77	6*7	N/D						
Q19B	Gp7 Dir. AALL				2.16					
	Gp2 Sci. Tech.				2.28					
	Gp5 R. Lib. (ARL)				2.57	5*7				
	Gp6 Law Deans AALS				2.59	6*7				
	Gp1 Lib.Sci.Prof. & Network				3.00	1*7,2	1*7			

Statistically Significant Differences

QUESTION	REVIEW GROUP	MEAN	AGREE GRP DIFF LSD	GRP DIFF SCHEFFE	MEAN	DESIRABLE GRP DIFF LSD	GRP DIFF SCHEFFE	MEAN	EVENT TIME GRP DIFF LSD	GRP DIFF SCHEFFE
Q20A&B-What percentage of the hard copy collection of basic library materials will be reduced to one copy by the year two thousand?	Gp7 Dir. AALL	2.12	N/D	N/D	2.13		N/D			
	Gp5 R. Lib. (ARL)	2.03	N/D	N/D	2.39		N/D			
	Gp2 Sci. Tech.	1.76	N/D	N/D	2.44	6*7	N/D			
	Gp6 Law Deans AALS	2.16	N/D	N/D	2.51		N/D			
	Gp1 Lib.Sci.Prof. & Network	2.15	N/D	N/D	2.56		N/D			
Q21-What type library materials do you envision for the library in future years once the basic book materials are available in automated form?		N/D			N/D		N/D	N/D	N/D	N/D
Q22-Policy for automated information budgeting will be set by:										
A. Librarian 1990		N/D	N/D	N/D	N/D	N/D	N/D	N/D	N/D	N/D
B. Dean 2000		N/D	N/D	N/D	N/D	N/D	N/D	N/D	N/D	N/D
C. Faculty Committee Post-2000		N/D	N/D	N/D	N/D	N/D	N/D	N/D	N/D	N/D
D. Combination of above; Never		N/D	N/D	N/D	N/D	N/D	N/D	N/D	N/D	N/D
Q23-Automated information budgets will be administered and managed by the librarian.										
A. Yes 1990		N/D	N/D	N/D	N/D	N/D	N/D	N/D	N/D	N/D
B. No 2000		N/D	N/D	N/D	N/D	N/D	N/D	N/D	N/D	N/D
C. If no, by whom? Post-2000		N/D	N/D	N/D	N/D	N/D	N/D	N/D	N/D	N/D
Never		N/D	N/D	N/D	N/D	N/D	N/D	N/D	N/D	N/D

The Twenty-First Century

QUESTION	REVIEW GROUP	MEAN	AGREE GRP DIFF LSD	GRP DIFF SCHEFFE	MEAN	DESIRABLE GRP DIFF LSD	GRP DIFF SCHEFFE	MEAN	EVENT TIME GRP DIFF LSD	GRP DIFF SCHEFFE
Q24A–Automated information budgets will be separated completely from budgets for library materials and binding.	Gp2 Sci. Tech.	2.70		N/D						
	Gp7 Dir. AALL	3.23	7*2	N/D						
	Gp6 Law Deans AALS	3.26		N/D						
	Gp5 R. Lib. (ARL)	3.36	5*2	N/D						
	Gp1 Lib.Sci.Prof. & Network	3.50	1*2	N/D						
Q24B&C	Gp2 Sci. Tech.				2.63		N/D	1.95	N/D	N/D
	Gp7 Dir. AALL				3.26	7*2	N/D	2.02	N/D	N/D
	Gp6 Law Deans AALS				3.27	6*2	N/D	1.91	N/D	N/D
	Gp5 R. Lib. (ARL)				3.40	5*2	N/D	2.03	N/D	N/D
	Gp1 Lib.Sci.Prof. & Network				3.59	1*2	N/D	2.48	N/D	N/D
Q25A,B&C–Institutional fiscal officers will continue to allocate substantial funds for automated information even though these expenditures generate no tangible hard copy additions to the library.	Gp1 Lib.Sci.Prof. & Network	2.32	N/D	N/D	1.91	N/D	N/D	1.57	N/D	N/D
	Gp2 Sci. Tech.	2.00	N/D	N/D	1.93	N/D	N/D	1.44	N/D	N/D
	Gp5 R. Lib. (ARL)	2.05	N/D	N/D	1.95	N/D	N/D	1.26	N/D	N/D
	Gp6 Law Deans AALS	2.02	N/D	N/D	1.81	N/D	N/D	1.30	N/D	N/D
	Gp7 Dir. AALL	2.00	N/D	N/D	1.88	N/D	N/D	1.47	N/D	N/D

Statistically Significant Differences

QUESTION	REVIEW GROUP	MEAN	AGREE GRP DIFF LSD	GRP DIFF SCHEFFE	MEAN	DESIRABLE GRP DIFF LSD	GRP DIFF SCHEFFE	MEAN	EVENT TIME GRP DIFF LSD	GRP DIFF SCHEFFE
Q26-Comparing the automated information budget with the library materials budget in year 1990 and beyond, the automated information budget will be:										
A. Less		N/D	N/D	N/D	N/D	N/D	N/D	N/D	N/D	N/D
B. The same		N/D	N/D	N/D	N/D	N/D	N/D	N/D	N/D	N/D
C. More		N/D	N/D	N/D	N/D	N/D	N/D	N/D	N/D	N/D
Q27-In light of the possible changes in book collecting policies, would you anticipate any special difficulty in acquiring the funding to build a new library building or addition?										
A. Yes		N/D	N/D	N/D	N/D	N/D	N/D	N/D	N/D	N/D
B. No		N/D	N/D	N/D	N/D	N/D	N/D	N/D	N/D	N/D
C. Don't know		N/D	N/D	N/D	N/D	N/D	N/D	N/D	N/D	N/D
Q28-In a year in which the allocations are reduced, the budget for automated information should be:										
A. Preserved at the present level		N/D	N/D	N/D	N/D	N/D	N/D	N/D	N/D	N/D
B. Increased		N/D	N/D	N/D	N/D	N/D	N/D	N/D	N/D	N/D
C. Decreased		N/D	N/D	N/D	N/D	N/D	N/D	N/D	N/D	N/D

THE TWENTY-FIRST CENTURY

QUESTION	REVIEW GROUP	AGREE			DESIRABLE			EVENT TIME		
		MEAN	GRP DIFF LSD	GRP DIFF SCHEFFE	MEAN	GRP DIFF LSD	GRP DIFF SCHEFFE	MEAN	GRP DIFF LSD	GRP DIFF SCHEFFE
Q29-In a year of reduced budgets, what types of materials should be reduced or cancelled first?										
A. Hard copy when information available in computer databases		N/D	N/D	N/D	N/D	N/D	N/D	N/D	N/D	N/D
B. Information system when hard copy available		N/D	N/D	N/D	N/D	N/D	N/D	N/D	N/D	N/D
C. Other materials		N/D	N/D	N/D	N/D	N/D	N/D	N/D	N/D	N/D
Q30-Who will absorb the costs of faculty access to automated information?										
A. Library		N/D	N/D	N/D	N/D	N/D	N/D	N/D	N/D	N/D
B. College or Department		N/D	N/D	N/D	N/D	N/D	N/D	N/D	N/D	N/D
C. Faculty		N/D	N/D	N/D	N/D	N/D	N/D	N/D	N/D	N/D
D. Combination of above; specify:		N/D	N/D	N/D	N/D	N/D	N/D	N/D	N/D	N/D
Q31A-A formula will be devised to determine the amount of access, hardware, and service that should be provided free to faculty.	Gp6 Law Deans AALS	2.19		N/D						
	Gp1 Lib.Sci.Prof. & Network	2.32		N/D						
	Gp7 Dir. AALL	2.36		N/D						
	Gp2 Sci. Tech.	2.48		N/D						
	Gp5 R. Lib. (ARL)	2.81	5*6,7	N/D						

Statistically Significant Differences

QUESTION	REVIEW GROUP	MEAN	AGREE GRP DIFF LSD	GRP DIFF SCHEFFE	MEAN	DESIRABLE GRP DIFF LSD	GRP DIFF SCHEFFE	MEAN	EVENT TIME GRP DIFF LSD	GRP DIFF SCHEFFE
Q31B&C	Gp6 Law Deans AALS				1.93			1.51	N/D	N/D
	Gp7 Dir. AALL				2.17		N/D	1.46	N/D	N/D
	Gp1 Lib.Sci.Prof. & Network				2.36		N/D	1.64	N/D	N/D
	Gp2 Sci. Tech.				2.52	2*6	N/D	1.60	N/D	N/D
	Gp5 R. Lib. (ARL)				2.65	5*6,7	N/D	1.91	N/D	N/D
Q32A–Faculty will have to pay for some of the costs to access online information beyond a pre-determined, reasonable, limited amount.	Gp1 Lib.Sci.Prof. & Network	1.92		N/D						
	Gp5 R. Lib. (ARL)	2.07		N/D						
	Gp7 Dir. AALL	2.39	7*1	N/D						
	Gp6 Law Deans AALS	2.40	6*1	N/D						
	Gp2 Sci. Tech.	2.43	2*1	N/D						
Q32B&C	Gp5 R. Lib. (ARL)				2.66	N/D	N/D	1.25	N/D	N/D
	Gp1 Lib.Sci.Prof. & Network				2.32	N/D	N/D	1.38	N/D	N/D
	Gp6 Law Deans AALS				2.65	N/D	N/D	1.55		N/D
	Gp7 Dir. AALL				2.31	N/D	N/D	1.57		N/D
	Gp2 Sci. Tech.				2.52	N/D	N/D	1.82	2*5	N/D
Q33A–Students will pay on a per use basis for the costs of information retrieval services.	Gp1 Lib.Sci.Prof. & Network	2.92		N/D						
	Gp2 Sci. Tech.	3.00		N/D						
	Gp5 R. Lib. (ARL)	3.19		N/D						
	Gp6 Law Deans AALS	3.35		N/D						
	Gp7 Dir. AALL	3.61	7*1,2,5	N/D						

177

The Twenty-First Century

QUESTION	REVIEW GROUP	MEAN	AGREE GRP DIFF LSD	AGREE GRP DIFF SCHEFFE	MEAN	DESIRABLE GRP DIFF LSD	DESIRABLE GRP DIFF SCHEFFE	MEAN	EVENT TIME GRP DIFF LSD	EVENT TIME GRP DIFF SCHEFFE
Q33B	Gp2 Sci.Tech.				3.31		N/D			
	Gp6 Law Deans AALS				3.51		N/D			
	Gp5 R.Lib. (ARL)				3.63		N/D			
	Gp7 Dir. AALL				3.80		N/D			
	Gp1 Lib.Sci.Prof. & Network				3.83	7*2	N/D			
Q33C	Gp1 Lib.Sci.Prof. & Network							1.58		
	Gp6 Law Deans AALS							1.92		
	Gp2 Sci.Tech.							2.00		
	Gp5 R.Lib. (ARL)							2.09		
	Gp7 Dir. AALL							2.73	7*1,6,2,5	7*1
Q34A—By 1990 most research university or law school student fees will cover the costs of automated information retrieval, word processing, and other related computer costs in the library.	Gp7 Dir. AALL	2.57		N/D						
	Gp6 Law Deans AALS	2.74		N/D						
	Gp2 Sci.Tech.	2.78		N/D						
	Gp1 Lib.Sci.Prof. & Network	2.96		N/D						
	Gp5 R.Lib. (ARL)	3.02	5*7	N/D						

Statistically Significant Differences

QUESTION	REVIEW GROUP	MEAN	AGREE GRP DIFF LSD	GRP DIFF SCHEFFE	MEAN	DESIRABLE GRP DIFF LSD	GRP DIFF SCHEFFE	MEAN	EVENT TIME GRP DIFF LSD	GRP DIFF SCHEFFE
Q34B	Gp7 Dir. AALL				2.14		N/D			
	Gp1 Lib.Sci.Prof. & Network				2.24		N/D			
	Gp6 Law Deans AALS				2.30					
	Gp2 Sci. Tech.				2.39		N/D			
	Gp5 R. Lib. (ARL)				2.75	5*7,1,6	N/D			
Q35A,B&C–The library will provide to students a limited amount of access to automated information free of charge.	Gp1 Lib.Sci.Prof. & Network	2.08	N/D	N/D	1.77	N/D	N/D	1.45	N/D	N/D
	Gp2 Sci. Tech.	2.20	N/D	N/D	1.96	N/D	N/D	1.40	N/D	N/D
	Gp5 R. Lib. (ARL)	2.09	N/D	N/D	1.93	N/D	N/D	1.21	N/D	N/D
	Gp6 Law Deans AALS	1.83	N/D	N/D	1.78	N/D	N/D	1.18	N/D	N/D
	Gp7 Dir. AALL	2.03	N/D	N/D	1.86	N/D	N/D	1.34	N/D	N/D
Q36A,B&C–The library will pay for the costs to access automated information for everyone when that information is available only online.	Gp1 Lib.Sci.Prof. & Network	3.44	N/D	N/D	2.54		N/D	2.37	N/D	N/D
	Gp2 Sci. Tech.	3.42	N/D	N/D	2.83		N/D	2.22	N/D	N/D
	Gp5 R. Lib. (ARL)	3.44	N/D	N/D	2.98		N/D	2.15	N/D	N/D
	Gp6 Law Deans AALS	3.55	N/D	N/D	3.07		N/D	1.89	N/D	N/D
	Gp7 Dir. AALL	3.55	N/D	N/D	3.33	7*1,2	N/D	2.42	N/D	N/D
Q37A,B&C–The library will furnish computers/terminals to patrons to access information and will collect the costs through coin or card operated machines or legal tender.	Gp2 Sci. Tech.	2.55	N/D	N/D	2.52		N/D	1.68	N/D	N/D
	Gp6 Law Deans AALS	2.51	N/D	N/D	2.54		N/D	1.89	N/D	N/D
	Gp7 Dir. AALL	2.57	N/D	N/D	2.67		N/D	1.87	N/D	N/D
	Gp5 R. Lib. (ARL)	2.50	N/D	N/D	2.68		N/D	1.42	N/D	N/D
	Gp1 Lib.Sci.Prof. & Network	2.65	N/D	N/D	3.04	1*6	N/D	1.68	N/D	N/D

THE TWENTY-FIRST CENTURY

QUESTION	REVIEW GROUP	MEAN	AGREE GRP DIFF LSD	GRP DIFF SCHEFFE	DESIRABLE MEAN	GRP DIFF LSD	GRP DIFF SCHEFFE	EVENT TIME MEAN	GRP DIFF LSD	GRP DIFF SCHEFFE
Q38A—In the future as there are changes in the library collection format and increased automation, the number and/or composition of library staff will change.	Gp2 Sci.Tech.	1.77		N/D						
	Gp5 R. Lib. (ARL)	1.84		N/D						
	Gp1 Lib.Sci.Prof. & Network	1.96		N/D						
	Gp6 Law Deans AALS	2.07		N/D						
	Gp7 Dir. AALL	2.08	7*2	N/D						
Q38B&C	Gp2 Sci.Tech.				1.79		N/D	1.46	N/D	N/D
	Gp5 R. Lib. (ARL)				1.85		N/D	1.36	N/D	N/D
	Gp1 Lib.Sci.Prof. & Network				2.00		N/D	1.39	N/D	N/D
	Gp7 Dir. AALL				2.04	6*2	N/D	1.42	N/D	N/D
	Gp6 Law Deans AALS				2.12		N/D	1.42	N/D	N/D
Q39—The number of administrative librarians will:										
A. Increase 1990		N/D	N/D	N/D	N/D	N/D	N/D	N/D	N/D	N/D
B. Decrease 2000		N/D	N/D	N/D	N/D	N/D	N/D	N/D	N/D	N/D
C. Remain unchanged Post-2000		N/D	N/D	N/D	N/D	N/D	N/D	N/D	N/D	N/D
Q40—The number of public service librarians will:										
A. Increase 1990		N/D	N/D	N/D	N/D	N/D	N/D	N/D	N/D	N/D
B. Decrease 2000		N/D	N/D	N/D	N/D	N/D	N/D	N/D	N/D	N/D
C. Remain unchanged Post-2000		N/D	N/D	N/D	N/D	N/D	N/D	N/D	N/D	N/D
Q41—The number of technical service librarians will:										
A. Increase 1990		N/D	N/D	N/D	N/D	N/D	N/D	N/D	N/D	N/D
B. Decrease 2000		N/D	N/D	N/D	N/D	N/D	N/D	N/D	N/D	N/D
C. Remain unchanged Post-2000		N/D	N/D	N/D	N/D	N/D	N/D	N/D	N/D	N/D

Statistically Significant Differences

QUESTION	REVIEW GROUP	MEAN	AGREE GRP DIFF LSD	GRP DIFF SCHEFFE	MEAN	DESIRABLE GRP DIFF LSD	GRP DIFF SCHEFFE	MEAN	EVENT TIME GRP DIFF LSD	GRP DIFF SCHEFFE
Q42-The number of support staff will:										
A. Increase	1990	N/D	N/D	N/D	N/D	N/D	N/D	N/D	N/D	N/D
B. Decrease	2000	N/D	N/D	N/D	N/D	N/D	N/D	N/D	N/D	N/D
C. Remain unchanged	Post-2000	N/D	N/D	N/D	N/D	N/D	N/D	N/D	N/D	N/D
Q43-The number of library trained professionals working in the libraries' information science program will:										
A. Increase	1990	N/D	N/D	N/D	N/D	N/D	N/D	N/D	N/D	N/D
B. Decrease	2000	N/D	N/D	N/D	N/D	N/D	N/D	N/D	N/D	N/D
C. Remain unchanged	Post-2000	N/D	N/D	N/D	N/D	N/D	N/D	N/D	N/D	N/D
Q44A-Library-trained professionals should be paid more for expertise in computer use.	Gp2 Sci. Tech.	2.48		N/D						
	Gp7 Dir. AALL	2.53		N/D						
	Gp6 Law Deans AALS	2.60		N/D						
	Gp1 Lib.Sci.Prof. & Network	2.77		N/D						
	Gp5 R. Lib. (ARL)	3.12	5*2,7,6	N/D						
Q44B&C	Gp6 Law Deans AALS				2.38			1.26	N/D	N/D
	Gp7 Dir. AALL				2.46			1.28	N/D	N/D
	Gp2 Sci. Tech.				2.48			1.41	N/D	N/D
	Gp1 Lib.Sci.Prof. & Network				2.77			1.28	N/D	N/D
	Gp5 R. Lib. (ARL)				3.22	5*6,7,2	5*6,7	1.31	N/D	N/D

THE TWENTY-FIRST CENTURY

QUESTION	REVIEW GROUP	MEAN	AGREE GRP DIFF LSD	GRP DIFF SCHEFFE	MEAN	DESIRABLE GRP DIFF LSD	GRP DIFF SCHEFFE	MEAN	EVENT TIME GRP DIFF LSD	GRP DIFF SCHEFFE
Q45A,B&C-Personnel without library but with computer science training should be paid commensurate with salaries in the computer specialty.	Gp2 Sci. Tech.	2.24		N/D	2.34	N/D	N/D	1.23	N/D	N/D
	Gp1 Lib.Sci.Prof. & Network	2.44		N/D	2.46	N/D	N/D	1.24	N/D	N/D
	Gp7 Dir. AALL	2.54		N/D	2.55	N/D	N/D	1.62	N/D	N/D
	Gp5 R. Lib. (ARL)	2.61		N/D	2.50	N/D	N/D	1.42	N/D	N/D
	Gp6 Law Deans AALS	2.80	6*2	N/D	2.65	N/D	N/D	1.48	N/D	N/D
Q46A&B-As a result of increased automation and changes in the library, the library will allocate funds for the training and re-education of library personnel.	Gp1 Lib.Sci.Prof. & Network	2.04	N/D	N/D	1.40		N/D			
	Gp5 R. Lib. (ARL)	2.02	N/D	N/D	1.73		N/D			
	Gp2 Sci. Tech.	1.97	N/D	N/D	1.75		N/D			
	Gp6 Law Deans AALS	2.12	N/D	N/D	1.81	6*1	N/D			
	Gp7 Dir. AALL	2.04	N/D	N/D	1.81	7*1	N/D			
Q47-By the year 1990 which department will be responsible for the computer operation, including budgets, personnel, and equipment?										
A. College or Departmental Library		N/D	N/D	N/D	N/D	N/D	N/D	N/D	N/D	N/D
B. College or Department		N/D	N/D	N/D	N/D	N/D	N/D	N/D	N/D	N/D
C. Computer Center		N/D	N/D	N/D	N/D	N/D	N/D	N/D	N/D	N/D
D. Parent institution library		N/D	N/D	N/D	N/D	N/D	N/D	N/D	N/D	N/D
E. Combination of above; identify		N/D	N/D	N/D	N/D	N/D	N/D	N/D	N/D	N/D
F. Other		N/D	N/D	N/D	N/D	N/D	N/D	N/D	N/D	N/D

Statistically Significant Differences

QUESTION	REVIEW GROUP	MEAN	AGREE GRP DIFF LSD	GRP DIFF SCHEFFE	MEAN	DESIRABLE GRP DIFF LSD	GRP DIFF SCHEFFE	MEAN	EVENT TIME GRP DIFF LSD	GRP DIFF SCHEFFE
Q48A,B&C-Each faculty member will own or be furnished a personal computer or a terminal for information access and word and data processing.	Gp6 Law Deans AALS	1.65		N/D	1.62	N/D	N/D	1.46	N/D	N/D
	Gp7 Dir. AALL	1.79		N/D	1.72	N/D	N/D	1.56	N/D	N/D
	Gp2 Sci. Tech.	1.81		N/D	1.57	N/D	N/D	1.45	N/D	N/D
	Gp1 Lib.Sci.Prof. & Network	1.88		N/D	1.65	N/D	N/D	1.58	N/D	N/D
	Gp5 R. Lib. (ARL)	2.09	5*6,7	N/D	1.80	N/D	N/D	1.60	N/D	N/D
Q49A&B-Most students enrolling in college will own personal computers.	Gp1 Lib.Sci.Prof. & Network	1.92	N/D	N/D	1.58		N/D			
	Gp2 Sci. Tech.	1.91	N/D	N/D	1.69	N/D	N/D			
	Gp6 Law Deans AALS	2.00	N/D	N/D	1.73	N/D	N/D			
	Gp7 Dir. AALL	2.16	N/D	N/D	1.93	7*1	N/D			
	Gp5 R. Lib. (ARL)	2.25	N/D	N/D	1.95	5*1	N/D			
Q49C	Gp1 Lib.Sci.Prof. & Network							1.38		N/D
	Gp5 R. Lib. (ARL)							1.50		N/D
	Gp2 Sci. Tech.							1.61		N/D
	Gp6 Law Deans AALS							1.76	6*1	N/D
	Gp7 Dir. AALL							1.84	7*1,5	N/D
Q50A&B-Each student who does not have a personal computer or a terminal will be furnished one for information access and word and data processing for individual use or in labs.	Gp2 Sci. Tech.	2.06	N/D	N/D	1.66		N/D			
	Gp1 Lib.Sci.Prof. & Network	2.27	N/D	N/D	1.84		N/D			
	Gp6 Law Deans AALS	2.42	N/D	N/D	2.00		N/D			
	Gp5 R. Lib. (ARL)	2.33	N/D	N/D	2.10	5*2	N/D			
	Gp7 Dir. AALL	2.45	N/D	N/D	2.18	7*2	N/D			

THE TWENTY-FIRST CENTURY

QUESTION	REVIEW GROUP	MEAN	AGREE GRP DIFF LSD	AGREE GRP DIFF SCHEFFE	MEAN	DESIRABLE GRP DIFF LSD	DESIRABLE GRP DIFF SCHEFFE	MEAN	EVENT TIME GRP DIFF LSD	EVENT TIME GRP DIFF SCHEFFE
Q50C	Gp5 R. Lib. (ARL)							1.49		N/D
	Gp2 Sci. Tech.							1.50		N/D
	Gp1 Lib.Sci.Prof. & Network							1.64		N/D
	Gp6 Law Deans AALS							1.83		N/D
	Gp7 Dir. AALL							1.95	7*5,2	N/D
Q51A—By 1900 each student will be required to have a personal computer.	Gp2 Sci. Tech.	2.82								
	Gp1 Lib.Sci.Prof. & Network	3.12								
	Gp5 R. Lib. (ARL)	3.37	5*2							
	Gp6 Law Deans AALS	3.37	6*2							
	Gp7 Dir. AALL	3.62	7*2,1	7*2						
Q51B	Gp2 Sci. Tech.				2.35					
	Gp5 R. Lib. (ARL)				2.79					
	Gp6 Law Deans AALS				2.90	6*2				
	Gp1 Lib.Sci.Prof. & Network				2.96	1*2				
	Gp7 Dir. AALL				3.30	7*2,5	7*2			

Appendix D

SELECTED COMMENTS OF RESPONDENTS

(The following comments were selected from the 224 returned questionnaires. The comments were taken from those questionnaires with the most well-developed and elaborate personal comments).

---

1. Publication of printed books will continue to increase in the future.

Comments

"I believe the post 1990s will witness a decrease in printed books." (law dean)

"Authors want to get information out beyond the owners and users of computer equipment. Also, printed books are usually better edited." (law dean)

"The technology will continue to be most helpful in the search part of research, but for [the] concentrated reading part of research, hard-copy books will be important." (law dean)

"Strongly agree, answer refers to law-related monographs." (law librarian)

"Books still provide better access and are more convenient." (law librarian)

"Despite rising costs?" (law librarian)

"Many people are not computer literate, or are even computer phobic; these people will not learn how to use computers necessarily. Also, in many ways books are less expensive and more familiar to use and work with (e.g., access, copying, etc.); I think the alternative resource approach--books, microforms, and computers--services library patrons the best. Increase in publication of books will likely respond to demand by private individuals." (law librarian)

"Depends on subject and nature of material (e.g., science or science fiction?)" (law librarian)

"Printed 'search tools' will dramatically decrease. All other books will stay about the same." (law librarian)

"[I] assume both will increase but be controlled by large mass-market vendors or publishers." (law librarian)

"All forms (print, computer, etc.) will continue to increase until post 2000)." (law librarian)

"'Because of the increase of publication of information in computerized and multimedia formats, automation actually stimulates print now, and will for some time." (ARL director)

"Increase will benefit scholarship but will create space problems and access problems for libraries." (ARL director)

"Increase will continue for some time to come." (ARL director)

"Books will remain popular especially for leisure activity." (library networker)

"Would agree more strongly if you hadn't used term 'books,' but had substituted 'material.'" (scientist)

"I don't know about increase. It also depends on what kind of book." (scientist)

---

2. Book collections of the libraries of the future will be reduced in size as more information becomes available in computerized and multimedia formats.

Comments

"By the year 2000, I believe libraries will begin to rely heavily on electronic media as a prime substitute. But I only agree somewhat that this will equate with reduced library collections; nevertheless, this proposition seems probable." (law dean)

Selected Comments of Respondents

"Books hog floor space. Videodiscs and computer terminals will not only make libraries physically smaller; they will enable greater dissemination (access in the office or home)." (law dean)

"The comparative size will reduce but not absolute reduction." (law dean)

"Answer refers to hard-copy book collections. (More than one-half of our present collection of books is in microform. While you did not specifically say so, I assume that the "book collections" which your question implies may be reduced in size are hard-copy book collections. Microform book collections may be reduced in size, ultimately, but I think that will take somewhat longer than indicated above.)" (law librarian)

"Certain kinds of books will cease to be published." (law librarian).

"Facility in use and searching must compensate for limitations! Case of use and costs." (law librarian)

"Book collection will probably decrease in size because of space problems. Space efficiency is an advantage of computerization, although there is a limit to the number of computers a library can set up or afford to maintain." (law librarian)

"Cost of housing depends on type of library. Major research library collections will continue to grow. Firm libraries will go to alternate formats and may reduce in size." (law librarian)

"Acquisition rates may drop, but the collection size itself will not be reduced." (law librarian)

"Though the rate of growth of book collections will almost certainly slow down." (law librarian)

"Book collections of institutional libraries will continue to increase in quantity, but this will not be true of law firm libraries. These will certainly be reduced in size before the year 2000. (Someday, post-2000, the printed book will be rediscovered and found to be an efficient, inexpensive form for information storage and retrieval)." (law librarian)

"As networks and consortia based on automated databases and modern communications link libraries together for information sharing." (ARL director)

"The need to archive recorded knowledge will be with us always. The form and size of the archive is difficult to predict. Book collections will continue to grow but growth rate may slow down." (ARL director)

The Twenty-First Century

"Technology and resources [are] not yet presently foreseen to do this." (ARL director)

"Financial constraints may force a diminution of acquisitions, but will not reduce collections." (ARL director)

"Rate of growth will surely diminish. Uncertain about reduction in total holdings for research collections--perhaps by 2000." (ARL director)

"Acquisitions of monographs may decrease, but collection size will continue to grow." (ARL director)

"Somewhat reduced." (library networker)

"I doubt if the size will be reduced--won't grow as fast; in fact may not need to grow at all." (library science professor)

"Have you tried reading copies from microfilm recently? White on black, for example??" (library science professor)

"Again, depends on what kind of book." (scientist)

"Why are these questions (1 & 2) focused on books when automation of journals offers such greater and more immediate promise?" (scientist)

"This question treats all collections as identical--some collections (e.g., small neighborhood public libraries) will be smaller; other (e.g., Harvard, Stanford U., other academic) collections will continue to grow." (scientist)

"[I agree], assuming that existing collections will not shrink but new information will be in computerized format. Also--until 2000 the amount published in print will be higher, along with increased electronic publishing." (scientist)

"What type of library? Special libraries--strongly agree, other academic school libraries--disagree, public libraries--disagree." (scientist)

"Event likely to happen because of budgetary restrictions on librarians." (scientist)

"Depends on the collection. Large research/university libraries will have lots of books. They may not grow as fast as they have in the past. Special information services won't have many books. Public libraries certainly won't disappear." (scientist)

"Different types of libraries will stabilize at different rates; some decrease in traditional collections will occur, not at a uniform rate. For law libraries, stability could occur by 2000, with some decline in traditional collections thereafter." (publisher)

Selected Comments of Respondents

> 3. In the future more people will buy the information they want to read in a computer-based or computer-generated format and will borrow less from a library.

Comments

"But the use of electronic databases may also stimulate borrowing." (law dean)

"There will be gradual, but fast, growth, noticeable before 1990 but taking [place] in most countries after 2000." (law dean)

"Lawyers will as looseleaf services become databases." (law dean)

"Not until technology allows for better screens, less eye strain, and people forget how cozy it is to curl up with a book." (law librarian)

"In some cases (nonfiction) yes--in others (fiction) no." (law librarian)

"Library--that's why we call them information centers and information specialists/brokers." (law librarian)

"It depends on how expensive and how accessible the programs become." (law librarian)

"For commentary on the information, the hard copy will be preferred." (law librarian)

"Information economics and economies of scale will probably mean libraries will continue to be used as resources/repositories of specialized information and services." (law librarian)

"They will do both until the 1990s or 2000." (law librarian)

"They will buy information through libraries rather than direct." (ARL director)

"More people will buy information and more people will also borrow information. Unlikely that an individual could afford to buy all the information he/she needs." (ARL director)

"Will not necessarily borrow less--may be different information." (ARL director)

"Purchases and interlibrary loans will increase. Libraries are also into providing access to databases and computer-generated data." (ARL director)

"Almost inevitable that this trend will increase. Extent is uncertain." (ARL director)

THE TWENTY-FIRST CENTURY

"This is really two separate questions--you are assuming cause and effect. Why can't libraries 'sell' the information?" (scientist)

"People might borrow diskettes--accumulate software." (scientist)

"Why will one medium supplant the other?" (scientist)

"Buy--'obtain' is my interpretation. Leasing and subscription agreements are also possible." (scientist)

"Depends on how 'the library' reacts to and uses technology." (scientist)

". . . More people will have access to computer-based information; frequently will have to buy." (scientist)

"Will depend on application and usage!" (scientist)

"Depends on type and time value of information!" (scientist)

"But [this] will not be inexpensive so I don't think borrowing will disappear." (scientist)

"This assumes that libraries do not develop local access services." (publisher)

---

4. In the future the services libraries provide patrons will be predominantly guidance in retrieving information in the nonbook format.

Comments

"Greater access will require greater skill to get to the materials on point." (law dean)

"I assume services mean actual assistance to the user provided by the staff, probably reference staff." (law dean)

"This will vary widely with type of library." (law dean)

"As patrons become more familiar with the format the need for reference service will decrease." (law dean)

"Too general. What about special libraries. I think patrons will continue to develop information 'found' by librarians." (law librarian)

"Isn't that the service they provide for book format?" (law librarian)

"To do it would be very desirable. To do it predominantly would be unfortunate." (law librarian)

Selected Comments of Respondents

"Great variation here by type of library." (law librarian)

"Many library patrons will be 'on-line' with home PCs." (law librarian)

"We are already seeing this trend. We call ourselves, accordingly and increasingly, 'information specialists.'" (law librarian)

"Until [the year] 2000 law school libraries will have to provide equal access and training to both print and computer materials." (law librarian)

"Libraries will evolve into information centers providing the needed information, not just bibliographic guidance." (ARL director)

"A great increase in this service is to be expected." (ARL director)

"No--it will be traditional. . . ." (ARL director)

"Guidance in retrieving nonbook format information will increase but will not predominate in at least public sector libraries." (ARL director)

"Desirable for some, not for others." (ARL director)

"Public libraries are likely to continue to emphasize recreational reading." (scientist)

"Again, highly sensitive to type of library." (scientist)

"Except for older information available only in print from earlier years." (scientist)

"Professional libraries (universities, companies) only." (scientist)

"Not sure it will be 'predominantly.'" (scientist)

"Again it depends on the library. I don't think public libraries will disappear." (scientist)

---

5. Microform will be replaced by a form of computer-based or computer-generated technology.

Comments

"The latter is easier to use." (law dean)

"OCR for all fonts in five years, I'd say. Then older materials can be put on videodisks." (law dean)

"Primarily because [microforms are] easier to read." (law dean)

"Optical digital storage will probably replace microforms." (law dean)

The Twenty-First Century

"This will vary widely with type of library." (law dean)

"Desirability will be determined by form of technology/cost/availability/desirability of present microform collections." (law librarian)

"Eventually, yes but optical disk technology still has a lot of bugs and computer time is expensive." (law librarian)

"Ease of use [is] the key." (law librarian)

"At least some will." (law librarian)

"Future historians will view microform as a temporary, stop-gap measure." (law librarian)

"Microforms as back-up copies should not be replaced." (law librarian)

"The sooner, the better." (ARL director)

"Microform is fragile; therefore, it has limited uses--unlikely to be completely replaced." (ARL director)

"[Libraries will] probably have both." (ARL director)

"Technologies such as optical disk will be used in preference to microforms but there will not be wholesale displacement/replacement of microforms." (ARL director)

"Role of microform will diminish, but computer produced microforms will play some role for a long time to come." (ARL director)

"Microform may continue to be useful for preserving older materials; new data will almost certainly be preserved on some computer-based archival storage." (ARL director)

"Short item and facts--yes; collections--no." (ARL director)

"And in fact, I really don't care--[it] probably will remain as a format for some storage." (ARL director)

"Maybe better--couldn't be worse. Have you tried reading copies from microfilm--recently? White on black, for example??" (library science professor)

"Provided costs of capturing and storing keep coming down." (scientist)

"Many products should not and need not be changed. Each medium has advantages for specific data usage pattern." (scientist)

"Probably laser disk technology--[which are] 1/10 the cost of microform." (scientist)

Selected Comments of Respondents

"To a considerable degree, but not entirely." (scientist)

"Microform = clay tablets" (scientist)

"Cost considerations!" (scientist)

"Laserdisk and CD ROM will compete in the area of interactive options, then slowly replace retrospective files. Perhaps not totally replaced for a long time." (publisher)

---

6. In the absence of published hard copy, automated information viewable only on a computer screen (with print-out available for permanent retention) will be widely accepted as readable format.

Comments

"Yes, but eyestrain may become the new disease." (law dean)

"Not "movable"--transportable and currently eye-straining."

"Desirable for some types of information." (law librarian)

"It depends on the quality, cost, etc., of print-out, and the training available to consumers. The problem I have with this is that people might be forced to accept this because of a lack in alternatives. Why is there an absence of hard copy?"

"If you accept the premise, you accept the conclusion. I don't think hard copy will disappear." (law librarian)

"Same situation as with microform--many who objected to it finally had to accept!" (law librarian)

"Unless hard copy is actually altogether unavailable." (law librarian)

"For some disciplines--predominantly sciences." (ARL director)

"Some information is suitable for this treatment. Most information will have some published version, for example, masses of data such as censuses, polls, economic statistics." (ARL director)

"On a limited basis." (ARL director)

"(In the absence of published hard copy . . .), what choice do we have?" (ARL director)

"Already true for database (e.g., directory and referral) information. Will become true for articles (e.g., encyclopedia articles) but not for book-length text." (ARL director)

"Desirable in some disciplines. Potentially damaging in others." (ARL director)

"The key phrase here is 'widely accepted.' Acceptance will depend on how badly people need the information." (ARL director)

"I'm not at all sure the absence of published hard copy will occur." (library science professor)

"Believe there will be multiple options including digesting, typeset quality output." (scientist)

"Again, this depends on what kind of material." (scientist)

"No one wants to read from a screen (VDT)." (scientist)

"Many assumptions in this question--there are other options." (scientist)

"This question is phrased to give choice between information and no information." (scientist)

"Will print to actually read unless factual or short text." (scientist)

"Cost considerations!" (scientist)

"The key is in the 'absence of hard copy.'" (scientist)

"Will be used but perhaps not widely acceptable." (scientist)

---

7. On-line information will be priced so that most people could afford to use on-line services.

Comments

"It's already cheaper to call up something on a PC than to drive downtown. That most people could afford it does not mean they will use it much. Note public library use today." (law dean)

"Much too early to tell; certainly not generally the case now." (law dean)

"Even with the funds I'm not sure 'most people' will be able to use on-line services." (law dean)

"This is something librarians must assure: to practice the right of all people to access information." (law librarian)

Selected Comments of Respondents

"If you're 'undecided' about an event, how can you predict when the event will happen?" (law librarian)

"It would be most desirable if priced so that all could afford it. If not, some mechanism is needed to subsidize the poor." (law librarian)

"This is the real problem with on-line information. The 'haves' and the 'have nots' will be distinguishable. The disadvantaged economically will suffer." (law librarian)

"I would hope presumably, greater economies of scale and technical efficiency will continue to be realized." (law librarian)

"I hope that pricing will become reasonable for most people." (law librarian)

"Remains to be seen." (ARL director)

"Doubtful, unless costs to access can be spread very widely. The nature of information is such that one needs a very large store (high capital investment) of which each individual requires a tiny portion." (ARL director)

"Some will not be able to afford; a real public policy issue must be how to deal with this." (ARL director)

"Not until it's a consumer driven market." (ARL director)

"Already true for very many public sector databases. Private sector mass market will develop by 2000." (ARL director)

"Market factors will dictate this." (ARL director)

"The trend is definitely elitist, and poor people will get screwed." (scientist)

"Costs will increase." (scientist)

"On-line is too expensive and too slow, but up-to-date!" (scientist)

"Many libraries will become local utilities with free access. On-line pricing will not serve 'most people,' but will come to serve majorities in selected market and product areas." (publisher)

---

8. Use of on-line public catalogs will significantly increase demands for document delivery.

Comments

"The reasons for and frequency of patrons going to a catalog will probably remain the same." (law dean)

"Library users don't use the catalog now." (law dean)

"No, but they'll reduce research time." (law dean)

"This is only a stepping-stone to full text retrieval." (law dean)

"Fairly unsophisticated patrons are showing success at retrieving bibliographical information from on-line catalogs--better than traditional!" (law dean)

"Probably an inevitable result of the facility that searching on-line catalogs offer users." (law librarian)

"Do you mean on-line union catalogs? If so, [then I disagree]." (law librarian)

"In itself it wouldn't--it would if the library doesn't stock the material." (law librarian)

"Witness Euronet experience--EEC emphasis now on document delivery." (ARL director)

"One of the biggest problems we'll face." (ARL director)

"Qualification--while desirable from scholar's point of view, libraries will have difficulty supplying document delivery. Costs too high--cannot have document gone, cannot always photocopy document." (ARL director)

"Assuming that the design of the catalog facilitates requesting document delivery, otherwise--no significant change." (scientist)

"Very desirable as a reasonable service but unlikely within existing budgets--at least as a free library service." (scientist)

"True only if holdings of multiple institutions are reflected in the on-line catalog database." (scientist)

"Local catalogs still reflect local holdings." (publisher)

---

9. In the future intelligent terminals, software, or other form of computer technology will be used to analyze and channel queries to appropriate databases for information.

Selected Comments of Respondents

Comments

"But this makes me nervous--as does using a digest." (law dean)

"Not completely, though, because computers cannot replace the weird interdisciplinary connections of the human mind." (law dean)

"It will probably vary, depending on the economics of use of the particular database." (law dean)

"I believe this will be only to some extent. The human interface will remain useful." (law dean)

"I should like to believe the the human mind will never be replaced." (law librarian)

"Probably, this is done now to an extent, if I understand your proposition; but I'm taking this to mean sophisticated analysis and channeling." (law librarian)

"If we're on the planet that long." (law dean)

"I have talked with A-1 researchers who have studied library questions. They say it is impossible at present because the intellectual processes of a reference librarian are very complex. Simple sorting may be possible by 1995." (ARL director)

"I'm sure they will, and I think it's too bad--this is one of the areas that libraries can serve best." (ARL director)

"There will be increasingly powerful local and remotely accessible directories." (ARL director)

"Very important for some types of researchers." (ARL director)

"Much more research into language/AI and information retrieval needs to be completed." (ARL director)

"It's already occurring." (library science professor)

"Only stupid people believe in 'intelligent' terminals." (scientist)

"Use won't be widespread in 1990, but it will be there." (scientist)

"Caution: Some already assume they are conducting a comprehensive search when they are not!" (scientist)

"This is already available. Further refinement is inevitable." (publisher)

The Twenty-First Century

> 10. Distributed databases (computer storage, e.g., tapes acquired for local or in-house computers) will replace remote on-line information sources.

Comments

"Too expensive, duplication [is] too costly for every library." (law dean)

"Not completely, we'll still require timely information." (law dean)

"Optical digital, this is [an] extremely important development." (law dean)

"Cut down on costly communication time and physical facilities." (law dean)

"It will probably vary, depending on the economics of use of the particular database." (law dean)

"Agree unless we find a way to reduce drastically the access charges, especially the communication costs." (law librarian)

"One hopes this would protect against wider information and thought control and support some degree of comparative pluralism." (law librarian)

"Some databases are appropriate, but not all." (law librarian)

"I think this has limited usefulness and desirability. But, overall I advocate shared information." (law librarian)

"Cost?" (law librarian)

"Probably not in the legal area." (law librarian)

"The trend is already there in light of increasing telecommunication costs." (law librarian)

"Only very large volume, rarely used sources will not be distributed." (ARL director)

"Local access to disk storage should certainly increase. It is in the best interests of users." (ARL director)

"There will be a great increase in local storage and processing, but this will not render remote access obsolete." (ARL director)

"The question is to what degree?" (ARL director)

"Suspect that this is partially true. Intense use of database would make local computer storage feasible. Decrease in telecommunications costs make remote access of database more feasible. (ARL director)

Selected Comments of Respondents

"Depends upon communication capabilities and costs." (ARL director)

"In many cases but not all." (library science professor)

"Both will be available--in-house and central. Depends on information content; timeliness, etc." (scientist)

"Too costly. Low cost local storage--laser CD ROM will change pattern of on-line." (scientist)

"In many cases, yes." (scientist)

"They'll coexist; a balance will work out depending on a variation of criticism." (scientist)

"Not tapes, of course--or words chiseled on stones." (scientist)

"They will replace some heavily used sources--but not all remote services, which will be needed on a lesser scale. Which database will vary according to the user." (scientist)

"Distributed database mainly for optical discs!" (scientist)

"As telecommunication costs increase this could surely happen." (scientist)

"Will supplement but not totally replace." (publisher)

---

11. The technology of disks (compact, digital, laser, optical, video) combined with microcomputers will provide an information retrieval capability superior to dial-up databases." (law dean)

Comments

"For small files, frequently used databases." (law dean)

"For some types of information." (law dean)

"Superior graphics and pictures." (law dean)

"On the one hand, telecommunications hassles are reduced; on the other, timeliness is lost." (law dean)

"Superior for certain types of information." (law librarian)

"Will not replace currency of dial-up. O.K. for retrospective research." (law librarian)

"Isn't this the same question as number 10?" (law librarian)

The Twenty-First Century

"Too early to tell." (law librarian)

"Cheaper?" (law librarian)

"Not necessarily disks." (law librarian)

"I don't know what this means; store more information? Retrieve the information faster? Be cheaper for the user? I would have a different answer for each interpretation." (ARL director)

"Local access is preferable because costs will not be so dependent on time." (ARL director)

"Superior in the sense of easier and more generous access." (ARL director)

"Superior for high quality video retrieval, and more economical for very high-rate material." (ARL director)

"Both will exist; I'm not sure when one will be superior." (ARL director)

"A gain for frequently accessed data." (ARL director)

"Superior because more accessible locally, but will not enhance sharing." (library networker)

"For many, but by no means all purposes." (library science professor)

"Not sure it will be 'superior'--again it will be appropriate with others. Both technologies will exist, side by side." (library science professor)

"Full circle?" (library science professor)

"'Superior' will be subjective. . . ." (scientist)

"Dial-up runs up the bill too fast for many." (scientist)

"Dynamic data only." (scientist)

"Superior for some purposes. Volatility of data is a major factor." (scientist)

"Disks? Maybe a new technology. . . ." (scientist)

"Allows graphics, sound, etc.--but won't cover all files." (scientist)

"Superior only in the sense that costs can be predicted. What about currency?" (publisher)

Selected Comments of Respondents

> 12. By the year 2000 disks (compact, digital, laser, optical, video) combined with microcomputers will provide an information retrieval capability superior to dial-up databases.

Comments

"Prospective or retrospective information? Answered on basis of prospective (current) information." (law dean)

"My guess is this may happen, but the timing will be more conservative than this." (law librarian)

"[I] have not yet received my distributable crystal ball." (law librarian)

"Not necessarily disks." (law librarian)

"That's my guess. Heavily used information will stay in hard format because it's more portable and more comfortable to use. Fiction will stay in hard copy. But reference works, studies, extensive status trial analysis, rarely. Consulted nonfiction works, etc., will probably be stored by the above means." (ARL director)

"Depends on whether it's current or retrospective current." (ARL director)

"There's still a lot of hard-copy information in the world, and unless we have a whole-scale book burning, there will still be a lot around by the year 2000." (ARL director)

"Who knows?" (ARL director)

"Will vary by discipline; sciences will progress more quickly than humanities and that is more desirable." (ARL director)

"Depends on your definition of information." (scientist)

"For some technical material." (scientist)

"Thought you were mostly concerned with 'books.'" (scientist)

"Primarily reference sources, journal articles--not 'books' such as novels and texts. Change in publishing industry will be cautious until then." (scientist)

"Not uniform for all types of libraries. For law very desirable." (publisher)

> 13. Interactive television, cable systems, or on-line systems like Viewtron or other videotex systems will replace the library as an information resource.

Comments

"Cost, amount, and use expertise will require library type organizations." (law dean)

"Supplement, not replace." (law dean)

"Probably not yet clear." (law dean)

"Unlikely for sophisticated legal research." (law dean)

"Perhaps to some extent but people are fixed in their ways and libraries will fill other voids." (law dean)

"Supplement not supplant." (law librarian)

"Seems to be same question as number 3." (law librarian)

"If you mean systems that are off-site and transmit very limited amounts of information or data, then 'Never.'" (law librarian)

"Although interactive videotex systems could replace libraries, I don't think they will because so far, people don't really like videotex." (ARL director)

"Not based on what we have seen so far." (ARL director)

"Viewdata/videotex systems will supplement libraries and AVCII on-line database services." (ARL director)

"Would be useful to some small degree." (ARL director)

"This will more likely replace newspapers, mail order catalogs, banking by mail, information with regard to community services, general information commonly found in basic textbooks, information for the basic needs of numbers of people. Libraries never did supply the information supplied by Viewtron." (ARL director)

"As information resources and formats increase information specialists will become more valuable." (ARL director)

"It will supplement the library probably." (library networker)

"It is not that I am a 'libraryophile'; it is just that I think libraries will always exist as one source of information access." (library science professor)

Selected Comments of Respondents

"Costs a huge potential problem; can't have guns and butter." (library science professor)

"Libraries will change, but will survive." (scientist)

"What kind of library? What kind of information? Can't answer without knowing." (scientist)

"Total replacement unlikely. To whatever extent replacement exists, it won't happen rapidly." (scientist)

"Technology today too primitive." (scientist)

"They will exist but not replace." (scientist)

"Agree if libraries don't start changing!" (scientist)

"Don't forget social factors. Television has not ruined the movie industry. Indeed more are going to movies now." (scientist)

"Libraries must restructure concepts of service, avoidability of resources, etc., or such services will become a major challenge." (publisher)

---

14. Other technologies will be developed that will permit access to information even faster and cheaper than those described above.

Comments

"For speed and cost." (law dean)

"Who knows?" (law dean)

"For example, oral compute commands." (law librarian)

"Don't know." (law librarian)

"Faster and cheaper should be better." (law librarian)

"Other technologies will come, using either on-site memory, or off-site memory with the ability to transmit great amounts of memory." (law librarian)

"Automated system costs per unit of output will continue to drop, and speeds will continue to increase." (ARL director)

The Twenty-First Century

---

15. By the year 2000 automated library technology will be characterized primarily by:
   A. Networks of personal computers or terminals
   B. Access of full-text databases, such as LEXIS and WESTLAW
   C. Video-disk technology
   D. Laser-disk technology
   E. Combination of above; identify
   F. Other:

Comments

"Depending upon technology, I would think we'd have PCs using laser disks for storage and accessing full-text databases." (law librarian)

"Laser disks will be replaced by newer, tighter technology, and other new developments will replace older ones." (law librarian)

"Options are not mutually exclusive. The one element that can be reasonably assured is the provision for greater personal access on a highly decentralized basis." (law librarian)

"Network of mainframe, mini, super micro, and microcomputers and terminals of varying intelligence plus local storage (e.g., diskette, optical disk, magnetic disk/tape and videodisk)." (ARL director)

"It seems to me . . . that laser disks will eventually supplant video disks, but I doubt that the transition will be complete by 2000." (library science professor)

"It's already hard to separate A and B easily. As for disks or the future technologies of number 14, I don't have strong feelings." (scientist)

"But large existing print collections will still exist from earlier years." (scientist)

---

16. What role and function for libraries do you envision in the years beyond 1990?
   A. Continued role as general information resource
   B. New role as computer-based information guide
   C. A and B above
   D. No role

Selected Comments of Respondents

Comments

"Librarians will continue to emphasize their function as educators in teaching patrons to use the new technologies." (law dean)

"There are other options--evaluation of resources too vast for researchers to analyze." (law dean)

"But we're really talking 2000 and beyond." (law dean)

"Libraries can and will serve as information/research centers, plus community organizations serving their special local patrons." (law librarian)

"Libraries will continue to exist as on-site repositories of knowledge and as access facilitators of off-site knowledge. They will also provide facilities for programmed learning in many areas and subjects." (law librarian)

"We're already there." (law librarian)

"Depends on library; some will become more 'B' than 'A'; others not." (ARL director)

"Research libraries will have a role as a source and a guide to all manner of specialized information." (ARL director)

"Libraries must become bridges between traditional information service and automated information service." (ARL director)

"Depends on type of libraries--public libraries will provide leisure reading; academic/special libraries will be computer information centers." (library networker)

"Again, what kind of libraries operating; what kind of institutions?" (scientist)

"However, libraries will always [be] useful as guides through [the] area of information [the] patron is unfamiliar with. 'A' role will not vanish." (scientist)

---

17. Increased automated information will slow the rate of growth in hard-copy acquisitions for the library.

Comments

"Particularly in time critical items like catalogs and looseleaf services." (law dean)

"Largely for financial reasons." (law librarian)

The Twenty-First Century

"It's happening now." (law librarian)

"More likely prices will slow rate of growth." (law librarian)

"Depends upon the library and type of material." (law librarian)

"Especially as regards serials. [It] should be cheaper." (law librarian)

"We won't need to maintain long backfiles of little-used journals nor to purchase their newest issues. But our acquisitions won't slow down a lot right away. Users will adjust to the change over a period of years." (ARL director)

"Libraries will choose to provide access to some information rather than buying the hard copy." (ARL director)+

"Will be a function of resources and allocations, not technology." (ARL director)

"Other factors may be more causative than automated information." (ARL director)

"Costs a huge potential problem; can't have guns and butter." (library science professor)

"Rate will be slowed by decreased budgets." (scientist)

"Cost of hard copy is already doing this." (scientist)

"Bad cause and effect inference is assumed; cost rather than availability is the driving force." (scientist)

"Dollars that would have been used for hard copy acquisitions will have to be used to meet demand for more information." (scientist)

"Desirable--if costs to access information do not create an 'information elite class' of society."

---

18. As access to automated information increases, annual hard-copy acquisitions of basic library materials will be reduced to one copy.

Comments

"Depends upon size of patron base and whether a goal of the library is instruction." (law dean)

"Monograph holdings for research libraries consist of only one copy now...." (law dean)

Selected Comments of Respondents

"Will vary according to user needs and vendor restrictions/costs of database access." (law dean)

"Depends on too many variants." (law librarian)

"Validity of statement depends on kind of library (research, etc.), patron base, etc." (law librarian)

"Basic library materials--what does this mean? Nutshells? Hornbooks? Study aids?" (law librarian)

"Or less." (law librarian)

"Subject to patron demand/needs multiple users." (law librarian)

"Also depends upon type of library/patrons." (law librarian)

"It all depends on why you need more than one copy in the first place. No one will want to read *Moby-Dick* on a television screen. But consulting a 15 page article is acceptable on a television screen." (ARL director)

"That is what we do now." (ARL director)

"It is precisely this material that is likely to be duplicated." (ARL director)

"Libraries should continue to buy as many copies of heavily used materials as are needed. Use on-line access for rarely needed items." (ARL director)

"Reductions have occurred, however, on multiple copies of some reference sources." (ARL director)

"May be some reductions, but not of most basic materials." (ARL director)

"We buy mainly one copy now." (ARL director)

"Not possible to generalize about this--libraries will still need several dictionaries, probably in hard copy for example." (library networker)

"Most items are already single copy; more will be, probably; but all? I doubt it." (library science professor)

"Depends on our needs; available access." (scientist)

"In most cases, we are already at one copy. Further reductions will not be caused by automation advances." (scientist)

"Depends on library, don't you think? What are 'basic library materials'?" (scientist)

"But not for novels--at least in public libraries." (scientist)

"Depends on type of library--academic--yes, public--no." (scientist)

"Need to compensate authors." (scientist)

"What's the relationship? Do you assume that some information is delivered in both forms? (publisher)

---

19. What percentage of the annual hard-copy acquisitions of basic library materials will be reduced to one copy by the year 2000?

Comments

"Forced by administrative limitations." (law dean)

"Space." (law librarian)

"I couldn't begin to guess, but I hope libraries will begin keeping records." (law librarian)

"Assuming [there will be] enough access to automated information systems." (law librarian)

"We will continue to need almost as many multiple copies of basic library materials as we get now." (ARL director)

"What is the percentage now?" (ARL director)

"But we only buy one copy of most titles now. This is a case where law libraries are very different from general academic libraries." (ARL director)

"Libraries change slowly!" (scientist)

---

20. What percentage of the hard-copy collection of basic library materials will be reduced to one copy by the year 2000?

Comments

"As materials wear out they won't be replaced." (law dean)

"Assuming enough access to automated information systems." (law librarian)

"As long as space costs and maintenance problems continue to rise!" (law librarian)

Selected Comments of Respondents

"One hard-copy (or more) of selected monographs and hornbooks; microform copy but no hard-copy of serials." (law librarian)

"No change will occur." (ARL director)

"In most cases, the multiple copies of things we have now are needed because of heavy use. I can't envision whole-scale weeding. In addition, for many items, we now hold only one copy." (ARL director)

"This represents no change." (ARL director)

"Basically one copy now in research libraries." (ARL director)

"Conversion of existing hard copy material [is] unlikely to proceed very fast." (scientist)

"Much of the older material will still be available only in print." (scientist)

"Will vary by type of library. Many academic libraries already show 76-90% of their titles [are] held in only one copy." (publisher)

---

21. What type library materials do you envision for the library in future years once the basic book materials are available in automated form?

Comments

"Items which use topic approach generally are hard to convert." (law dean)

"This question is unclear." (law librarian)

"What does this mean? What physical formats? What kind of bibliographic forms?" (ARL director)

"I do not accept [this] statement." (ARL director)

"Very gradual change from present form." (ARL director)

"A mix, as at present. (Poor question)." (library science professor)

"Sorry, I don't know what 'type' means--is this media or something else?" (scientist)

"Basic books will never be eliminated." (scientist)

THE TWENTY-FIRST CENTURY

> 22. Policy for automated information budgeting will be set by:
>   A. Librarian
>   B. Dean
>   C. Faculty committee
>   D. Combination of above, identify

Comments

"It's a dirty, thankless job, but someone's got to do it." (law librarian)

"No change in present procedure." (law librarian)

"Depends on the law school. I would like to set the policy myself, and have the faculty approve it." (law librarian)

"I hope the library will always control its budget." (ARL director)

"Statewide planning including legislature." (ARL director)

"This combination (librarian, dean, and faculty committee) is already at work. (University and other administration also important.)" (ARL director)

"Other factors will determine some policies: 1. cost of external information, 2. availability of research grants, and 3. 'lease versus own' information databases, 4. networking arrangements." (ARL director)

"D would be best, but requires considerable educational effort of A-C." (scientist)

"I assume you're talking about college libraries."

"Librarian, as [an] expert, should be consulted but should not have absolute control." (scientist)

"There is now no one pattern. Why should one develop?" (publisher)

> 23. Automated information budgets will be administered and managed by the librarian.

Comments

"Just like now." (law dean)

"Often in conjunction with in-house computer information specialist." (law librarian)

Selected Comments of Respondents

"No change!" (law librarian)

"Providing we don't drop the ball now, we should be able to continue this." (ARL director)

"Some will be, some won't. Computer center directors manage some now, graduate deans, research project directors, etc." (ARL director)

"Yes and no--smart librarians will have a role--some will get left out." (library networker)

"Who else would be qualified? DP managers might assume responsibility if librarian does not." (scientist)

"Sometimes." (scientist)

"Who knows?" (scientist)

"Not for some sources used outside the library." (scientist)"

"[Yes,] if the librarian is smart!" (scientist)

"Depends on the librarian's skills and respect with which he or she is held." (scientist)

---

24. Automated information budgets will be separated completely from budgets for library materials and binding.

Comments

"These budgets will be a separate line item perhaps, but not completely separate from other library budgets." (law dean)

"After 1990 some libraries will begin to merge the budget lines." (law librarian)

"A.B.A. standards revision--suggest to library." (law librarian)

"I hope not. We need the flexibility to choose between formats without regard for how much was 'set aside' at [the] beginning of year." (law librarian)

"For accurate budgeting and planning, there should be separate line items included in library nonpersonal budget." (law librarian)

"Could be, but should not be unless we want to give up our role as the center of information resources." (ARL director)

"Practical considerations will probably require separate budgets, though findings may be shifted from materials budget." (ARL director)

"I don't know what 'separated completely' means. There probably will be an 'access' budget made up of different parts."

"Not entirely, unless we merge all information service agencies on campus: Libraries, computer centers, communications, presses, etc." (ARL director)

"We should have information access budgets, not book budgets." (ARL director)

"Depends on what organization we have in mind." (scientist)

"Information, not technology, is the key issue." (scientist)

"I assume you mean separately identifiable as a line item in an acquisitions budget." (scientist)

"Who knows?" (scientist)

"Will be separate budget items to track use--but increase in one will affect the other. But we do need a change allowing flexibility regardless of whether using a service or purchasing a tangible permanent addition to the collection." (scientist)

"Two separate issues: the system and the data (information) stored in the system." (scientist)

"It will be impossible to separate automated information and materials budgets." (scientist)

"Total information and resource needs should be evaluated, questions considered, and budgets allocated accordingly. This philosophy may not prevent the separation if libraries don't develop requisite skills." (publisher)

---

25. Institutional fiscal officers will continue to allocate substantial funds for automated information even though these expenditures generate no tangible hard-copy additions to the library.

Comments

"Access to current information in the product purchased." (law dean)

"The contrary result would be ludicrous." (law dean)

"Information budgets--not book budgets." (law dean)

Selected Comments of Respondents

"By 1990, institutions will ask for guidance from ABA and AALS." (law dean)

"In some ways, automated is more 'glamorous' than books." (law librarian)

"It depends on how extensive the automation and what kind of information at what cost." (law librarian)

"Universities are in the business of producing knowledge. This is why they have always supported libraries. Since electronic journals will soon be widely distributed, faculty will be much more familiar with the format. Since university administrators come from the faculty, it seems likely that they will accept it as an important format that their university must have access to." (ARL director)

"I do not accept the statement." (ARL director)

"Much library activity is presently intangible." (ARL director)

"This hits on a key problem of electronic access--costs must be paid again for every user, in contrast to long-term benefits from hard copy acquisition costs." (ARL director)

"They will want some recovery of costs." (ARL director)

"Unless amazing proselytizing takes place!" (ARL director)

"If access is available and as users become accustomed to using automated sources (which they will) this won't be an issue. Preservation is an issue." (scientist)

"Information valuable. Form? Not so material." (scientist)

"Many ARL libraries are not yet allocating 'substantial' funds--but the amounts will likely increase." (scientist)

---

26. Comparing the automated information budget with the library materials budget in year 1990 and beyond, the automated information budget will be:
   A. Less
   B. The same
   C. More

Comments

(Less) "Maybe by 2000." (law dean)

"Hopeful that although information will cost more, it can be more selectively provided." (law librarian)

"Obviously depends on development of technology/communication v. cost and number of other library materials." (law librarian)

(More) "This will be a sad event for the future of education." (ARL director)

"[The] question is, how will the rest of the budget change?" (ARL director)

"Proportion of dollars for the former will increase over time." (ARL director)

"At research universities it will be more." (ARL director)

"The question implies a pre-1990 transition to some other state." (scientist)

"More information, more cost." (scientist)

"Depends on type and size of library." (scientist)

---

27. In light of the possible changes in book collecting policies, would you anticipate any special difficulty in acquiring the funding to build a new library building or addition?

Comments

"Unless the accrediting agencies are of some help." (law dean)

"We've worried about this, but our legislature hasn't." (law dean)

"... probably not quite yet--5 years away." (law dean)

"Difficulty--pressure for book storage space is less." (law dean)

"Depends upon local conditions (e.g., availability of space, money, enrollment, etc.)." (law librarian)

"Provided building program reflects the state of the art and realities of the period." (law librarian)

"Books scream for space more loudly than the terminals do." (law librarian)

"We are beginning to plan for an addition." (law librarian)

"Who would want it!" (law librarian)

Selected Comments of Respondents

"I don't think there will be any change in book collecting policies. We will still collect information to support the academic program. Other departments on campus get new buildings for reasons other than expanding collections. We will just have to make a good case for why we need a new building." (ARL director)

"No, not on this account--other factors such as land and building costs and need to limit government expenditures are much more important." (ARL director)

"Collection policy would not be decisive factor." (ARL director)

"Collections will still grow; uses of collections and services change." (ARL director)

"If those responsible for funding believe that books will be replaced shortly by automated forms, then building to hold books will not be funded." (ARL director)

"I will base building needs on actual services, and expect to build the kind of building needed in the automated environment." (ARL director)

"For what? Warehouse more books? Add space for terminals whereby more users learn more?" (scientist)

"But I think it is a misconception--the change won't come that fast for ARL libraries." (scientist)

---

28. In a year in which the allocations are reduced, the budget for automated information should be:
   A. Preserved at the present level
   B. Increased
   C. Decreased

Comments

"Today they are similar to continuation of fixed fee. If there is a hit or per use charge they are easier to cut." (law dean)

"Impossible to answer in the abstract." (law dean)

"This is hard to answer in abstract--depends on what trade-offs are available." (law dean)

"I presume you are referring to the ratio of hard copy to automated programs." (law librarian)

"Depends on the current levels." (law librarian)

(Decreased) "Since it generally is more expensive, and we would want to stretch the budget as far as possible." (law librarian)

"Depends: why/how long?" (law librarian)

(Preserved) "Too valuable to cut." (law librarian)

(Decreased) "This is what I desire--it probably won't happen." (ARL director)

"The automated information budget should be adjusted to meet demand, which will probably mean an increase." (ARL director)

"May need to make fuller collection of costs from users, and maintain/increase services." (ARL director)

"Really depends on institutional academic priorities." (ARL director)

"Cannot make a general response: depends on circumstances." (ARL director)

"The allocations?" (ARL director)

"Depends on the marginal cost and value of available services." (scientist)

"Changed, as the same effect has caused allocations to change." (scientist)

"As a general a priori assumption." (scientist)

"Depends if the information is also available in print and whether the most significant sources are in print, automated, or both." (scientist)

"Automation becomes a fixed cost." (scientist)

---

29. In a year of reduced budgets, what types of materials should be reduced or canceled first?
   A. Hard copy when information available in computer databases.
   B. Information system when hard copy available.
   C. Other materials

Selected Comments of Respondents

Comments

"Providing information is still available at same cost to patron. For example, cutting shepards or digests is intriguing but what of our responsibility to alumni and per se. (law dean)

"Depends on relative cost." (law dean)

"Depends on use patterns." (law dean)

"Good question!" (law dean)

"Duplicative materials, including duplicative database services, that is, Westlaw or Lexis if library has both." (law librarian)

"Many factors based on type of materials and policy considerations." (law librarian)

"It would really depend on the information and whether we would have access to it through computers at all times. It would also depend on what other information we would lose on the computers that we don't have in hard copy." (law librarian)

"Confusing answers." (law librarian)

"Those materials in whatever format that are most peripheral to the academic program." (law librarian)

"This should not be a tradeoff between machine-readable and hard-copy sources; rather, little used materials of either form should be eliminated." (ARL director)

"A. Where usage is reasonably light and hardcopy costs substantial. C. Would continue to examine low use materials, duplication, and materials available elsewhere." (ARL director)

"Information provision less central to national library mandate than collection/preservation of national literature and cultural materials." (ARL director)

"Depends on any number of things: institutional priorities; how entrenched computerized access is; how big the bang is per dollar." (ARL director)

"Cannot make a general response: cuts must be related to the various research and instruction programs, and the needs of the academic community." (ARL director)

"Depends on the discipline, type of use, continuity, anticipated ability to recover in future years, etc." (ARL director)

"Cut down on junk, whether hard-copy or machine-readable." (scientist)

"Lowers total costs--storage, etc.--unless the materials are used frequently." (scientist)

"Depends on which is used less, and upon subject area and type (e.g., primary, secondary) of information." (scientist)

"Depends upon what is available, what is used, and what is needed. Seventy-five percent of books never get used." (scientist)

"One would not expect this to be administered in a procrustean manner." (scientist)

"Assuming access is provided free for the computer databases." (scientist)

---

30. Who will absorb the costs of faculty access to automated information?
    A. Library
    B. College or department
    C. Faculty
    D. Combination of above; specify:

Comments

"Today--as yet unsettled." (law dean)

"Terminals in faculty offices [should be] paid by college. Central costs [should be] paid by library." (law dean)

"In the absence of ABA/AALS guidelines, various schools will set various policies in accordance with local resources." (law librarian)

"Question should read 'should' rather than 'will.'" (law librarian)

"A or B (it's ultimately the same. Probably better to have a librarian or 'information director' in charge, not the dean." (law librarian)

"University currently pays on-line faculty research charges." (law librarian)

"Depends on the school." (law librarian)

"The library will probably purchase and mount large and widely used databases. Colleges and departments will budget funds for searching databases needed by their discipline that are not supplied by the library (S.S. departments already do this). Individual faculty with distinctive needs will

Selected Comments of Respondents

write it into their grants or negotiate departmental support for their access to unique databases, just as they do now." (ARL director)

"Library--any fixed costs, Faculty/patrons--variable costs (e.g., on-line connect charges)." (ARL director)

(Combination of A, B, C) "Happening now." (ARL director)

"Will vary from institution to institution." (library science professor)

"Depends on what resources. If only one department needs, that department pays." (scientist)

"If on-line (local or remote) data is a substitute for local paper products; and access is requisite to the function of the institution, (hence faculty) cost should be borne as in the other specialized areas, by the institution/library." (publisher)

---

31. A formula will be devised to determine the amount access, hardware, and service that should be provided free to faculty.

Comments

"We are already at this stage." (law dean)

"Their needs vary too much." (law librarian)

"Guidelines only." (law librarian)

"At each school maybe--but I think some guidelines might be nice." (law librarian)

"Too many variables--I'd hate to be on the committee that would devise the formula." (law librarian)

"Probably not. Need will continue to vary for years depending on the specific research and the databases available." (ARL director)

"Formula approach has not succeeded in the past. Too much variation in need and means of satisfying requirements." (ARL director)

"Not desirable--libraries will have to become more accountable on costs, and more cost effective." (ARL director)

"Why prejudice access?" (library science professor)

"Will be required to assure equity." (scientist)

"Don't know what you mean by 'free.' Changed to overhead? Subsidized? Nonproject accounts?" (scientist)

"Many formulae will be devised; some used." (scientist)

"What information? Can professors justify as to university purpose?" (scientist)

"Balancing access may acquire guidelines; formulas may well develop, but such trends retard scholarship and do not reward quality." (publisher)

---

32. Faculty will have to pay for some of the costs to access on-line information beyond a predetermined, reasonable, limited amount.

Comments

"Faculty accounts or budgets." (law dean)

"But that amount will be generous." (law dean)

"Probably time for relatively esoteric, expensive databases, at least." (law dean)

"Faculty or the school. It depends on funds (grants) for research purposes." (law dean)

"Not if I can avoid it!" (law librarian)

"Out of their salaries?" (law librarian)

"The key is what is reasonable." (law librarian)

"What is reasonable? Is Harvard's 'reasonable' or the University of Florida's 'reasonable'? I think individual faculty will fight for and get what they need. This question seems to presuppose that every faculty will get the same thing. They don't now and never have so I doubt that they will in the future. Law and the hard sciences get a lot more support than social scientists and humanists in terms of automated support." (ARL director)

"Complex; someone has to pay for it, although libraries don't like to see scholars pay." (ARL director)

"Done now, and will broaden." (ARL director)

"Should be fully absorbed and distributed." (library science professor)

"Faculty or departments or colleges." (scientist)

"Assume you mean 'out of their own pockets.'" (scientist)

Selected Comments of Respondents

"Value for value. Information has value--and users should pay something for it or it has no value." (scientist)

"Base not on amount but on kind of information and purpose of research. Airline guide--for whose travel? Why? Westlaw? More likely to have academic purpose." (scientist)

"Budgets won't allow unlimited use." (scientist)

"Perhaps!" (scientist)

"Have to set some limit." (scientist)

"Do faculty now have to pay for interlibrary loan requests? What are the qualitative objectives of an institution?" (publisher)

---

33. Students will pay on a per use basis for the costs of information retrieval services.

Comments

"Depends on database--if they have to pay, the majority won't use them or will use them infrequently...." (law dean)

"This depends on the budget of the institution." (law dean)

"Perhaps, if their demands exceed broad, generous limits." (law dean)

"Depends on project student working on and database access sought." (law dean)

"Basis for a power structure based on the economics of information access." (law dean)

"Though a portion, at least, of these costs would undoubtedly be built into tuitions. Students will probably be asked to bear their own costs." (law librarian)

"Some schools will subsidize (or use specially earmarked student fees) for a reasonable amount of student use." (law librarian)

"Should be equivalent to what a student is provided to do as a library service--based on 'library fee.'" (law librarian)

"The rich would get richer and the poor poorer." (law librarian)

"Varies as to database." (law librarian)

"In some cases." (law librarian)

THE TWENTY-FIRST CENTURY

"Should be available as other services." (law librarian)

"Students should not be required to pay for access to basic legal databases, but, perhaps, for general interdisciplinary databases." (law librarian)

"I think a certain amount will be included in their tuition because it will be necessary for them to do their academic work." (ARL director)

"Only out of pocket expenses--not usual services, that is, card catalog." (ARL director)

"Depends on the service--remote database access--yes." (ARL director)

"Probably only part of the costs, and after time, probably less and less." (ARL director)

"Use will be subsidized up to a certain point; users will pay for additional services." (ARL director)

"I assume you mean access to outside vendors' wares? I think this approach will change." (scientist)

"May have 'information credits' to use to assure equity, but payment for information access goes against concept of learning, and discourages curiosity." (scientist)

"Out of their own pockets? Or charged to a set-aside 'funny money' account like campus computer services?" (scientist)

"One way or another. Increased tuition, or...." (scientist)

"This is a probable trend for remote access; not for local on-line access." (publisher)

---

34. By 1990 most research university or law school student fees will cover the costs of automated information retrieval, word processing, and other related computer costs in the library.

Comments

"I see a distinction between information access/retrieval and word processing for personal use." (law dean)

"As is usual for the cost of all institutional services." (law dean)

"Most equitable." (law librarian)

Selected Comments of Respondents

"Subject to getting fees." (law librarian)

"I hope so." (law librarian)

"We instituted such a fee last year. This year it is included in tuition." (law librarian)

"Fees will include an element but cannot cover all per-use charges." (ARL director)

"States and institutions will pay major cost (society at large)." (ARL director)

"Should be general fund which supports above." (library science professor)

---

35. The library will provide to students a limited amount of access to automated information free of charge.

Comments

"'Free' meaning included in institutional support, that is, tuition." (law dean)

"Don't most of us do this already, either directly (Lexis, Westlaw) or indirectly (OCLC, RLIN, other automated administrative services)?" (law librarian)

"Most libraries already do so with Lexis and Westlaw, but as use and number of computer stations increase, student fees will have to be imposed." (law librarian)

"Failure to do so would make the 'poor' student ('economically')--a second class citizen." (law librarian)

"We already do." (law librarian)

"Course related." (law librarian)

"Most access should be completely free--only the 'unusual' request should be charged." (law librarian)

"Access should be unlimited and free, to students, if use is course-related." (law librarian)

"About the same amount of access they now provide to books. Rich libraries will provide more and poor libraries will provide less." (law librarian)

The Twenty-First Century

"Only out of pocket expenses." (ARL director)

"Depends on financial constraints and student/faculty pushing." (ARL director)

"Is the case; will increase rapidly." (ARL director)

"Still don't know what you mean by this term--(free)." (scientist)

---

36. The library will pay for the costs to access automated information for everyone when that information is available only on-line.

Comments

"Duty to private education?" (law dean)

"A worthy goal but not likely in my opinion." (law dean)

"For most of our libraries, many access costs will probably be paid for directly from budgeted funds, but of course, in nonpublic institutions which are tuition-dependent, these funds will be augmented by increases in tuition (assuming we are still in business)." (law librarian)

"Even the public at large? (We are private)." (law librarian)

"Depends on the type of subscription: flat charge or usage-based." (law librarian)

"Depends on the cost of information, but generally the answer is no." (law librarian)

"Depends on library/institution, private or public, etc." (law librarian)

"The library or law school should pay access costs for faculty and students, if course-related, but certainly not 'for everyone.'" (law librarian)

"The library will pay only where it owns the computer and the database involved so that essentially the cost is free to the library. That is, there is no out-of-pocket cost to the library for additional use of hardware, software, and data it has already purchased." (ARL director)

"I feel patrons should pay for part of these costs, above a threshold of free information service." (library science professor)

"What type of library? How is it supported?" (scientist)

"Depends on type of library: public, special law library in corporation? For an academic law library, I doubt that free services will be extended beyond defined constituencies." (publisher)

Selected Comments of Respondents

---

37. The library will furnish computers/terminals to patrons to access information and will collect the costs through coin- or card-operated machines or legal tender.

Comments

"Librarians will probably continue to do the searching where appropriate." (law dean)

"Some of us are doing this now, particularly with regard to WP services and for 'outside' patrons (i.e., not students or faculty)." (law librarian)

"Personally, I believe that hardware will be so cheap by [the year] 2000 that it will be no more a financial burden for the library to provide use of hardware without charge--than to provide books, etc." (law librarian)

"We are looking into this now." (law librarian)

"Perhaps with word processors particularly." (law librarian)

"Depends on library--we offer our students PCs completely free; but others are not allowed to use them." (law librarian)

"But library should collect costs only from outside users (lawyers and lay users), not from faculty and students." (law librarian)

"I doubt that it will provide these for exclusive use. It will provide terminals for access to basic data (card catalog), etc., just as it provides micro readers for fiche and film." (law librarian)

"To some degree." (ARL director)

"It's already happening." (library science professor)

"Some no doubt will. Ugh!" (scientist)

"Multiple question--however, could be analogous to coin-operated copiers." (scientist)

---

38. In the future as there are changes in the library collection format and increased automation, the number and/or composition of library staff will change.

Comments

"I doubt that the number will increase because I don't think universities can afford it. I do think the composition will continue to evolve toward highly

The Twenty-First Century

trained specialists on both the professional and nonprofessional levels." (ARL director)

"Composition probably will change much more than number." (ARL director)

---

39. The number of administrative librarians will:
A. Increase
B. Decrease
C. Remain unchanged

Comments

"Define administrative, but probably remain unchanged." (ARL director)

"Not much basis to speculate on." (ARL director)

"The administrative pyramid will flatten." (ARL director)

"To deal with changing technology." (scientist)

"This probably won't change much, as long as the library remains a vital institution." (publisher)

---

40. The number of public service librarians will:
A. Increase
B. Decrease
C. Remain unchanged

Comments

"And their credentials will rise--I see more librarians with J.D.s in public services." (law librarian)

"Include more technical functions." (law librarian)

"Definitions will change." (ARL director)

"This will depend entirely on skills and role." (publisher)

Selected Comments of Respondents

---

41. The number of technical service librarians will:
    A. Increase
    B. Decrease
    C. Remain unchanged

Comments

"There will be more in-depth cataloging perhaps locally done, probably more centrally done." (ARL director)

"Include more public service. Related functions." (ARL director)

"Definition? Can they cross lines?" (scientist)

"Unless libraries assume responsibilities for creating and maintaining other types of databases." (scientist)

"Hardware requires technical support. How do you define this: cataloging, acquisitions, serials, etc.? There will be change the further you look into the future." (publisher)

---

42. The number of support staff will:
    A. Increase
    B. Decrease
    C. Remain unchanged

Comments

"Slightly increase, slightly." (law librarian)

"Total library use will increase." (ARL director)

"Less reshelving [and] circulation demands." (scientist)

"Role will change: software and hardware support needs will evolve but not disappear in a dynamic institution." (publisher)

---

43. The number of library-trained professionals working in the libraries' information science program will:
    A. Increase
    B. Decrease
    C. Remain unchanged

The Twenty-First Century

Comments

"What does this mean?" (law dean)

"'Library-trained,' meaning M.L.S.?" (ARL director)

". . . increase likely to come from more involvement of present staff." (ALR Director)

"'Library trained' will mean something different in the future." (ARL director)

"I don't understand the question." (library networker)

"What is an 'information science program'?" (scientist)

"Depends whether library-trained professionals acquire critical skills." (publisher)

---

44. Library-trained professionals should be paid more for expertise in computer use.

Comments

"Private sector will force this on educational institutions." (law dean)

"All professionals should be paid more. Computer use is part of a librarian's job." (law dean)

"They should be paid more but not because they have different skills (although, of course, in the beginning they will be paid for technical skills.)" (law dean)

"All professionals should be paid according to their skills and duties; if computer person has more responsibilities--salary should reflect it." (law librarian)

"Paid more than whom?" (ARL director)

"Such skills should become part of everyone's professional skills to some degree. Higher salaries now might help expedite such knowledge and skill development." (ARL director)

"Professionals are paid to do a job. Increasingly, a library information job requires computer use." (ARL director)

"They should be paid for their expertise in information acquisition, organization, retrieval, and management regardless of what tools they use to

Selected Comments of Respondents

carry out these activities: computers, bookdealers' catalogs, card catalogs, or magicians' wands." (library science professor)

"Irrelevant. 'Paid more, period.'" (scientist)

"Just goes with the territory!" (scientist)

"All information professionals should be paid more." (scientist)

"Paid more than whom or more than what?" (scientist)

"Value of information." (scientist)

"Generalization; isn't possible. This is a bad question which might have totally different answers depending on the time-frame selected for the answer. Other situational variables are also relevant." (scientist)

"Why is computer expertise worth more than hard-copy expertise? No magic in computers." (scientist)

"All library-trained professionals should have such skills; those without should be paid less, and should seek alternative types of library service--children's librarian, etc." (publisher)

---

45. Personnel without library but with computer science training should be paid commensurate with salaries in the computer specialty.

Comments

"Total benefits should be similar." (law dean)

"Libraries will never pay competitively with industry for computer specialists." (law dean)

"Market factors at work." (law dean)

"I presume these people have engineering and programming skills." (law librarian)

"As much as any, library salaries are commensurate." (law librarian)

"We already have such a person--wonderful help!" (law librarian)

"If libraries don't, they won't attract any." (ARL director)

"Not relevant." (ARL director)

"Wrong comparison--depends on what they do." (ARL director)

"You have to compete! Though, I think this will change as computer training becomes more wide-spread." (ARL director)

"Provided they perform the same kind of work for the library setting. Otherwise, no." (ARL director)

"I don't understand the question." (library science professor)

"Depends on the function." (scientist)

"Just goes with the territory!" (scientist)

"If you don't, you lose them." (scientist)

"Value of information." (scientist)

"But the need for such staff may be exceedingly limited. What is 'the computer specialty'?" (scientist)

"Equal work, equal pay." (scientist)

"What are you asking? Computer specialty in the library? Or industry? Academic institutions probably won't be able to match industry, but such is surely desirable." (publisher)

---

46. As a result of increased automation and changes in the library, the library will allocate funds for the training and reeducation of library personnel.

Comments

"Continuing education benefits the employee, which benefits the library." (law dean)

"At least during a reasonable 'grandfathering' period for present librarians and until there is a significant pool of computer-trained personnel with special training and career orientation in the area of provision of information services that are specifically relevant to our programs (academic and research)." (law librarian)

"Currently available for workshops." (law librarian)

"We do this now. Question of how extensively it can be undertaken in the future." (ARL director)

"[It] is going on right now." (ARL director)

"It is happening already." (library science professor)

Selected Comments of Respondents

"Funds should come from federal, state, [and] private university sources--for retraining. Distribute the costs." (library science professor)

"It should but most won't." (scientist)

"Where libraries have such funds already, they will be used in that way by those who care. Most of the change will come as vacancies are filled with younger staff with newer training and fresh attitudes." (scientist)

"Some--but probably not for all, unless the university allows free tuition to employees." (scientist)

---

47. By the year 1990 which department will be responsible for the computer operation; including budgets, personnel, and equipment?
    A. College or departmental library
    B. College or department
    C. Computer center
    D. Parent institution library
    E. Combination of above; identify
    F. Other

Comments

"(A), for a law library." (law dean)

"(A, B), no change." (law librarian)

"(A), the law library in most law schools, but local considerations will apply." (law librarian)

"(B), what is 'the computer operation'? Microcomputers? Mainframe? Really too ambiguous to answer." (law librarian)

"(F), no change." (law librarian)

"(All), use and operation in library by library. Mainframes and communications by computer center." (law librarian)

"(C, D), there will be both centralized and distributed responsibilities; but local situations will dictate." (ARL director)

"Major libraries will be in charge of their own computer and database access services. This will be closely coordinated with access via LAN to all other computers." (ARL director)

"Surely this will continue to vary with the institution." (library science professor)

The Twenty-First Century

"Patterns will vary, depending on the institution." (scientist)

"(C, D, B), the library should!" (scientist)

"Computer operation is less and less a centralized business." (scientist)

---

48. Each faculty member will own or be furnished a personal computer or a terminal for information access and word and data processing.

Comments

"Already furnished." (law librarian)

"We have done so already--wonderful help!" (law librarian)

"Each will certainly have access--some more than others." (ARL director)

"By 1987, over 90% of white collar workers will have access via terminal or microcomputer--would not want university faculty to be underprivileged." (scientist)

"This is certain to happen in many places by 1990. If it doesn't happen by the year 2000, the institution will probably be in trouble." (scientist)

---

49. Most students enrolling in college will own personal computers.

Comments

"Essentially irrelevant." (law dean)

"But their PCs may or may not have sufficient software for legal research or study." (law librarian)

"We see that already, too." (law librarian)

"Many will own their own; institution will provide others, and 'computers' will change." (ARL director)

"Access will be necessary to some degree, I don't know how widespread private ownership will be." (scientist)

---

50. Each student who does not have a personal computer or a terminal will be furnished one for information access and word and data processing for individual use or in labs.

Selected Comments of Respondents

Comments

"Unnecessary to have a 1:1 ratio." (law dean)

"This will probably be considered a private cost to be borne by the individual, although computers will be available in labs or libraries or on a shared-access basis, whether for free or not.

"Otherwise the school will fail in its educational role and purpose resulting in computer illiterates." (law librarian)

"Labs are available now." (law librarian)

"Each will have some means of access but not necessarily their own computer." (ARL director)

"Will be provided access to one." (ARL director)

"In labs, at least, it is already happening." (library science professor)

---

51. By 1990 each student will be required to have a personal computer.

Comments

"There will not be enough programs available by 1990 for student use-- at least not enough to justify having students buy their own PCs." (law librarian)

"This is only five years away. Remember that a substantial proportion of American families are still unacquainted with computer technology, and surely personal computers and expensive peripherals and software are still beyond the means of many people. Access to public information must not be dependent on affluence." (law librarian)

"Yes, by 2000. By 1990 the economics will not be such that colleges will be able to impose such a requirement." (law librarian)

"Each student should have access, ownership is not necessary." (law librarian)

"Depends on course of study chosen." (ARL director)

"But individuals will not each have their own or be required to own their own." (ARL director)

"But I would agree that by 2000, say, each student will be required to have access to a personal computer. (I'm planning to teach a course in 1986 that will require each student to have such access.)" (library science professor)

The Twenty-First Century

"May be too early for some schools." (scientist)

"I think that the cost of such equipment will still, in 1990, be a sufficiently significant percent of educational cost that it won't be made a requirement in most places. Have your students been required to own typewriters? Pocket calculators?" (scientist)

"But each student will use a personal computer." (scientist)

"Every student should have virtually unlimited access to one. They should not be required to buy one, unless financial aid is readily provided." (publisher)

The Authors

BETTY W. TAYLOR is a director of the Legal Information Center and professor of law at the College of Law of the University of Florida. She received an M.A. degree from the University of Florida in 1962. She has been employed in the library system at the University of Florida since 1950 and has been director of the Legal Information Center since 1962. She is the author of many publications and is a frequent speaker on the subject of libraries, law, and computers. As a board member of both the American Association of Law Libraries and SOLINET, the Southeastern Library Network, and a member of the American Bar Association's Committee on Law Libraries, she has been influential in the development of automation of law libraries.

ROBERT J. MUNRO has been a law librarian at the Legal Information Center since 1975. He earned an M.A. in political science and a J.D. from the University of Iowa, an M.L.S. at Louisiana State University, and a Ph.D. in higher education at the University of Florida in 1981. He and his wife, Louise, reside in Gainesville, Florida.

ELIZABETH B. MANN is an associate professor at Florida State University, School of Library and Information Studies. She joined the faculty in 1978 following a career in public, school, and special libraries. She earned an M.L.S. at Carnegie and a Ph.D. in library science at Florida State University.